# F5
## PERFORMANCE MANAGEMENT
**QUESTION BANK**

# ACCA

Edition 3, Version 1

ISBN No. 978-1-84808-241-0

Published by

Get Through Guides Ltd.
Unit – 2, 308A Melton Road
Leicester LE47SL
United Kingdom


Website: www.GetThroughGuides.com

Email: info@GetThroughGuides.com

Student Support Forum: http://GetThroughGuides.co.uk/forum


The publisher is grateful to the Association of Chartered Certified Accountants for permission to reproduce past examination questions. The answers to past examination questions have been prepared by Get Through Guides Ltd.

Limit of liability / Disclaimer of warranty: While the publisher has used its best efforts in preparing this book, it makes no warranties or representations with respect to the accuracy or completeness of contents of this book and specifically disclaims any implied warranties of merchantability or fitness for any specific or general purpose. No warranty may be created or extended by sales or other representatives or written sales material. Each company is different and the suggestions made in this book may not suit a particular purpose. Companies/individuals should consult professionals where appropriate. The publisher shall not be liable for any loss of profit or other commercial damages including but not limited to special, incidental, consequential or other damages.

All rights reserved. No part of this publication may be reproduced, stored in a retrieval system or transmitted, in any form or by any means, electronic, mechanical, photocopying, scanning or otherwise, without the prior written permission of Get Through Guides Ltd.

No responsibility for any loss to anyone acting or refraining from action as a result of any material in this publication can be accepted by the author, editor or publisher.

Please check the back of this book for any updates / errata. Further live updates / errata may also be found online on the Get Through Guides Student Support Forum at: http://GetthroughGuides.co.uk/forum. Students are advised to check both of these locations.





© Get Through Guides 2011

# QUESTION CONTENTS

## F5-PERFORMANCE MANAGEMENT

About the paper      i - vi

| Question number | Topic | Name | Marks | Page Numbers Question bank | Page Numbers Solution bank |
|---|---|---|---|---|---|

### Section A — Specialist Cost and Management Accounting Techniques

| Question number | Topic | Name | Marks | Question bank | Solution bank |
|---|---|---|---|---|---|
| 1 | Traditional method and activity based costing | Egale Ltd | 20 | 1 - 1 | 51 - 53 |
| 2 | Traditional method and activity based costing | Northern High – Tech Inc | 20 | 2 - 2 | 53 - 55 |
| 3 | Cost drivers | Pearl | 20 | 2 - 3 | 55 - 58 |
| 4 | Activity based costing | Matrix Ltd | 20 | 3 - 4 | 58 - 60 |
| 5 | Product life cycle | Target Inc | 20 | 4 - 5 | 60 - 63 |
| 6 | Product life cycle | Santa's Workshop Plc | 20 | 5 - 6 | 63 - 66 |
| 7 | Target cost | Comfort Ltd | 20 | 6 - 7 | 67 - 69 |
| 8 | Throughput accounting | Boots Footwear Ltd | 20 | 7 - 7 | 70 - 73 |
| 9 | Activity based costing | Jola Publishing | 20 | 8 - 9 | 73 - 75 |
| 10 | Activity based costing | Triple Ltd | 20 | 9 - 9 | 75 - 77 |
| 11 | Target costing | Edward Co | 20 | 10 - 10 | 78 - 80 |

### Section B — Decision-Making Techniques

| Question number | Topic | Name | Marks | Question bank | Solution bank |
|---|---|---|---|---|---|
| 12 | Sensitivity analysis | Smart Kids Ltd | 20 | 11 - 11 | 81 - 84 |
| 13 | Production planning and decision-making | Almora Engineers | 20 | 12 – 12 | 84 - 86 |
| 14 | Marginal costing | Albion Plc | 20 | 13 - 13 | 87 - 89 |
| 15 | Production planning and shadow pricing | Chivassa Ronald | 20 | 14 - 14 | 89 - 92 |
| 16 | Decision making | Spice Shock | 20 | 14 - 15 | 93 - 94 |
| 17 | Profit forecasting model |  | 20 | 15 - 15 | 95 - 97 |
| 18 | Swot analysis, pricing strategies | Alocin Plc | 20 | 16 - 16 | 97 - 99 |
| 19 | Shut down vs. continue and make vs. buy | Mariam Inc and Fast Pro | 20 | 17 - 18 | 99 - 103 |
| 20 | Expected value | Shifters haulage | 20 | 18 - 18 | 103 - 105 |
| 21 | Contribution | Higgins | 20 | 19 - 19 | 105 - 108 |
| 22 | Budgeted sales mix | Nerville | 20 | 19 - 20 | 109 - 111 |
| 23 | Contribution per limiting factor | Bookem Co | 20 | 20 - 21 | 111 - 113 |
| 24 | Profit forecasting | Recco | 20 | 21 - 22 | 113 - 115 |
| 25 | Relevant cost | PF201 | 20 | 22 - 23 | 115 - 116 |
| 26 | Make or buy | Culum Ltd | 20 | 23 - 24 | 116 - 118 |

# CONTENTS

**F5-PERFORMANCE MANAGEMENT**

| Question number | Topic | Name | Marks | Page Numbers ||
|---|---|---|---|---|---|
| | | | | Question bank | Solution bank |
| **Section C** | **Budgeting** | | | | |
| 27 | Zero-based budgeting | NN Ltd | 20 | 25 - 25 | 119 - 121 |
| 28 | Budget preparation | Sine Ltd | 20 | 25 - 26 | 121 - 123 |
| 29 | Sales forecasting | Storrs Plc | 20 | 26 - 26 | 123 - 125 |
| 30 | Learning rate | Sole Ltd | 20 | 27 - 27 | 126 - 128 |
| 31 | Learning curve concept | Labnew Ltd | 20 | 27 - 28 | 128 - 130 |
| 32 | Learning curve | Richard Designs | 20 | 28 - 28 | 131 - 132 |
| 33 | Learning curve and net cash flow | BFG Ltd | 20 | 28 - 29 | 133 - 135 |
| 34 | Learning curve | Henry Co | 20 | 29 - 30 | 135 - 137 |
| 35 | Budgeting and forecasting | Track Co | 20 | 30 - 30 | 138 - 140 |
| **Section D** | **Standard Costing and Variance Analysis** | | | | |
| 36 | Analysis of variances | Smart Ltd | 20 | 31 - 31 | 141 - 143 |
| 37 | Variances and budgeting | Morse Plc | 20 | 32 - 32 | 143 - 145 |
| 38 | Operational changes | Woodezer Ltd | 20 | 33 - 33 | 145 - 148 |
| 39 | Revised budget and variances | Jackson Plc | 20 | 34 - 34 | 148 - 150 |
| 40 | Sales variances | Simple Co | 20 | 34 - 35 | 151 - 153 |
| 41 | Analysis of variances | Tasty Treat Inc | 20 | 35 - 36 | 153 - 156 |
| 42 | Variances | Lumina Inc | 20 | 36 - 37 | 156 - 160 |
| 43 | Variances | Nice-look Ltd | 20 | 37 - 38 | 160 - 162 |
| 44 | Planning and operational variances | Kid-world | 20 | 38 - 39 | 163 - 165 |
| 45 | Reconciliation of budgeted and actual profit | Ash Plc | 20 | 39 - 39 | 165 - 169 |
| 46 | Sales variances | Spike Co | 20 | 40 - 40 | 169 - 172 |

# QUESTION CONTENTS

## F5-PERFORMANCE MANAGEMENT

### Section E — Performance Measurement and Control

| | | | | | |
|---|---|---|---|---|---|
| 47 | Performance Evaluation | Serene Bay | 20 | 41 - 41 | 173 - 175 |
| 48 | Balanced scorecard and building block | Fresh Foods | 20 | 42 - 42 | 175 - 178 |
| 49 | Not-for profit organisations, behavioural issues | Osho Spiritual Centre | 20 | 42 - 43 | 179 - 180 |
| 50 | Financial and non-financial performance indicators | Concept Academy | 20 | 43 - 44 | 181 - 184 |
| 51 | Divisional performance assessment and ROI | Mystique Ltd | 20 | 45 - 45 | 184 - 186 |
| 52 | Transfer pricing and external considerations in performance measurement | Elegant Ltd | 20 | 45 - 46 | 187 - 189 |
| 53 | Return on investment | Smart Mart | 20 | 46 - 46 | 189 - 192 |
| 54 | Performance management | Lavender | 20 | 47 - 48 | 192 - 195 |
| 55 | Performance measurement | Pace Co | 20 | 48 - 49 | 196 - 198 |
| 56 | Non-financial performance indicators | Ties | 20 | 49 - 50 | 199 - 200 |

### Appendix

| | | |
|---|---|---|
| Formulae sheet | | 1 - 2 |

**Total Page Count : 210**

### Examination structure

Paper F5, Performance Management, seeks to examine candidates' understanding of how to manage the performance of a business.

The paper builds on the knowledge acquired in Paper F2, Management Accounting, and prepares those candidates who choose to study Paper P5, Advanced Performance Management, at the Professional level.

The syllabus is assessed by a three-hour paper-based examination. The examination will contain five compulsory 20 marks questions. There will be calculation and discursive elements to the paper with the balance being broadly in line with the pilot paper. The pilot paper contains questions from four of the five syllabus sections. Generally, the paper will seek to draw questions from as many of the syllabus sections as possible.

### Reading and planning time

For all three hour examination papers, ACCA has introduced 15 minutes reading and planning time.

This additional time is allowed at the beginning of each three-hour examination to allow candidates to read the questions and to begin planning their answers before they start writing in their answer books. This time should be used to ensure that all the information and exam requirements are properly read and understood.

During reading and planning time candidates may only annotate their question paper. They may not write anything in their answer booklets until told to do so by the invigilator.

### Effective time management – a key to success

Remember you have 1.8 minutes per mark.
Aim to solve a 20 marks question in 36 minutes.

## About the GTG Question Bank

This Question Bank of 56 questions covers all important topics of the syllabus.

The Solution Bank has the following features, in addition to solutions to the questions:

| Strategy | to help you tackle the question |
| --- | --- |
| Callouts and tips | to give you additional guidance |
| Score More | where students lose marks even when they have the required knowledge and notes how to avoid these mistakes |
| Answer plan | to help you plan the answers for longer questions |

# QUESTION BANK

## SECTION A: SPECIALIST COST AND MANAGEMENT ACCOUNTING TECHNIQUES

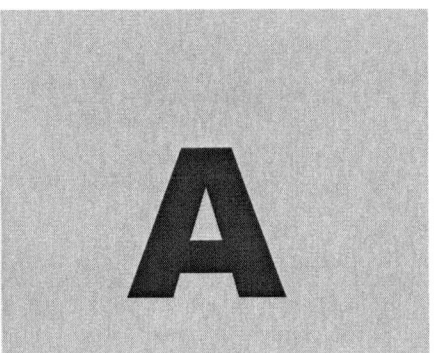

### 1. Traditional method and activity based costing - Egale Ltd

Egale Ltd is engaged in the production of different types of cooling systems. It manufactures and sells cooling systems using almost the same production methods and equipment for each system. It also specialises in processing and replacing old parts of systems. Egale Ltd traditionally determines its prices by adding a 10% mark-up to the budgeted full cost of the system. The fixed overheads are absorbed on the basis of machine hours using a predetermined rate.

**Egale Ltd Operating and Financial Data for 20X8**

|  | Mist cooling | Water mist | Total |
|---|---|---|---|
| Average hours per unit | 3 hours | 3.6 hours |  |
| Number of systems produced (units) | 996 | 1,270 | 2,266 |
| Variable cost per system | $1,450 | $1,254 |  |
| Total Costs |  |  | $14,376,780 |

**Required:**

(a) Calculate the cost per unit and the prices that Egale would have charged for each system using the traditional system of allocation.

(4 marks)

David is a new management accountant appointed this year. He reviewed the cost accounting system and found that irrelevant overheads were allocated to the system. The inappropriate allocation of overheads had a direct impact on the cost and prices of the systems. Therefore, he has recommended activity based costing (ABC) for allocation of the overhead costs to the systems.

However, directors are not aware of the activity based costing (ABC) system. Therefore, they are worried about the impact of switching to an activity based costing (ABC) system to assign overheads to the system. David has gathered the following additional information after analysing the cost accounting records maintained by the organisation:

| Activity | Cost Driver | Mist cooling | Water mist | Fixed overheads $ |
|---|---|---|---|---|
| Set ups | Number of set ups | 3,000 | 2,000 | 8,780,000 |
| Materials handling | Number of movements of materials | 6,200 | 6,200 | 1,500,400 |
| Inspection costs | Number of inspections | 7,860 | 23,580 | 1,059,600 |
| **Total overheads** |  |  |  | **11,340,000** |

**Required:**

(b) Explain the concept of activity based costing and also discuss the benefits that may arise from introducing the ABC for the allocation of overhead costs.

(6 marks)

(c) Calculate the cost per unit and the prices that Egale would have charged for each system using the ABC to assign overhead costs.

(7 marks)

(d) Compare the results of your calculated prices in (a) and (c) and suggest with reasons what pricing decisions you would recommend to the organisation.

(3 marks)
**(20 marks)**

## 2. Traditional method and activity based costing – Northern High – Tech Inc

Northern High Tech Inc has successfully produced and sold two quality printers. Assume the company has the following financial and cost data for the two products:

|  | Deluxe | Regular |
|---|---|---|
| Production volume | 5,000 | 15,000 |
| Direct material per unit | $120 | $48 |
| Labour costs per unit | $80 | $32 |
| Direct labour hours | 25,000 | 75,000 |

The company's management accountant has identified the following activities, budgeted cost pools and activity drivers:

| Activity | Budgeted Cost Pool $ | Activity Driver |
|---|---|---|
| Engineering | 125,000 | Engineering hours |
| Setups | 300,000 | Number of setups |
| Machine running | 1,500,000 | Machine hours |
| Packaging | 75,000 | Number of packaging orders |
| Total | 2,000,000 |  |

These are the actual units or transactions for both products:

| Activity drivers | Deluxe | Regular | Total |
|---|---|---|---|
| Engineering hours | 5,000 | 7,500 | 12,500 |
| Number of setups | 200 | 100 | 300 |
| Machine hours | 50,000 | 100,000 | 150,000 |
| Number of packaging orders | 5,000 | 10,000 | 15,000 |

**Required:**

(a) Calculate the cost per unit for each product using labour hours to absorb the overhead costs.

(4 marks)

(b) Calculate the unit cost of each product under an activity based costing (ABC) system.

(12 marks)

(c) Compare and comment on the costs computed under the above methods.

(4 marks)
**(20 marks)**

## 3. Cost drivers – Pearl

Pearl owns several home furnishing stores. In each store, consultations, if needed, are undertaken by specialists. They also visit potential customers in their homes, using specialist software to help customers realise their design objectives. Customers visit the store to make their selections from the wide range of goods offered. Then administration staff process the purchase orders and sales staff collect the payment. Customers collect their self-assembly goods from the warehouse, using the purchase order as authority for collection.

Each store operates an absorption costing system. Costs other than the cost of goods sold are apportioned on the basis of the sales floor area.

Results for one of Pearl's stores for the last three months are as follows:

|  | Kitchens $ | Bathrooms $ | Dining Rooms $ | Total $ |
|---|---|---|---|---|
| Sales | 210,000 | 112,500 | 440,000 | 762,500 |
| Cost of goods sold | 63,000 | 36,000 | 176,000 | 275,000 |
| Other costs | 130,250 | 81,406 | 113,968 | 325,624 |
| Profit | 16,750 | (4,906) | 150,032 | 161,876 |

Pearl's management accountant is concerned that the Bathrooms department has been showing a loss for some time. He is considering a proposal to close it down in order to concentrate on the more profitable departments like Kitchens and Dining rooms. He has found that other costs for this store for the last three months are made up of:

|  | $ | Employees |
|---|---|---|
| Sales staff wages | 64,800 | 12 |
| Consultation staff wages | 24,960 | 4 |
| Warehouse staff wages | 30,240 | 6 |
| Administration staff | 30,624 | 4 |
| General overheads (light, heat, rates, etc.) | 175,000 |  |
| Total | 325,624 |  |

He has collected the following additional information for the last three months:

| Department | Kitchens | Bathrooms | Dining Rooms |
|---|---|---|---|
| Number of items sold | 1,000 | 1,500 | 4,000 |
| Purchase orders | 1,000 | 900 | 2,500 |
| Floor area (Sq. meters) | 16,000 | 10,000 | 14,000 |
| Number of consultations | 798 | 200 | 250 |

The management accountant believes that he can use this information, to review the store's performance in the last three months, from an activity-based costing (ABC) perspective.

**Required:**

(a) Discuss the management accountant's belief that the information provided can be used in an activity-based costing analysis.

(4 marks)

(b) Illustrate using supporting calculations, how an ABC profit statement might be produced from the information provided. Clearly explain the reasons behind your choice of cost drivers.

(9 marks)

(c) Evaluate and discuss the proposal to close the Bathrooms department.

(7 marks)
**(20 marks)**
**(Adapted from Paper 2.4 June 2004)**

### 4. Activity based costing – Matrix Ltd

Matrix Ltd manufactures and installs complex satellite navigation systems in cars on its national depots. It also sells these systems to a few car dealers. A navigation system acquires position data to locate the user on a road in the unit's map database. Matrix Ltd manufactures three models based on the different satellite navigation maps used in the system. It assembles Model X (CARIN Database Format), Model Y (S-Dal) and Model Z (Physical Storage Format). The navigation system is manufactured using machines; however, labour plays a key role in the installation process.

Neo, the management accountant of the company, is concerned that not all navigation systems produced are as profitable as they should be. Hence, he has suggested adopting activity based costing (ABC) for the allocation of overheads. Earlier, Matrix Ltd had allocated overhead costs using a traditional method i.e. direct labour hours. Below are some of the figures extracted from the financial statements of Matrix Ltd:

|  | Annual Output (units) | Annual Direct Labour Hours | Selling Price ($ per unit) | Raw material cost ($ per unit) |
|---|---|---|---|---|
| Model X | 800 | 100,000 | 5,850 | 3,000 |
| Model Y | 1,500 | 220,000 | 8,000 | 1,250 |
| Model Z | 2,500 | 180,000 | 5,000 | 1,000 |

The three cost drivers that generate overheads are:

| Deliveries to car retailers | The number of deliveries of the system made to different car retailers. |
|---|---|
| Machine set up costs | The number of times the machine is reset to accommodate the production run of a different type of navigation system. |
| Quality testing costs | The number of quality tests performed. |

Cost per driver for each type of navigation system:

|  | Number of deliveries to car retailers | Number of machine set-ups | Number of quality test controls |
|---|---|---|---|
| Model X | 150 | 45 | 40 |
| Model Y | 100 | 50 | 65 |
| Model Z | 200 | 35 | 90 |

The annual overhead costs relating to these activities are as follows:

|  | $ |
|---|---|
| Deliveries to retailers | 2,250,000 |
| Set-up costs | 2,650,000 |
| Quality test controls | 1,000,000 |
| **Total overhead costs** | **5,900,000** |

**Note**: direct labour is charged at $8 per hour. The company does not hold any inventory.

The managers of the finance and accounting department of the company had a meeting to decide whether to adopt activity based costing in the company or not. Below are a few aspects of the discussion:

➤ information on incremental costs is needed to identify the amount of discount that can be allowed to clients placing huge orders. However, incremental costs cannot be calculated under activity based costing.

➤ Activity based costing can only help them to derive information about the use of labour hours in assessing the viability of each product. But it may not be helpful to gain any further information.

➤ if the labour force repeats a certain activity, they gain knowledge. Hence, the labour time is reduced and thereby the costs. However, this is not considered in activity based costing. Also, some costs remain fixed irrespective of the labour hours worked and any other cost driver.

➤ a few people did not see the use of getting this costing system into the organisation. They were of the opinion that no matter what type of costing was adopted, the overall profit remained the same, whereas some people were in the favour of introducing activity based costing into the organisation.

**Required:**

(a) Calculate the total profit on each of Matrix Ltd's three types of products using both the following methods to attribute overheads:
  (i) Traditional method
  (ii) Activity based costing

(12 marks)

(b) Comment on the result of the meeting and state whether you agree with all the points that have come up.

(8 marks)
**(20 marks)**

## 5. Product life cycle – Target Inc

Target Inc sells medical instruments to many hospitals. Its instruments are also sold in the open market. These medical instruments are designed, developed and manufactured solely by Target. They have a life cycle ranging from 3 to 10 years. Target has a centralised research lab where all the design and development work is carried out, before forwarding the equipment to the sales and distribution department so that they can market and distribute the product.

Target measures the performance of the instruments according to profits made each year during the product's life cycle. Recently, Target developed a blood pressure monitor. However, it only has a life cycle of 5 years.

Data relating to the blood pressure monitor regarding life cycle costs and revenues is given below:

Expected net profit percentage: 20% of turnover considered reasonable.
Rate of contribution (sales price- variable costs): 60% considered reasonable.
Selling price: $45 per monitor

Cost analysis of the monitor reveals the following information:

| Units | Expected costs (excluding marketing and design costs) |
|---|---|
| 5,000 | $150,000 |
| 9,000 | $230,000 |

Fixed cost will remain the same for both the activity levels, as mentioned above. However, if production increases beyond the activity level of 10,000 units, then the fixed cost will increase by 40%.

The budgeted sales volume and costs are as follows:

| Years | Units |
|---|---|
| 1 | 8,000 |
| 2 | 12,000 |
| 3 | 15,000 |
| 4 | 10,000 |
| 5 | 6,000 |

|  | Year 0 ($) | Year 1($) | Year 2($) | Year 3($) |
|---|---|---|---|---|
| Market costs |  | 70,000 | 60,000 | 40,000 |
| Design and development costs (written off to the income statement before the launch of the product.) | 325,000 |  |  |  |

**Required:**

(a) Elaborate on the concept of the product life cycle.

(3 marks)

(b) Explain how implementation of the life cycle principles will be helpful to Target.

(2 marks)

(c) Assess the budgeted results for the monitor as against the expected profitability.

(15 marks)
**(20 marks)**

## 6. Product life cycle - Santa's Workshop Plc

Santa's workshop Plc makes toys for children. Since its inception, Santa's workshop has introduced innovative toys in the market. Within a very short span of time Santa's has captured a big share of the market. Santa has a policy of introducing an innovative toy in the market every Christmas. The Managing Director of Santa's workshop, Brian, thinks this is the best time to introduce new toys as almost every one wants to buy Christmas gifts for their loved ones around this time.

Santa has its own research lab where the new toys are designed. After introducing all these toys, Brian wants to introduce educational T.V. and Video games for children. He has asked the management accountant to prepare a life cycle budget without considering the time value of money for this new toy. He is thinking of starting the development of this new toy very soon.

Related estimates about its revenues and costs are given below for your reference.

| Life-cycle units to be manufactured and sold | 350,000 |
|---|---|
| Selling price per toy | $100 |
| Life-cycle costs: |  |
| R & D and design costs | $8,000,000 |
| **Manufacturing** |  |
| Variable cost per toy | $50 |
| Variable cost per batch | $150 |
| Toys batch | 100 |
| Fixed costs | $900,000 |
| **Marketing** |  |
| Variable cost per toy | $10 |
| Fixed costs | $200,000 |
| **Distribution:** |  |
| Variable cost per batch | $80 |
| Fixed costs | $320,000 |
| Toys per batch | 200 |
| Customer-service cost per toy | $2.00 |

## 6: Specialist Cost and Management Accounting Techniques

**Required:**

(a) Prepare a statement showing a budgeted life-cycle operating income for the new toy.

(4 marks)

(b) Calculate the percentage of the budgeted total product life-cycle costs that will be incurred by the end of the R & D and design stages.

"80% of the budgeted total product life-cycle costs of the new toy will be locked/ committed in at the R & D and design stage." What effect will this have on the management of costs of the new toy?

(2 marks)

(c) The Market Research Department of Santa's workshop has proposed to reduce the price of the new toy by $10. According to their analysis it will increase the forecasted sales of the new toy by 20%. However if the forecasted sales increased by 20%, Brian plans to increase the manufacturing and distribution batch sizes by 20%.

Evaluate the Market research department's proposal and advise Brian on whether he should accept the Market research department's proposal.

(12 marks)

(d) If the target price of the new toy is $80 per toy, then calculate the target cost of producing 350,000 units and the cost gap. Santa's Workshop expects to earn a profit at 20% on sales.

(2 marks)
**(20 marks)**

### 7. Target cost - Comfort Ltd

Comfort Plc manufactures office chairs. It has been observed that sales for the current year have fallen, compared to the previous year. Therefore, Tom Warne, the marketing manager at Comfort conducted a market research to find out the reasons for the decrease. He discovered that a competitor has started selling a set of 10 chairs at a lower price i.e. $2,000. He estimated that in order to maintain the demand, the company will need to rework the pricing decisions and cost structures.

Therefore, the directors asked the accounting team to compare Comfort's cost accounting system with the competitors' system. Jim, the accountant at Comfort Ltd, analysed the competitors' cost accounting system. He determined that the competitor has adopted a target costing approach for its product. Hence, the directors have decided to implement target costing to manage costs and maintain the market position.

However, Jim is not aware of the target costing concept.

**Required:**

As a management accountant you are required to:

(a) Describe the target costing process that Comfort Ltd should take on.

(4 marks)

(b) Explain the implications of using target costing on cost control.

(4 marks)

Currently Comfort sells a set of 10 chairs for $2275. In order to meet the competition, Comfort's management has decided to sell each set for $2000. The management expects to maintain a 25% return on its sales. It has budgeted the sale of 10,000 sets of chairs at $2000 per set for the coming period.

Due to fluctuations in the business volume, Comfort has more labour than what is required. Comfort's cost department has estimated that 5% of the hourly rate is paid to the carpenters for idle time.

The following is a cost structure for Comfort.

(i) Raw material i.e. wooden sheets required to make one set of chairs has been purchased for $ 20 per sheet. 10 sheets are required to make one set of 10 chairs.
(ii) Polish that is used to finish the chairs is purchased at $15 per bottle. One complete bottle is required to polish one chair.
(iii) Other accessories used for the chair are brought in at the rate of $12 per chair.
(iv) 5 hours are needed to complete one chair. Carpenters are paid at the rate of $5 per hour.
(v) Assembly workers are paid at the rate of $4 per hour for assembling one chair. 30 minutes are needed to assemble one chair.
(vi) Overheads are absorbed on the basis of total labour hours worked on carpentry work. Comfort's carpentry department generally works for 80,000 hours per year.

The following data relates to the last two month's production overheads:

| Month | Production overheads | Labour hours in Carpentry department |
|---|---|---|
| 1 | $80,000 | 5000 |
| 2 | $120,000 | 9000 |

**Required:**

(c) From the above cost data, calculate the expected cost per unit of each set. Also identify the difference between the expected cost and the target cost per unit of each set.

(12 marks)
**(20 marks)**

## 8. Throughput accounting – Boots Footwear Ltd

Boots Footwear Limited (BFL) is a company that manufactures footwear. They innovate and develop their designs on a continuous basis in order to provide more choice and range for their customers. Two of their products are: 'Trainers' and 'Trekkers'. They are sports shoes meant for professional use, however, the target market for these shoes differ. Trainers are designed to offer superb fit for professional runners. While Trekkers is designed to provide exceptional comfort for professional hikers.

Given below is data for the year ending 31 December, 2008.

Selling price and cost information:

|  | Trainers ($) | Trekkers ($) |
|---|---|---|
| Selling price | 100 | 150 |
| Material cost | 40 | 50 |
| Variable production conversion | 10 | 30 |

The fixed production overheads incurred in the manufacture of footwear is $2,025,000.

BFL expects the demand of these shoes to be:

|  | Units |
|---|---|
| Trainers | 75,000 |
| Trekkers | 35,000 |

Both the sports shoes need to go through the finishing department before they can be sold in the market. The data below provides information relating to the number of shoes that can be completed in an hour by the finishing department:

|  | Number of shoe pairs |
|---|---|
| Trainers | 4 |
| Trekkers | 2.50 |

The finishing department has a total of 25,000 hours available.

BFL follows the just in time (JIT) manufacturing system. They intend to hold negligible work-in-progress and no finished goods stocks.

**Required:**

(a) Calculate the optimum product mix that will maximize the profit. State the value of the projected profit by applying the marginal costing principles.

(6 marks)

(b) Calculate the throughput accounting ratios for both types of shoe. Assume that the variable overheads cost incurred in part (a) is fixed in the short-term. Comment on the answer.

(5 marks)

(c) Calculate the optimum product mix that will maximise the profit. State the value of the projected profit by using throughput accounting principles.

(5 marks)

(d) How does the concept of contribution in marginal costing differ from the concept of contribution in throughput accounting?

(4 marks)
**(20 marks)**

## 9. Activity based costing - Jola Publishing Co

Jola Publishing Co publishes two forms of book.

The company publishes a children's book (CB) which is sold in large quantities to government controlled schools. The book is produced in only four large production runs but goes through frequent government inspections and quality assurance checks.

The paper used is strong, designed to resist the damage that can be caused by the young children it is produced for. The book has only a few words and relies on pictures to convey meaning.

The second book is a comprehensive technical journal (TJ). It is produced in monthly production runs, 12 times a year. The paper used is of relatively poor quality and is not subject to any governmental controls and consequently only a small number of inspections are carried out. The TJ uses far more machine hours than the CB in its production.

The directors are concerned about the performance of the two books and are wondering what the impact would be of a switch to an activity based costing (ABC) approach to accounting for overheads. They currently use absorption costing, based on machine hours for all overhead calculations. They have accurately produced an analysis for the accounting year just completed as follows:

|  | CB | | TJ | |
| --- | --- | --- | --- | --- |
|  | $per unit | $per unit | $per unit | $per unit |
| Direct production costs |  |  |  |  |
| Paper | 0·75 |  | 0·08 |  |
| Printing ink | 1·45 |  | 4·47 |  |
| Machine costs | 1·15 |  | 1·95 |  |
|  |  | 3·35 |  | 6·50 |
| Overheads |  | 2·30 |  | 3·95 |
| Total cost |  | 5·65 |  | 10·45 |
| Selling price |  | 9·05 |  | 13·85 |
| Margin |  | 3·40 |  | 3·40 |

The main overheads involved are:

| Overhead | % of total overhead | Activity driver |
| --- | --- | --- |
| Property costs | 75·0% | Machine hours |
| Quality control | 23·0% | Number of inspections |
| Production set up costs | 2·0% | Number of set ups |

If the overheads above were re-allocated under ABC principles then the results would be that the overhead allocation to CB would be $0·05 higher and the overhead allocated to TJ would be $0·30 lower than previously.

**Required:**

(a) Explain why the overhead allocations have changed in the way indicated above.

(8 marks)

The directors are keen to introduce ABC for the coming year and have provided the following cost and selling price data:

1. The paper used costs $2 per kg for a CB but the TJ paper costs only $1 per kg. The CB uses 400g of paper for each book, four times as much as the TJ uses.
2. Printing ink costs $30 per litre. The CB uses one third of the printing ink of the larger TJ. The TJ uses 150ml of printing ink per book.
3. The CB needs six minutes of machine time to produce each book, whereas the TJ needs 10 minutes per book. The machines cost $12 per hour to run.
4. The sales prices are to be $9·30 for the CB and $14·00 for the TJ

As mentioned above there are three main overheads, the data for these are:

| Overhead | Annual cost for the coming year $ |
| --- | --- |
| Property costs | 2,160,000 |
| Quality control | 668,000 |
| Production set up costs | 52,000 |
| **Total** | **2,880,000** |

The CB will be inspected on 180 occasions next year, whereas the TJ will be inspected just 20 times.

Jola Publishing will produce its annual output of 1,000,000 CBs in four production runs and approximately 10,000 TJs per month in each of 12 production runs.

**Required:**

(b) Calculate the cost per unit and the margin for the CB and the TJ using machine hours to absorb the overheads.

(4 marks)

(c) Calculate the cost per unit and the margin for the CB and the TJ using activity based costing principles to absorb the overheads.

(8 marks)
**(20 marks)**
**(Adapted from June 2008)**

### 10. Activity based costing – Triple Ltd

Triple Limited makes three types of gold watch – the Diva (D), the Classic (C) and the Poser (P). A traditional product costing system is used at present; although an activity based costing (ABC) system is being considered. Details of the three products for a typical period are:

|           | Hours per unit |               | Materials Cost per unit ($) | Production Units |
|-----------|----------------|---------------|-----------------------------|------------------|
|           | Labour hours   | Machine hours |                             |                  |
| Product D | ½              | 1½            | 20                          | 750              |
| Product C | 1½             | 1             | 12                          | 1,250            |
| Product P | 1              | 3             | 25                          | 7,000            |

Direct labour costs $6 per hour and production overheads are absorbed on a machine hour basis. The overhead absorption rate for the period is $28 per machine hour.

**Required:**

(a) Calculate the cost per unit for each product using traditional methods, absorbing overheads on the basis of machine hours.

(3 marks)

Total production overheads are $654,500 and further analysis shows that the total production overheads can be divided as follows:

|                                       | %   |
|---------------------------------------|-----|
| Cost relating to set-ups              | 35  |
| Costs relating to machinery           | 20  |
| Costs relating to materials handling  | 15  |
| Costs relating to inspection          | 30  |
| Total production overhead             | 100 |

The following total activity volumes are associated with each product line for the period as a whole:

|           | Number of set ups | Number of movements of materials | Number of inspections |
|-----------|-------------------|----------------------------------|-----------------------|
| Product D | 75                | 12                               | 150                   |
| Product C | 115               | 21                               | 180                   |
| Product P | 480               | 87                               | 670                   |
|           | 670               | 120                              | 1,000                 |

**Required:**

(b) Calculate the cost per unit for each product using ABC principles (work to two decimal places).

(12 marks)

(c) Explain why costs per unit calculated under ABC are often very different to costs per unit calculated under more traditional methods. Use the information from Triple Limited to illustrate.

(5 marks)
**(20 marks)**
**(Adapted from Pilot paper)**

## 10: Specialist Cost and Management Accounting Techniques

### 11. Target costing – Edward Co

Edward Co assembles and sells many types of radio. It is considering extending its product range to include digital radios. These radios produce a better sound quality than traditional radios and have a large number of potential additional features not possible with the previous technologies (station scanning, more choice, one touch tuning, station identification text and song identification text etc.).

A radio is produced by assembly workers assembling a variety of components. Production overheads are currently absorbed into product costs on an assembly labour hour basis.

Edward Co is considering a target costing approach for its new digital radio product.

**Required:**

(a) Briefly describe the target costing process that Edward Co should undertake.

(2 marks)

(b) Explain the benefits to Edward Co of adopting a target costing approach at such an early stage in the product development process.

(4 marks)

(c) Assuming a cost gap was identified in the process, outline possible steps Edward Co could take to reduce this gap.

(4 marks)

A selling price of $44 has been set in order to compete with a similar radio on the market that has comparable features to Edward Co's intended product. The board have agreed that the acceptable margin (after allowing for all production costs) should be 20%.

Cost information for the new radio is as follows:

Component 1 (Circuit board) – these are bought in and cost $4·10 each. They are bought in batches of 4,000 and additional delivery costs are $2,400 per batch.

Component 2 (Wiring) – in an ideal situation 25 cm of wiring is needed for each completed radio. However, there is some waste involved in the process as wire is occasionally cut to the wrong length or is damaged in the assembly process. Edward Co estimates that 2% of the purchased wire is lost in the assembly process. Wire costs $0·50 per metre to buy.

Other material – other materials cost $8·10 per radio.

Assembly labour – these are skilled people who are difficult to recruit and retain. Edward Co has more staff of this type than needed but is prepared to carry this extra cost in return for the security it gives the business. It takes 30 minutes to assemble a radio and the assembly workers are paid $12·60 per hour. It is estimated that 10% of hours paid to the assembly workers is for idle time.

Production Overheads – recent historic cost analysis has revealed the following production overhead data:

|         | Total production overhead $ | Total assembly labour hours |
|---------|-----------------------------|-----------------------------|
| Month 1 | 620,000                     | 19,000                      |
| Month 2 | 700,000                     | 23,000                      |

Fixed production overheads are absorbed on an assembly hour basis based on normal annual activity levels. In a typical year 240,000 assembly hours will be worked by Edward Co.

**Required:**

(d) Calculate the expected cost per unit for the radio and identify any cost gap that might exist.

(10 marks)
**(20 marks)**
**(Adapted from December 2007)**

# QUESTION BANK

## SECTION B: DECISION MAKING TECHNIQUES

### 12. Sensitivity analysis – Smart Kids Ltd

**(a)** Smart Kids Limited (SKL) designs and sells soft toys for kids. Its marketing policy involves innovation and as a result each year SKL comes up with a new innovative character in soft toys.

This year the company has come up with a character called 'Bobby D' for kids. They expect to sell 30,000 Bobby Ds at the rate of $40 per unit. The direct cost of labour associated with the manufacturing of soft toys is $20 per unit. The overhead costs associated with the project are $6 per unit and the direct materials used is $7 per unit.

**Required:**

**(i)** Calculate the cash flow from the project. Also, evaluate the sensitivity of the project's cash flow to a change in the following project variables:

- an increase in the overhead cost by 2%
- a decrease in the labour cost by 5%
- a decrease in the selling price by $0.50 and a following increase in the sales volume by 4%

Discuss using sensitivity analysis as a way of evaluating project risk.

(8 marks)

**(ii)** 'Risk and uncertainty should be considered in making decisions with regard to investment projects'. Explain the importance of this statement in the context of Smart Kids and how these may affect their markets since they launch a new character every year. Also mention the qualitative techniques that can help Smart Kids to reduce uncertainty.

(7 marks)

### (b) Expected value of profit – Better Budgets Ltd

Better Budgets Ltd is preparing its budget for 20X0. In the preparation of the budget, it does not want to take any chances but would like to envisage all sorts of possibilities and incorporate them in the budget. Their considered estimates are as follows:

(i) If the worst possible happens, sales will be 8,000 units at a price of $19 per unit, the material cost will be $9.5 per unit, direct labour $2 per unit and the variable overhead will be $1 per unit. The fixed cost will be $60,000 per annum.

(ii) If the best possible happens, sales will be 15,000 units at price of $20 per unit. The material cost will be $7 per unit, direct labour $3 per unit and the variable overhead will be $1 per unit. The fixed cost will be $48,000 p.a.

(iii) It is most likely, however, that sales will be 2,000 units above the worst possible level at a price of $20 per unit. The material cost will be $8 per unit, direct labour $3 per unit and the variable overhead will be $1 per unit. The fixed cost will be $50,000 p.a.

(iv) There is 20% probability that the worst will happen, a 10% probability that the best will happen and a 70% probability that the most likely outcome will occur.

**Required:**

What will the expected value of profit be according to the budget for 20X0?

(5 marks)
**(20 marks)**

# 12: Decision Making Techniques © GTG

## 13. Production planning and decision-making - Almora Engineers

(a) Almora Engineers manufactures special motor spares used for water pumps in buildings that have over 25 storeys. These products are in heavy demand, since the construction industry is flourishing. There are two main departments in the factory - welding and pressing departments. There are four products, namely WT4, WT6, PL1 and PL7. Whilst WT4 and WT6 are produced by welders in the welding department, PL1 and PL7 are produced by press-operators in the pressing department. Due to very specific training by the company during induction, welders and press-operators cannot work interchangeably.

Details of the per unit resource consumption, cost and selling price are given below:

|  | WT4 | WT6 | PL1 | PL7 |
|---|---|---|---|---|
| Hours required | 7.2 | 7.2 | 9.0 | 3.6 |
| Selling price per unit ($) | 86.4 | 90 | 138.6 | 124.2 |
| Direct material per unit ($) | 32.4 | 39.6 | 57.6 | 79.2 |
| Direct labour rate per hour ($) | 7.2 | 7.2 | 7.2 | 7.2 |
| Variable overhead per unit ($) | 3.6 | 3.6 | 5.4 | 5.4 |
| Minimum demand to be met according to management decision (units) | 3,600 | 4,500 | 3,240 | 3,960 |

The maximum hours available for welders are 60,000 and for press-operators are 45,000. In addition to the above costs, the company also incurs fixed costs of $90,000.

The company is likely to experience an additional demand for some of their products in the coming quarter. However, since the workmen cannot interchange their jobs and cannot support each other, Almora can cater only to the demand for the product of one department at a time. The newly appointed manager has suggested a special training course which will ensure that workers perform both jobs. This will lead to an increase in fixed costs by $9,000.

**Required:**

(i) Prepare a product mix to maximise profits, assuming that workers are not given any special training. Also calculate the maximum possible profit.

(10 marks)

(ii) Evaluate whether the manager's recommendation of special training to be given to workmen is advisable for the company. Provide appropriate calculations.

(4 marks)

(b) A manufacturer makes a product in which the principal ingredient is chemical X. Presently, the manufacturer spends $1,000 p.a. on his supply of X. However, there is a strong possibility that the price may soon increase to four times its current price due to a worldwide shortage of the chemical. There is another chemical, Y, which the manufacturer could use in conjunction with a third chemical, Z, in order to give the same effect as chemical X. Chemical Y and Z would together cost the manufacturer $3,000 p.a. Their prices are unlikely to rise.

**Required:**

What action should the manufacturer take? Apply the maximin and minimax criterion for decision making and give two sets of solutions.

(6 marks)
**(20 marks)**

## 14. Marginal costing – Albion Plc

The managers of Albion Plc are reviewing the operations of the last month of the company in order to make operational decisions for the following month. Details of some of the products manufactured by the company are given below.

| Product | AR2 | GL3 | HT4 | XY5 |
|---|---|---|---|---|
| Selling price ($/unit) | 21 | 28.5 | 27.3 | |
| Material R2 (kg/unit) | 2 | 3 | 3 | |
| Material R3 (kg/unit) | 2 | 2.2 | 1.6 | 3 |
| Direct labour (hours/unit) | 0.6 | 1.2 | 1.5 | 1.7 |
| Variable production overheads ($/unit) | 1.1 | 1.3 | 1.1 | 1.4 |
| Fixed production overheads ($/unit) | 1.5 | 1.6 | 1.7 | 1.4 |
| Expected demand for next month (units) | 950 | 1,000 | 900 | |

Products AR2, GL3 and HT4 are sold to Albion's customers. Product XY5 is a component that is used in the manufacture of other products. Albion Plc manufactures a wide range of products in addition to those detailed above.

Material R2, which is not used in any other of Albion's products, is expected to be in short supply next month due to industrial action at a major producer of the material. Albion Plc has just received a delivery of 5,500 kg of Material R2. This is expected to be the amount held in stock at the start of next month. The company does not expect to be able to obtain further supplies of Material R2 unless it pays a premium price. The normal market price is $2·50 per kg.

Material R3 is available at a price of $2·00 per kg. Albion Plc does not expect any problems in securing supplies of this material. Direct labour is paid at a rate of $4·00 per hour.

Folam Limited has recently approached Albion Plc with an offer to supply a substitute for Product XY5 at a price of $10·20 per unit. Albion Plc would need to pay an annual fee of $50,000 for the right to use this patented substitute.

**Required:**

(a) Determine the optimum production schedule for Products AR2, GL3 and HT4 for the following month, on the assumption that additional supplies of Material R2 are not purchased.

(8 marks)

(b) If Albion Plc decides to purchase further supplies of Material R2 to meet demand for Products AR2, GL3 and HT4, what should be the maximum price per kg that the company is prepared to pay?

(3 marks)

(c) Discuss whether Albion Plc should manufacture Product XY5 or buy the substitute offered by Folam Limited. Your answer must be supported by appropriate calculations.

(7 marks)

(d) 'Fixed costs are irrelevant for short-term decision-making' – does this make marginal costing less reliable as a decision-making technique?

(2 marks)
**(20 marks)**
(Adapted from Paper 2.4 June 2003)

## 14: Decision Making Techniques

### 15. Production planning and shadow pricing - Chivassa Ronald

Chivassa Ronald is a company that manufactures catalysts that uses a very scarce mineral powder. Its two main catalysts are caramium and corrum. The mineral powder, available at select pharmaceutical manufacturers, is in short supply. The supply is restricted to 8,100 kg and costs $60 per kg.

CR specialises in manufacturing these catalysts which are widely used by doctors for medical research. The skilled workmen who are involved in preparing the catalysts are trained for one year, by the only two experienced specialists who have the knowledge of the original chemical combination. In the current budget period these workmen can work for only 18,000 hours. They are paid at $27 per hour.

The products are prepared in boxes of 1 kg each. There is generally a ready market available for it. However this year the market has gone down. They can now sell only 16,000 boxes of caramium and 12,000 boxes of corrum in the current period.

The selling price and the resource requirements per box are given below:

|  | Caramium | Corrum |
| --- | --- | --- |
| Selling price | $61.5 | $103.50 |
| Workman time per box (hrs) | 0.75 | 1.125 |
| Mineral powder per box | 405 g | 405 g |
| Other variable costs | $1.80 | $7.05 |

**Required:**

(a) Using the graphical approach to solving linear programming problems, prepare an optimal production plan for CR. Identify the optimal product mix of caramium boxes and corrum boxes that will maximise contribution.

(15 marks)

(b) What is shadow pricing? Calculate the per unit shadow price for workmen time and mineral powder in the above case?

(5 marks)
**(20 Marks)**

### 16. Decision making – Spice Shock

Spice Shock is a manufacturer of a spice mix that is made from a combination of 20 different herbs and spices which makes a unique blend which is used in the preparation of curry. The blend that the company prepares is a well-guarded secret. The various ingredients are ordered from different suppliers so that no single supplier can identify all the ingredients. Its spice mix is an established brand in the market and sells at a price of $71.97 per 100g pack.

Spice Shock is in the process of preparing a new blend, Spice Magic (SM), by altering the existing spice combination. In doing this it intends to add a rare flavour enhancer, MHA. It is known to induce a unique flavour and aroma to food. A market survey costing $4,500 has revealed that the aroma of this spice is difficult to resist. The product can hence be sold in the market at a higher price of $134.5 per 100g pack.

However, the ill effects of this additive have been a topic of debate in health organisations, since it is known to induce an addictive habit amongst the users and hence can be harmful neurologically. Being an established brand Spice Shock may have to consider the adverse effects on the brand image.

The company wishes to produce the new spice mix Spice magic (SM) on a test basis for some part of its production capacity. The normal production capacity is 10,000 kgs per month. The company wants to produce an output of 1,000 kgs of the new spice mix in the coming month.

The existing spice mix contains 98% of the base and 2% spices. The base costs $36 per kg and the spices blend costs $20,000 per kg. The labour required for 1,000 kg is 2,000 hours @ $27. The new spice blend SM will contain 10 kgs of MHA costing $35,550 to the existing spice blend which will accordingly increase the volume by 10 kgs. The process losses are assumed to be zero in all stages.

Spice Shock currently has the extra machine capacity to complete this production. Since the product is new and the existing labour does not have knowledge of the spice mix a senior manager will spend 40% of his time supervising the project. The salary of the senior manager is $63,000. Spare labour capacity is, however, not available and hence existing labour will have to be diverted to prepare the SM. 1200 labour hours will be required to produce SM. Overhead allocation is $45 per kg for all products.

**Required:**

(a) Without providing any calculations, list the various considerations that should be taken into account while deciding whether to manufacture SM.

(4 marks)

(b) Evaluate whether manufacturing SM would be profitable for Spice Shock using the given information.

(14 marks)

(c) Calculate the selling price per kg if Spice magic wants to earn an incremental profit of $250,000.

(2 marks)
**(20 marks)**

### 17. Profit forecasting model

An essential aspect of financial and business planning is concerned with estimating costs and revenues and deciding the optimum output and price levels. A company produces a single product and operates in a market where it has to lower the retail price of all its units, if it wishes to sell more. The company's costing and marketing departments currently use the following cost and revenue model (all output is sold in the current period).

**Current Model**

Total Costs = 5,000 + 0·6x
Total Revenue = 20x - 0·01$x^2$

Where x = the number of units sold
The company has recently updated its cost and revenue model:

**Revised model**

Total Costs = 4,750 + 0·8x
Total Revenue = 19x - 0·009$x^2$

The acceptability of the current model and the proposed changes as a basis for profit planning and for monitoring performance is to be reviewed.

**Required:**

(a) Explain the structure of the current and the revised model.

(4 marks)

(b) It has been estimated that the revised model will result in an optimal output of 1,011 units being produced and sold.

(i) Suggest two alternative ways to determine the optimal level of output.

(3 marks)

(ii) Discuss the extent to which adherence to this output target is a satisfactory indicator of managerial performance.

(3 marks)

(c) Name and comment on cost and revenue factors which should be considered in order to improve the validity of the model, as a profit forecasting model.

(10 marks)
**(20 marks)**
(Paper 3.3 December 2002)

## 18. Swot analysis, Pricing strategies – Alocin Plc

Alocin Plc is a well-established manufacturer of high quality consumer durables. The company has recently developed a state of the art 'travel system' i.e. baby carriage for infant children. The travel system, named the 'Cruiser' is manufactured from a rare substance (CLO), which gives it superior strength, to any other travel system that is currently on the market. The marketing director believes that the fact the 'Cruiser' weighs less than half of the weight of all currently available travel systems will give the company a considerable competitive advantage. Alocin plc also manufactures another travel system called the 'Glider' which is manufactured from material DMP.

The following information is available in respect of the year ending 31 December 20X5:

(i) Each Cruiser requires 2 kilograms of CLO.

(ii) Each kilogram of CLO costs $60.

(iii) The labour cost of manufacturing a 'Cruiser' is estimated at $40 per unit.

(iv) Variable overheads are estimated to be $20 per unit.

(v) Incremental fixed costs relating to the 'Cruiser' are estimated to be $31·5 million.

(vi) The marketing director has estimated that at a selling price of $500 per Cruiser, an annual sales volume of 500,000 units would be achieved. He has further estimated that an increase/decrease in price of $20 will cause quantity demanded to decrease/increase by 25,000 units. He has provided you with the following formulae:

Price function: $P_q = P_0 - bq$

Total revenue (TR) function: $= P_0 q - bq^2$

Marginal revenue (MR) function: $= P_0 - 2bq$

**Where,**

$P_0$ = Price at zero units of demand,
$P_q$ = Price at q units of demand,
b = price: demand relationship,
q = Units of demand.

**Required:**

(a) Calculate the profit maximising output level for sales of the 'Cruiser' and the profit that would arise from those sales during the period ending 31 December 2009.

(6 marks)

(b) Explain the ways in which each of the following may affect the pricing strategies that the management of Alocin plc might adopt for the 'Cruiser':

(i) Cost leadership
(ii) Product differentiation

(6 marks)

(c) Explain the benefits and potential limitations of the use of SWOT analysis by the management of Alocin Plc. Your answer should include a brief comment with respect to the formulation of a pricing strategy for the 'Cruiser'.

(8 marks)
**(20 marks)**
**(Adapted from Paper 3.3 December 2004)**

## 19. Shut down vs. continue and make vs. buy – Mariam Inc and Fast Pro

(a) Mariam Inc manufactures a special electronic equipment which it sells for $150. Having its head office in New York it has factories at New Jersey, Chicago and Dallas.

Recession has caused the market for the product to decline and as a result the sales manager has forecast that this year sales will be 16.67% lower than that for the year ended 31 December 20X8. Neither the selling price nor the cost will change during the year.

Management is considering closing down the factory at one of the locations and changing / increasing the output levels of one or both of the remaining locations to maintain the same sales level. This will however be subject to the change in the market demand.

The income statement for the year ended 31 December 20X8 is given below:

|  | Factories ($'000) | | |
|---|---|---|---|
|  | New Jersey | Chicago | Dallas |
| Direct Materials | 1,200 | 4,800 | 2,400 |
| Direct Wages | 600 | 3,000 | 1,440 |
| Prime cost | 1,800 | 7,800 | 3,840 |
| Variable production overhead | 150 | 840 | 360 |
| Fixed production overhead | 750 | 2,640 | 1,200 |
| Production cost | 2,700 | 11,280 | 5,400 |
| Administrative overhead | 300 | 1,800 | 840 |
| Variable selling overhead | 300 | 1,440 | 480 |
| Fixed selling overhead | 450 | 1,560 | 1,080 |
| Head office costs | 300 | 1,200 | 600 |
| Total costs | 4,050 | 17,280 | 8,400 |
| Profit | 450 | 720 | 600 |
| Sales | 4,500 | 18,000 | 9,000 |

**Additional data**

1. Costs of closing down each factory can be ignored; it has been forecast that the cost will be offset by the sale of the plant etc.,

2. In general, there is sufficient capacity available at each factory to undertake additional production, if required. Each factory could increase its output up to twice the past year's level without a need for major investment. However additional supervision and storage will be required. This will result in additional cost forecast as follows:

    New Jersey: $500,000, Chicago: $1,000,000 and Dallas: $700,000

3. Transport costs would be affected if one of the factories were closed down. This is because incremental transport costs would have to be incurred in order to cater to the customers of the area where the factory has closed down. The transport of materials will be from a central warehouse. The incremental costs associated with transport to each area are as follows:

    |  | $ |
    |---|---|
    | To factory New Jersey area | 10 |
    | To factory Chicago area | 15 |
    | To factory Dallas area | 12 |

**Required:**

You are required to evaluate the possibility of closing down one of the factories, and changing the output of one or both of the remaining two factories, to maximise profits.

(8 marks)

(b) Fast Pro Inc produces four different products, the demand for which keeps fluctuating. The company has been able to raise its production from 6,450 tonnes in 20X7 to 8,650 tonnes in 20X8. Even though the demand is rising the company has almost reached the full capacity. It cannot increase its production over the levels achieved in 2008 as there is an acute shortage of the type of skilled labour required by Fast Pro.

## 18: Decision Making Techniques

The following data relates to 20X6:

| Products | A | B | C |
|---|---|---|---|
| Output (Tonnes) | 2,280 | 3,400 | 1,740 |
|  | $ per tonne | $ per tonne | $ per tonne |
| Selling price | 64,800 | 46,560 | 39,680 |
| **Costs:** | | | |
| Direct wages | 7,840 | 5,200 | 3,960 |
| Direct materials | 26,080 | 19,600 | 16,400 |
| Direct packing | 3,360 | 2,960 | 2,240 |
| Fixed overheads (on basis of direct wages) | 15,680 | 10,400 | 7,920 |
| **Total** | **52,960** | **38,160** | **30,520** |

Another company, PQR has recently offered to supply 1,000 tonnes of product B. It would charge a price equivalent to 90% of the selling price of Fast Pro Inc. Due to this, Fast Pro will be able to produce an extra quantity of product A so that it utilises its full capacity.

**Required:**

(i) Advise, with supporting calculations, whether Fast Pro Inc should accept PQR Inc's offer.

(4 marks)

(ii) If PQR Inc's offer was not restricted to product B, but was equally valid for the other products, advise which combination of sub-contracting 1,000 tonnes of one of its products would be most profitable.

(8 marks)
**(20 marks)**

## 20. Expected value – Shifters Haulage

Shifters Haulage (SH) is considering changing some of the vans it uses to transport crates for customers. The new vans come in three sizes; small, medium and large. SH is unsure about which type to buy. The capacity is 100 crates for the small van, 150 for the medium van and 200 for the large van.

Demand for crates varies and can be either 120 or 190 crates per period, with the probability of the higher demand figure being 0·6.

The sale price per crate is $10 and the variable cost $4 per crate for all van sizes subject to the fact that if the capacity of the van is greater than the demand for crates in a period then the variable cost will be lower by 10% to allow for the fact that the vans will be partly empty when transporting crates.

SH is concerned that if the demand for crates exceeds the capacity of the vans then customers will have to be turned away. SH estimates that in this case goodwill of $100 would be charged against profits per period to allow for lost future sales regardless of the number of customers that are turned away.

Depreciation charged would be $200 per period for the small, $300 for the medium and $400 for the large van.

SH has in the past been very aggressive in its decision-making, pressing ahead with rapid growth strategies. However, its managers have recently grown more cautious as the business has become more competitive.

**Required:**

(a) Explain the principles behind the maximax, maximin and expected value criteria that are sometimes used to make decisions in uncertain situations.

(5 marks)

(b) Prepare a profits table showing the SIX possible profit figures per period.

(9 marks)

(c) Using your profit table from (b) above discuss which type of van SH should buy taking into consideration the possible risk attitudes of the managers.

(6 marks)
**(20 marks)**
**(Adapted from December 2008)**

## 21. Contribution - Higgins

Higgins Co (HC) manufactures and sells pool cues and snooker cues. The cues both use the same type of good quality wood (ash) which can be difficult to source in sufficient quantity. The supply of ash is restricted to 5,400 kg per period. Ash costs $40 per kg.

The cues are made by skilled craftsmen (highly skilled labour) who are well known for their workmanship. The skilled craftsmen take years to train and are difficult to recruit. HC's craftsmen are generally only able to work for 12,000 hours in a period. The craftsmen are paid $18 per hour.

HC sells the cues to a large market. Demand for the cues is strong, and in any period, up to 15,000 pool cues and 12,000 snooker cues could be sold. The selling price for pool cues is $41 and the selling price for snooker cues is $69.

Manufacturing details for the two products are as follows:

|  | Pool cues | Snooker cues |
|---|---|---|
| Craftsmen time per cue | 0·5 hours | 0·75 hours |
| Ash per cue | 270 g | 270 g |
| Other variable costs per cue | $1·20 | $4·70 |

HC does not keep inventory.

**Required:**

(a) Calculate the contribution earned from each cue.

(2 marks)

(b) Determine the optimal production plan for a typical period assuming that HC is seeking to maximise the contribution earned. You should use a linear programming graph (using the graph paper provided), identify the feasible region and the optimal point and accurately calculate the maximum contribution that could be earned using whichever equations you need.

(13 marks)

Some of the craftsmen have offered to work overtime, provided that they are paid double time for the extra hours over the contracted 12,000 hours. HC has estimated that up to 1,200 hours per period could be gained in this way.

(c) Explain the meaning of a shadow price (dual price) and calculate the shadow price of both the labour (craftsmen) and the materials (ash).

(5 marks)
**(20 marks)**
**(Adapted from June 2008)**

## 22. Budgeted sales mix - Nerville

(a) Nerville makes and sells a range of three gardening products.

Budgeted data for the next year are:

| Product | E375 | F294 | G142 |
|---|---|---|---|
| Sales volume (units) | 20,000 | 17,000 | 16,000 |
| Selling price per unit | $250·00 | $300·00 | $170·00 |
| Direct costs per unit: |  |  |  |
| Materials | $47·50 | $52·75 | $38·30 |
| Labour | $28·88 | $32·80 | $21·32 |
| Royalties | $5·00 | $7·00 | $4·80 |
| Production overheads | $73·92 | $95·04 | $42·24 |

Production overheads are absorbed on a machine hours basis, at a rate of $52·80 per machine hour. 40% of overheads are estimated to be fixed.

A total of 73,000 machine hours are available for the next year.

## 20: Decision Making Techniques

**Required:**

Based on the budgeted sales mix, calculate:

(i) the number of units of each product which will be sold at the break-even point;

(10 marks)

(ii) the margin of safety, expressed as a % of budgeted sales revenue.

(2 marks)

(b) Following the collation of the budgeted data provided in (a), new safety legislation was introduced. The following changes will apply as a result of the legislation:

(i) additional features must be incorporated into all products at a cost of $8 per unit;
(ii) the machinery must be upgraded at a cost of $80,000;
(iii) the upgrade will not create any additional machine hours;
(iv) the machine hours required for each product will increase by 5%

The marketing manager has stated that the selling price of E375 and F294 cannot be changed, but that an increase of $2 per unit in the selling price of product G142 will be possible.

**Required:**

Calculate the number of units of each product which should be produced in order to maximise the profit for the next year.

(8 marks)
**(20 marks)**
**(Paper Dip FM December 2008)**

### 23. Contribution per limiting factor – Bookem Co

Bookem Co offers customers an on-line booking service for package holidays, tickets for events, and flights.

The projected results for the current year are:

|  | Holidays $000 | Tickets for events $000 | Flights $000 |
|---|---|---|---|
| Sales revenue | 7,685 | 3,770 | 3,045 |
| Direct costs | (5,870) | (2,670) | (2,260) |
| Share of central costs | (1,157) | (845) | (767) |
| **Profit** | **658** | **255** | **18** |

The direct costs are made up of the cost of buying the various services from the providers and other costs incurred by Bookem to operate and promote that line of business. With the exception of advertising costs of $2,972,900, the direct costs are considered to be variable. The price charged to the customer is calculated by adding a standard mark up to the cost of buying the service from the provider.

The analysis of the advertising costs is:

| Holidays $000 | Tickets $000 | Flights $000 |
|---|---|---|
| 1,766·21 | 773·69 | 433·00 |

The central costs, which are considered to be fixed, are allocated to the lines of business on the basis of the usage of the central computer system, at a rate of $65 per processing hour.

The directors are considering whether to undertake a further investment in the booking system. They have received a quote of $819,000 for the upgrade, which will have a useful life of three years and will increase processing capacity by 13%. They estimate that the following cost increases will occur in the incoming year:

**Advertising**

| | |
|---|---|
| Holidays | $160,000 |
| Tickets | $55,000 |
| Flights | $35,000 |
| Central costs before system upgrade | $215,000 |

© GTG                                                                                                                                         Question Bank: 21

The directors have asked you to investigate:

(i)   the profitability of each line of business, based on the contribution per processing hour;
(ii)  the total revenue which must be generated in the incoming year to increase the company's profit by 10%; and
(iii) whether the booking system upgrade will provide sufficient processing hours to generate the revenue required to achieve the profit target

For the purposes of your investigation, the directors do not anticipate any change in either:

(i)  the proportion of total revenue which is generated by each line of business; or
(ii) the contribution per processing hour for each line of business

**Required:**

(a) Calculate:
   (i) the profitability of each line of business, based on the contribution per processing hour;

   (5 marks)

   (ii) the total revenue which Bookem must generate to meet the directors' target of a 10% increase in profit in the incoming year; and

   (5 marks)

(b) whether the upgraded system will provide sufficient processing hours to generate the revenue required to achieve the profit target.

   (6 marks)

(c) Briefly discuss the limitations of your analysis in (a).

   (4 marks)
   **(20 marks)**
   **(Paper Dip FM June 2007)**

### 24. Profit forecasting - Recco

Recco, a limited liability company, makes three products which are sold to manufacturers of luxury cars. The company's profitability has been declining recently and the directors are considering a number of possible options.

The following product data has been collected:

| Product                | Robin    | Eagle    | Hawk     |
|------------------------|----------|----------|----------|
| Selling price per unit | $400·00  | $470·00  | $320·00  |
| Material cost per unit | $92·60   | $83·20   | $57·90   |
| Labour hours per unit  | 1·2      | 0·9      | 1·4      |
| Machine hours per unit | 4·0      | 5·5      | 2·5      |

The labour cost is $54·50 per labour hour. Variable overheads are incorporated into product cost on a machine hour basis at a pre-determined rate of $34·70 per hour.

At present, capacity is 44,000 machine hours per annum.

Fixed costs are $680,000 per annum.

Three possible options to halt the decline in profitability have been suggested:

**1. Increase production capacity**

An investment of $1,400,000 would provide an additional 11,200 machine hours per annum. The investment would have a useful life of three years.

The marketing director estimates that if the selling price of each product is maintained at the present level, annual sales volumes will be:

Robin – 5,200 units; Eagle – 3,100 units; Hawk – 6,700 units.

## 2. Improve product quality

A change in the production process would increase the machine hours for each unit produced by:

Robin – 0·2 hours; Eagle – 0·3 hours; Hawk – 0·1 hours

This would improve product quality, and would allow sales prices to be increased by 5%. To ensure that customers are aware of the improved quality, a marketing campaign would be required. This campaign will cost $875,000 in the next year and $640,000 per annum for each of the next two years.

The anticipated annual sales volumes would be:

Robin – 5,800 units; Eagle – 4,400 units; Hawk – 7,900 units.

## 3. Preferred supplier contract

The marketing director is aware that one of Recco's customers would be interested in entering into a 'preferred supplier' contract. It would be a term of the contract that Recco would not sell the same product to any other manufacturer.

The customer has indicated that they would contract to purchase 5,200 Eagle units per annum, and as many units of either Robin or Hawk as Recco can produce.

**Required:**

(a) Calculate the profit which would be generated by each of the three options under consideration.
(Note: marks are equally divided across each option. The time value of money should be ignored.)

(18 marks)

(b) Briefly indicate the action the directors should take, based on the available information.

(2 marks)
**(20 marks)**
**(Paper Dip FM December 2006)**

## 25. Relevant cost – PF201

You are part of a project team working on the development of an improved design for the warning system for a passenger ferry. This project has been given the code PF201. An impending change in legislation means that a modification to the fire warning system is required. This modification will add $2·4m to the development costs and will also require an engineering team to be transferred from another project (BR156) which is close to completion.

The engineering team will be required to work on the ferry project for four weeks at cost of $112,500 per week. The transfer of the team will delay the completion of project BR156, reducing the number of units which will be sold. Data relating to the two projects is given below:

| Project | Note | PF201 | BR156 |
|---|---|---|---|
| Cost to date | 1 | $3·35m | $32·86m |
| Costs to complete | 2 | $31·14m | $0·75m |
| Expected sales volumes (units): | | | |
| Year 1 | 3 | 40 | 25 |
| Year 2 | | 55 | 30 |
| Year 3 | | 50 | 20 |
| Selling price per unit | | $1·43m | $2·86m |
| Variable cost per unit | | $1·12m | $1·96m |
| Standard hours per unit | 4 | 700 | 1,100 |

| Note 1 | It is the company's policy to recover development costs over the first three years of a project's life. If the project is abandoned, costs incurred to date cannot be recovered and must be written off against profit in the accounting period in which the project is abandoned. |
|---|---|
| Note 2 | The costs relating to Project PF201 are before the transfer of the engineering team. |
| Note 3 | Expected sales volumes do not take into account the effect of the transfer of the engineering team. The delay resulting from the transfer of the engineering team is expected to lead to a loss of the sale of three units of Project BR156 in the first year. The sale of these units will not be recovered in subsequent periods. |
| Note 4 | The company absorbs fixed costs on the basis of standard hours at a rate of $100 per standard hour. |

The project manager has shown you a memo from the Managing Director which includes the following comments:

'You will be aware that the company requires all projects to generate a profit over the first three years in which sales are made. The calculation of profit should include the full write off of development costs. When external factors lead to a major change in the resources required for a project, a revised assessment should be carried out. This is to establish if the profit objective is still likely to be achieved. Such an assessment should take full account of sunk costs and opportunity costs. If the revised assessment indicates that the project will not generate a profit over the first three years, it should not be continued.

Please let me have your assessment of Project PF201, based on these criteria.'

The project manager does not know what is meant by the terms 'sunk costs' and 'opportunity costs'. He has asked you to explain these terms and to prepare the revised assessment.

**Required:**

(a) Define, and in relation to Project PF201, give an example of:
  (i) sunk cost
  (3 marks)
  (ii) opportunity cost
  (2 marks)
  (iii) relevant cost
  (2 marks)

(b) Prepare the revised assessment of Project PF201, and indicate whether or not it should be continued.
  (13 marks)
  **(20 marks)**
  **(Paper Dip FM June 2004)**

### 26. Make or buy – Culum Ltd

Culum Ltd produces three products. The company has an established, but static, domestic market for its products.

The management team is concerned that the market may have reached maturity with the result that, while demand is expected to remain stable for the foreseeable future, the long term outlook is difficult to predict.

You are a member of a project team which has been asked to consider the options available to the company and report to the management team.

Your team has undertaken market research which confirms the view of domestic demand. In addition, a potential export market has been researched. This has indicated that the level of demand can be influenced by marketing activity. The research has provided the following data with regard to marketing expenditure and potential sales in the export market for the next year:

| Annual Demand (units) ||| Marketing expenditure | Probability |
|---|---|---|---|---|
| Standard | Premium | Deluxe | | |
| 1,300 | 800 | 600 | $60,000 | 0·55 |
| 1,100 | 600 | 550 | $40,000 | 0·35 |
| 900 | 500 | 400 | $20,000 | 0·10 |

The market research has indicated that customers are likely to be strongly influenced by their perception of the company's commitment to a particular market and consequently the company must decide whether to serve the domestic market or the export market.

Last year's sales in the domestic market were:

| Standard | 1,200 units |
|---|---|
| Premium | 700 units |
| Deluxe | 500 units |

Cost and product data is:

|  | Standard | Premium | Deluxe |
|---|---|---|---|
| Labour hours per unit | 1·8 | 2·6 | 3·2 |
| Material cost per unit | $102 | $165 | $180 |
| Selling price per unit | $400 | $700 | $900 |

Labour costs are $50 per labour hour and variable overheads are absorbed on a labour hour basis at a rate of $40 per hour. Fixed costs are $120,000 per annum.

**Required:**

(a) Calculate the profit which the company can expect from:
  (i) continuing to sell in the domestic market; and

(5 marks)

  (ii) entering the export market.

(7 marks)

(b) Draft a brief report to the Managing Director which discusses the options that are available to the company and highlights issues which should be considered before a final decision is made.

(8 marks)
**(20 marks)**
**(Paper Dip FM December 2003)**

# QUESTION BANK

## SECTION C: BUDGETING

### 27. Zero-based budgeting – NN Ltd

NN Ltd manufactures and markets a range of electronic office equipment. The company currently has a turnover of $40 million per annum. The company has a functional structure and currently operates an incremental budgeting system. The company has a budget committee that is comprised entirely of members of the senior management team. No other personnel are involved in the budget-setting process.

Each member of the senior management team has enjoyed an annual bonus of between 10% and 20% of their annual salary for each of the past five years. The annual bonuses are calculated by comparing the actual costs attributed to a particular function with budgeted costs for that function during the twelve month period ending 31 December in each year.

A new Finance Director, who previously held a senior management position in a 'not for profit' health organisation, has recently been appointed. Whilst employed by the health service organisation, the new Finance Director had been the manager responsible for the implementation of a zero-base budgeting system which proved highly successful.

**Required:**

(a) As the new Finance Director, prepare a memorandum to the senior management team of NN Ltd which identifies and discusses factors to be considered when implementing a system of zero-based budgeting within NN Ltd. State how NN Ltd will benefit from this.

(16 marks)

(b) Explain how the implementation of a zero-based budgeting system in NN Ltd may differ from the implementation of such a system in a 'not for profit' health organisation.

(4 marks)
**(20 marks)**
**(Paper 3.3 June 2004)**

### 28. Budget preparation - Sine Ltd

Sine Ltd produces a single product, Product DG, and is preparing budgets for the next three-month period, July to September. The current cost data for Product DG is as follows:

|  |  | $ |
|---|---|---|
| Direct Material X | 1.5kg at 3·50 per kg | 5·25 |
| Direct Material P | 2.0kg at 4·50 per kg | 9·00 |
| Direct labour | 12minutes at $8·00 per hour | 1·60 |
| Variable production overhead | $1.00 per unit | 1·00 |
| Fixed production overhead | $3.00 per direct labour hour | 0·60 |
|  |  | **17·45** |

Sine Ltd experiences seasonal changes in sales volumes, and forecast sales for the next four months are expected to be as follows:

| Month | July | August | September | October |
|---|---|---|---|---|
| Sales (units) | 30,000 | 35,000 | 60,000 | 20,000 |

It has been decided that opening stocks of finished goods in August and September must be 20% of the expected sales for the coming month. Closing stocks of finished goods in September must be 10% of the expected sales in October. Stocks of finished goods at the start of July are expected to be 4,000 units. Opening stocks of finished goods in July are valued at $69,800.

There will be 30,000 kg of Material X and 40,400 kg of Material P in stock at the start of July. These stocks will be bought in June at the current prices per kilogram for each material. Further supplies of Material X and Material P will need to be purchased for higher prices of $3·80 per kg for Material X and $4·80 per kg for Material P due to supplier price increases. Opening stocks of each material will remain at the same level as at the start of July.

In any given month, any hours worked in excess of 8,000 hours are paid at an overtime rate of $12·00 per hour.

Sine Ltd operates a FIFO (first in, first out) stock valuation system.

**Required:**

(a) Prepare the following budgets for July, August and September and in total for the three-month period:
  (i) Production budget, in units;
  (ii) Material usage budget, in kilograms;
  (iii) Production budget, in money terms.

(10 marks)

(b) Calculate the value of the closing stocks of finished goods at the end of the three-month period, and the value of cost of sales for the period.

(4 marks)

(c) Discuss the concept activity based budget and the limitations of this type of budget.

(6 marks)
**(20 marks)**
**(Adapted from Paper 2.4 June 2006)**

## 29. Sales forecasting – Storrs Plc

It is mid-June and the new managing director of Storrs Plc is reviewing sales forecasts for Quarter 3 of 2003, which begins on 1 July, and for Quarter 4. The company manufactures garden furniture and experiences seasonal variations in sales, which has made forecasting difficult in the past. Sales for the last two calendar years were as follows:

| Year | Quarter 1 $ | Quarter 2 $ | Quarter 3 $ | Quarter 4 $ |
|---|---|---|---|---|
| 2001 | 2,700,000 | 3,500,000 | 3,400,000 | 3,000,000 |
| 2002 | 3,100,000 | 3,900,000 | 3,600,000 | 3,400,000 |

Sales in Quarter 1 of 2003 were $3,600,000. There are two weeks to go until the end of Quarter 2 and the managing director of Storrs Plc is confident that it will achieve sales of $4,400,000 in this quarter.

The existing sales forecasts for the two remaining quarters of the year were made by the sales director (who has been with the company for several years) during last year's budget-setting process. These forecasts are $3,800,000 for Quarter 3 and $3,600,000 for Quarter 4. Budgets within Storrs Plc have traditionally been prepared and agreed by the directors of the company before being implemented by junior managers.

As a basis for revising the sales forecasts for the two remaining quarters of 2003, the management accountant of Storrs Plc has begun to apply time series analysis in order to identify the seasonal variations in sales. He has so far calculated the following centred moving averages, using a base period of four quarters.

| Year | Quarter 1 $ | Quarter 2 $ | Quarter 3 $ | Quarter 4 $ |
|---|---|---|---|---|
| 2001 | | | 3,200,000 | 3,300,000 |
| 2002 | 3,375,000 | 3,450,000 | 3,562,500 | 3,687,500 |

**Required:**

(a) Using the sales information and centred moving averages provided, and assuming an additive model, forecast the sales of Storrs Plc for Quarter 3 and Quarter 4 of 2003, and comment on the sales forecasts made by the sales director.
  (**Note:** that you are NOT required to use regression analysis)

(8 marks)

(b) Discuss the limitations of the sales forecasting method used in part (a).

(5 marks)

(c) Discuss the top-down and bottom-up approaches to budget setting. Briefly discuss the limitations of using these methods.

(7 marks)
**(20 marks)**
**(Adapted from Paper 2.4 June 2003)**

## 30. Learning rate - Sole Ltd

Sole Ltd produces shoes for children and supplies them to various schools. This year they have received a contract proposal from Marigold High School for 18,000 pairs of shoes in 12 equal batches. The management of Sole has decided to accept the proposal, only if it yields a net cash flow of $43,000.

The cost accountant of Sole Ltd had prepared estimates of the costs that would be incurred to complete the above order. Details of this estimate, along with the proposed sales price are given below.

|  | $ |  |
|---|---|---|
| Selling Price | 30,000 | per batch |
| Direct materials cost for the 1st batch | 12,500 | (adjusted for the cash discount) |
| Direct labour for first batch | 10,000 | per batch (1,000 hours at $10 per hour) |

The project manager of Sole Ltd. highlighted a few areas that need to be looked into:

1. As Marigold has placed a large order, they have negotiated the contract price as $30,000 per batch.
2. Sole Ltd. will require additional space. Hence, rent will rise to $5,000 per month.
3. Direct material costs for the production of the first three batches will be the same. The second three batches will cost 95% of the cost per batch of the first three batches. Thereafter, all the batches will cost 95% of the cost of the second three batches. All the purchases are made in cash; therefore the company can avail of 2% cash discount on the total cost.
4. The variable cost per pair of shoes is $1.75.
5. For the first seven batches a 90% learning curve will apply to the labour costs. After which the labour time utilized for production would be equal to the time of the 7th batch.

Note: at the learning rate of 0.9 (90%), the learning factor (b) would be -0.1520.

**Required:**

(a) Prepare a report showing the estimated net cash flows of the project.

(12 marks)

(b) Should Sole Ltd. accept the project? What measures can it take to increase the net cash flow of the project?

(5 marks)

(c) Calculate the time taken by the second batch if the actual rate of learning is:
- 80%
- 70%

Briefly explain which learning rate is faster, and quicker.

(3 marks)
**(20 marks)**

## 31. Learning curve concept - Labnew Ltd

Labnew Ltd is a company that manufactures products required by laboratory and testing technology companies. Recently they designed an advanced product. This machine can be used to test the tearing resistance of films, foils, paper, textiles, and laminated films. Hence, the company is expecting a large market share.

**Below are the figures showing the estimated cost and selling price of the first machine:**

|  | $ |
|---|---|
| Cost of material and components | 2,550 |
| Labour cost (150 hours @ $10 per hour) | 1,500 |
| Overheads (50% of labour cost) | 750 |
| Profit (25% of cost) | 1,200 |
| Selling price | 6,000 |

The manager of Labnew has identified some aspects related to the sale of the new product:

- The selling price of the equipment will be determined by the total cost plus 25%.
- The cost of material required per product will not change, even if greater quantities are produced.
- The management expects that the workers will learn and improve regularly. They anticipate a learning curve of 80%.

Labnew has been approached by a textile company, which is interested in purchasing the new product. The textile company has requested a quotation covering the following aspects:

- If we decide to buy the first eight machines assembled, what would be the price per machine?
- If we purchase the first machine manufactured, and immediately place an order for the second one, what would be the price for the second machine?
- If we are ready to wait for a while until Labnew sells two machines to other buyers, and then place an order for the third and the fourth machine, what would be the average price of these two machines?

**Required:**

(a) Explain how the selling price of a product can be established with the help of the learning curve. Also, point out, in brief, the other advantages of this theory, for managers, in relation to preparing budgets.

(4 marks)

(b) Identify the potential limitations of the learning curve concept.

(6 marks)

(c) For the above enquiries of the textile company, prepare price quotations.

(10 marks)
**(20 marks)**

## 32. Learning curve - Richard Designs

Richard Designs is a company that manufactures furniture. A furniture wholesaler, Ben Home Décor, has approached them to provide 200 identical sets of bedroom furniture. The bedroom set must include one king size bed, two side tables, one wardrobe and one dressing table. The wholesaler has asked Richard Designs to submit their tender for this proposal.

The material required for production will include wood, screws, etc. The estimated cost of material for 10 sets is $4,625.

According to the specifications of the order, Richard Designs have concluded that it will take 36 hours to craft out each bedroom set. A 85% learning curve will apply for further productions. Once the $75^{th}$ set is produced, the learning rate will cease. The time taken for the 75 set will apply to the remaining productions. Labour is available at the rate of $10 per hour. The company usually works 40,000 labour hours per annum.

The company usually utilises the high low method to analyse overheads. Overheads are accounted on the basis of labour hours worked. Below are the overhead costs for the past four months:

|         | Hours worked | Overhead cost $ |
|---------|--------------|-----------------|
| Month 1 | 3,720        | 46,000          |
| Month 2 | 3,680        | 45,440          |
| Month 3 | 3,760        | 46,440          |
| Month 4 | 3,840        | 46,720          |

**Note**: at the learning rate of 0.85 (85%), the learning factor (b) would be -0.2345

**Required:**

(a) As a manager of Richard Designs, calculate the total cost of the project in order to prepare the tender.

(13 marks)

(b) With a learning rate of 95%, it is given that the second bedroom set will take 32.4 hrs for production. Justify the calculation.

(2 marks)

(c) Incremental budgeting is often used while budgeting; however it has its own limitations. Justify the statement.

(5 marks)
**(20 marks)**

## 33. Learning curve and net cash flow – BFG Ltd

BFG Limited is investigating the financial viability of a new product the S-pro. The S-pro is a short-life product for which a market has been identified at an agreed design specification. The product will only have a life of 12 months.

© GTG	Question Bank: 29

The following estimated information is available in respect of S-pro:

1. Sales should be 120,000 in the year in batches of 100 units. An average selling price of $1,050 per batch of 100 units is expected. All sales are for cash.

2. An 80% learning curve will apply for the first 700 batches after which a steady state production time will apply, with the labour time per batch after the first 700 batches being equal to the time for the 700th batch. The cost of the first batch was measured at $2,500. This was for 500 hours at $5 per hour.

3. Variable overhead is estimated at $2 per labour hour.

4. Direct material will be $500 per batch of S-pro for the first 200 batches produced. The second 200 batches will cost 90% of the cost per batch of the first 200 batches. All batches from then on will cost 90% of the batch cost for each of the second 200 batches. All purchases are made for cash

5. S-pro will require additional space to be rented. These directly attributable fixed costs will be $15,000 per month.

A target net cash flow of $130,000 is required in order for this project to be acceptable.

**Note:** The learning curve formula is given on the formulae sheet. At the learning rate of 0.8 (80%), the learning factor (b) is equal to -0.3219.

**Required:**

(a) Prepare detailed calculations to show whether product S-pro will provide the target net cash flow.
(12 marks)

(b) Calculate what length of time then second batch will take if the actual rate of learning is:
   (i) 80%;
   (ii) 90%.

   Explain which rate shows the faster learning.
(3 marks)

(c) Suggest specific actions that BFG could take to improve the net cash flow calculated above.
(5 marks)
**(20 marks)**
**(Adapted from Pilot Paper)**

## 34. Learning curve – Henry Co

Henry Company (HC) provides skilled labour to the building trade. They have recently been asked by a builder to bid for a kitchen fitting contract for a new development of 600 identical apartments. HC has not worked for this builder before. Cost information for the new contract is as follows:

Labour for the contract is available. HC expects that the first kitchen will take 24 man-hours to fit but thereafter the time taken will be subject to a 95% learning rate. After 200 kitchens are fitted the learning rate will stop and the time taken for the 200th kitchen will be the time taken for all the remaining kitchens. Labour costs $15 per hour.

Overheads are absorbed on a labour hour basis. HC has collected overhead information for the last four months and this is shown below:

|         | Hours worked | Overhead cost $ |
|---------|--------------|-----------------|
| Month 1 | 9,300        | 115,000         |
| Month 2 | 9,200        | 113,600         |
| Month 3 | 9,400        | 116,000         |
| Month 4 | 9,600        | 116,800         |

HC normally works around 120,000 labour hours in a year.

HC uses the high low method to analyse overheads.

The learning curve equation is $y = ax^b$, where $b = \dfrac{\text{Log LR}}{\text{Log 2}} = -0.074$

# 30: Budgeting

**Required:**

(a) Describe THREE factors, other than the cost of labour and overheads mentioned above, that HC should take into consideration in calculating its bid.

(6 marks)

(b) Calculate the total cost including all overheads for HC that it can use as a basis of the bid for the new apartment contract.

(12 marks)

(c) If the second kitchen alone is expected to take 21·6 man-hours to fit demonstrate how the learning rate of 95% has been calculated.

(2 marks)
**(20 marks)**
**(Adapted from December 2008)**

## 35. Budgeting and forecasting – Track Co

Track Co provides raw cotton to textile mills. Robbie is appointed as an assistant management accountant in Track Co. He has been instructed by management to introduce a new forecasting technique with a view to improving the accuracy of the budgeting for the next budget to be produced for the year ended 31 December 20Y0.

Robbie used time series analysis and presented the following relationship between the quantum of raw cotton sold (S) and the required time frame (in quarters) (T) in which raw cotton has been sold.

S = 46.25 + 0.25T

Market trend analysis is predicted as shown below:

| Quarter | 1 | 2 | 3 | 4 |
|---|---|---|---|---|
| Raw cotton (tonne) | (2) | 2.5 | 1.5 | (1) |

Once T is predicted, Robbie hopes to use the values to predict the variable operating costs and fixed operating costs that Track Co will be subjected to in 20Y0.

To this end, he has provided the following operating cost data for 20X9.

| Raw cotton sold (tonne) | 47 | 49 | 40 | 32 |
|---|---|---|---|---|
| Total operating expenses incurred | 10,000,000 | 12,000,000 | 950,000 | 975,000 |

Inflation for the operating cost is expected to be 3.25% during 20X9 and 20Y0.

**Required:**

(a) Calculate the expected sales of raw cotton in the calendar year 20Y0.

(4 marks)

(b) Calculate the total expected operating cost for the year 20Y0, using regression analysis on the 20X9 data and allowing for inflation as appropriate.

(10 marks)

Note: the regression formula is given in the formula sheet.

Track Co operates incremental budgeting as one of their main budgeting techniques. They take a previous period's actual spend, adjust for any known changes to operations and then add a percentage for expected inflation in order to set the next period's budget.

(c) Describe two advantages and two disadvantages of Track Co in using incremental budgeting as its main budgeting technique.

(6 marks)
**(20 marks)**

# QUESTION BANK

## SECTION D: STANDARD COSTING AND VARIANCE ANALYSIS

### 36. Analysis of variances – Smart Ltd

Smart Ltd is a cable television company which operates from a number of locations in London. The accounting staffs regularly prepare financial control reports. The following is the budget related to the first three months of the current period.

|  |  | $ | $ |
|---|---|---|---|
| Sales | $16.55 x 25,000units |  | 413,750 |
| Direct material | AP 2.5kg @ $1.80 per kg | 112,500 |  |
| Direct material | AQ 1.25 kg @ $1.40 per kg | 43,750 |  |
| Direct labour | 2.20hrs @ $1.50 per hour | 82,500 |  |
| Fixed overheads |  | 31,250 | (270,000) |
| Profit |  |  | 143,750 |

Robin, the management accountant, recently reviewed the accounting operations, and has undertaken a cost investigation. He gathered the following actual data for a three month period:

|  |  | $ |
|---|---|---|
| Material AP | 61,838 Kg | 108,835 |
| AQ | 31,525 kg | 40,352 |
| Labour | 50,500 hours | 80,800 |
| Sales and production | 24,250 units | 394,790 |
| Fixed production overheads |  | 32,500 |

Robin has suggested adopting the variance analysis system to examine the performance of Smart Ltd. After conducting an investigation the following additional information was obtained:

➢ the purchasing manager purchased cheaper quality material from a new supplier to control the purchase cost

➢ the production manager increased the wages of labour in an expectation of an increase in labour efficiency and thereby an increase in sales revenue

**Required:**

(a) Calculate the following variances

 (i) Material price and usage variances,
 (ii) Labour rate and efficiency variances,
 (iii) Fixed overhead expenditure variances,
 (iv) Sales volume and price variances.

(12 marks)

(b) Comment on the performance of the purchasing manager and production manager, using the variances calculated in part (a).

(4 marks)

(c) Discuss the behavioural problems resulting from using standard costs, and ways to prevent them.

(4 marks)
**(20 marks)**

## 37. Variances and budgeting – Morse Plc

Morse Plc manufactures and sells a range of small kitchen appliances. Morse Plc has a budgetary control system to monitor revenue and costs and therefore exercise control.

The company is recovering from the recent recessions. Therefore, the company is operating at only 65% of normal capacity, producing 65,000 units in the current year. The directors of the company expect that the company will operate at 85% of its normal capacity.

Hence, Lewis, the management accountant, has recommended developing the current budgeting system and including a flexed budget.

The standard costs and selling price are as follows:

|  | $ |
|---|---|
| Direct material | 318,500 |
| Direct labour | 364,000 |
| Semi-variable overheads | 313,950 |
| Fixed production overheads | 227,500 |
| Sales | 1,625,000 |

**Note:** variable overhead included in semi-variable overheads is $3.71 per unit.

**Required:**

(a) Explain the importance of flexing budgets in performance management.

(4 marks)

(b) Prepare a revised budget at the new level of activity using a flexible budgeting approach.

(5 marks)

Morse Plc uses a standard costing system to ascertain the efficiency and effectiveness of cost performance. It compares actual results with standards to find out discrepancies and take corrective actions.

The fixed production overheads are allocated to the product on a machine hour basis. A total of 19,500 standard machine hours were budgeted for 65,000 units. A total of 25,700 machine hours were actually used in the three-month period.

The following actual results for 85% capacity were obtained at the end of three months:

|  | Actual | |
|---|---|---|
|  | $ | $ |
| Sales (a) |  | 2,210,000 |
| Less: Cost of sales |  |  |
| Direct material | 431,800 |  |
| Direct labour | 467,500 |  |
| Variable production overheads | 318,750 |  |
| Fixed production overheads | 381,130 |  |
| Total costs (b) |  | (1,599,180) |
| **Profit (a-b)** |  | **610,820** |

(c) Calculate the following variances:

(i) Direct material total cost variance,
(ii) Direct labour total cost variance,
(iii) Variable overhead total variance,
(iv) Fixed overhead efficiency variance,
(v) Fixed overhead capacity variance,
(vi) Fixed overhead expenditure variance.

(11 marks)
**(20 marks)**

## 38. Operational changes – Woodeezer Ltd

Woodeezer Ltd makes quality wooden benches for both indoor and outdoor use. Results have been disappointing in recent years and a new managing director, Peter Beech, was appointed to raise production volumes. After an initial assessment Peter Beech considered that budgets had been set at levels which made it easy for employees to achieve. He argued that employees would be better motivated by setting budgets which challenged them more in terms of higher expected output.

Other than changing the overall budgeted output, Mr Beech has not yet altered any part of the standard cost card. Thus, the budgeted output and sales for November 20X8 was 4,000 benches and the standard cost card below was calculated on this basis:

|  |  | $ Per unit |
|---|---|---|
| Wood | 25 kg @ $3.20 per kg | 80 |
| Labour | 4 hours @ $8 per hour | 32 |
| Variable overheads | 4 hours @ $4 per hour | 16 |
| Fixed overheads | 4 hours @ $16 per hour | 64 |
|  |  | 192 |
| Selling price |  | 220 |
| Standard profit |  | 28 |

Overheads are absorbed on the basis of labour hours and the company uses an absorption costing system. There were no inventories at the beginning of November 20X8. Inventories are valued at standard cost.

Actual results for November 20X8 were as follows:

|  | $ |
|---|---|
| Wood (80,000 kg @ $3.50) | 280,000 |
| Labour (16,000 hours @ $7) | 112,000 |
| Variable overhead | 60,000 |
| Fixed overhead | 196,000 |
| Total production cost (3,600 benches) | 648,000 |
| Closing inventory (400 benches @ $192) | 76,800 |
| Cost of sales | 571,200 |
| Sales (3,200 benches) | 720,000 |
| Actual profit | 148,800 |

The average monthly production and sales for some years prior to November 20X8 had been 3,400 units and budgets had previously been set at this level. Very few operating variances had historically been generated by the standard costs used.

Mr Beech has made some significant changes to the operations of the company. However, the other directors are now concerned that Mr Beech has been too ambitious in raising production targets. Mr Beech had also changed suppliers of raw materials to improve quality, increased selling prices, begun to introduce less skilled labour, and significantly reduced fixed overheads.

**Required:**

(a) Prepare an operating statement for November 20X8. This should show all operating variances and should reconcile budgeted and actual profit for the month for Woodeezer Ltd.

(14 marks)

(b) In so far as the information permits, examine the impact of the operational changes made by Mr Beech on the profitability of the company. In your answer, consider each of the following:

(i) Motivation and budget setting; and
(ii) Possible causes of variances.

(6 marks)
**(20 marks)**
**(Adapted from Paper 2.4 December 2002)**

## 39. Revised budget and Variances – Jackson Plc

Jackson Plc manufactures and retails leather bags. It follows the standard costing method for performance analysis. It accordingly calculates the variances, analyses the performance and identifies the reasons thereof. According to the marketing report, the raw material and labour prices are increasing, due to inflation. Therefore, Brown, the accounting manager, has come up with a suggestion for a revision of the budget plan to maintain the market share.

**Required:**

(a) Describe the circumstances under which a budget can be revised, and comment on Brown's suggestion of revising the budget plan.

(5 marks)

The budgeted output and sales of Jackson Plc are 5,000 units for 20X7. The selling price has been set at $390 per unit. The following is the budgeted production cost and selling prices of Jackson Plc for the year ended 31 December 20X7:

|  |  | $ |
|---|---|---|
| Material per unit | 15 metres @ $13.64 per metre | 204.60 |
| Labour charges per unit | 6.25 hours @ $6 per hour | 37.50 |
| Variable overheads per unit | 6.25 hours @ $3.15 per hour | 19.69 |
| **Fixed overheads** |  |  |
| Administrative expenses |  | 165,000 |
| Selling expenses |  | 51,000 |
| Distribution expenses |  | 64,000 |

In preparing the budget for the year 20X8, the company predicted the following increase in the cost and prices.

1. The material price per metre is expected to rise by 10% of the current price.

2. It is predicted that the cost of labour per hour will go up by $3. The variable overheads are expected to rise by 15% of the hourly labour rate.

3. A 20% growth is expected in the selling price per unit. Additional selling expenses of $40,000 will be incurred to maintain the current volume of sales.

(b) Prepare a revised budgeted statement showing expected profitability for 20X8 after taking into account the anticipated inflation effect on cost and price.

(5 marks)

The following actual results for the year ended 20X8 have been obtained:

|  |  | $ |
|---|---|---|
| Direct material per unit | (14 metres @ $16.75 per metre) | 234.50 |
| Labour charges per unit | (6.5 hours @ $8.20 per hour) | 53.30 |
| Variable overheads per unit | (7 hours @ $4.75 per hour) | 33.25 |
| Actual output | 4,500 units |  |

(c) Calculate the variances for 20X8 in detail with the use of the above information.

(10 marks)
**(20 marks)**

## 40. Sales variances – Simple Co

Simple Co manufactures and sells standard quality fuel pumps. Other companies integrate these pumps in their production of petrol engines. At present Simple Co manufactures only three different types of fuel pumps – oil pump, gas pump and diesel pump. Simon, the management accountant, allocates fixed overheads to these pumps on an absorption costing system.

The standard selling price and cost data for these three products for the last period are as follows:

|  | Oil Pump | Gas pump | Diesel pump |
|---|---|---|---|
| Direct material per unit | $35.10 | $26.65 | $31.52 |
| Selling price per unit | $91.00 | $97.50 | $117.00 |
| Direct labour per unit ($6.50 per hour) | 3.25 hrs | 5.20 hrs | 4.55 hrs |
| Machine hours per unit | 1.95 hrs | 3.90 hrs | 5.20 hrs |
| Budgeted production and sales (units) | 10,000 | 13,000 | 9,000 |

The total fixed production overhead for the last period was estimated in the budget to be $526,500. This was absorbed on a machine hour basis.

The board of directors has decided to calculate the variances for the period to analyse the sales performance of the company.

Therefore, the following information of actual volumes and selling prices for the three products in the last period was obtained:

| Products | Actual selling price per unit | Actual production and sales (units) |
|---|---|---|
| Oil Pump | $94.25 | 9,500 |
| Gas pump | $100.75 | 13,500 |
| Diesel pump | $123.50 | 8,500 |

**Required:**

(a) Calculate the following variances for overall sales for the last period:

    (i) Sales profit margin variance;
    (ii) Sales volume profit variance;
    (iii) Sales mix profit variance; and
    (iv) Sales quantity profit variance.

(9 marks)

(b) Prepare a statement showing the reconciliation of budgeted profit for the period to actual sales less standard cost.

(4 marks)

(c) Discuss the significance of the sales mix profit variance and comment on whether useful information would be obtained by calculating mix variances for each of these three products.

(4 marks)

(d) Comment on the sales performance of the business.

(3 marks)
**(20 marks)**

### 41. Analysis of variances – Tasty Treat Inc

Tasty Treat Inc bakes and sells chocolate chip cookies for children. The cookies are made using a highly standardised process. The main ingredients consist of wheat flour, butter and sugar. The company has a standard costing and variance system in place to control the manufacturing process. Tasty Treat employs a Purchase Manager, a Sales Manager, and a General Manager, but recognises a need for management at the production level.

So, in August, a new production manager, Jill, was recruited. She was to be in charge of the whole production process. In addition to her salary, Jill was to get a bonus, based on the directly attributable variances involved in the production process.

In October, during Jill's 3-month appraisal, it was observed that on the whole, the cost variances were favourable. However, the sales manager, John, in his sales report, brought to the managements notice that the sale of the cookies was decreasing significantly. This decrease in sales had an impact on the overall profitability of the company.

The following is the standard cost information for the three month period:

|  | $ |
|---|---|
| 1.35 kg of wheat flour @ $ 0.8 per kg | 1.080 |
| 0.075 kg of butter @ $4 per kg | 0.300 |
| 1.65 kg of sugar @ $ 0.50 per kg | 0.825 |
| **Total cost of production of 1 kg of cookies** | **2.205** |

The actual level of activity was approximately the same for every month during the three month period.

The following are the variances for the period under review:

|  | August $ | September $ | October $ |
|---|---|---|---|
| Material Price Variance | 450(F) | 1,350(A) | 3,300(A) |
| Material Mix Variance | 2,700(F) | 3,379.5(F) | 4,200(F) |
| Material Yield Variance | 3,189(F) | 8,766(F) | 14,628(F) |
| Total Variance | 6,339(F) | 10,795.5(F) | 15,528(F) |

**Required:**

(a) Explain material price, mix and yield variances. Discuss whether each type of variance is controllable by the production manager, and to what extent.

(6 marks)

(b) Evaluate the performance of the production manager, taking into account, the variances, as well as the sales report.

(5 marks)

The management wants to check the performance of the company in the fourth month, for which, it needs to know the variances for the month of November.

Actual production was 102,500 kg of cookies. Actual costs for the month of November were:

|  | $ |
|---|---|
| 123,000 kg of wheat flour | 104,550 |
| 7,350 kg of butter | 31,605 |
| 183,000 kg of sugar | 87,840 |

(c) Calculate the following variances with the use of the above information:

(i) Material Price Variance
(ii) Material Mix Variance
(iii) Material Yield Variance

**Note:** You are not required to comment on the performance of the company for the month of November.

(9 marks)
**(20 marks)**

## 42. Variances – Lumina Inc

Lumina Inc is a company engaged in manufacturing miniature lamps, used for Christmas decoration. Lamps are made on fully automatic machines, using two chief raw materials, tungsten filaments and glass tubing. The company employs semi-skilled labour to work the machines.

To survive in the competitive market, the management has decided to review the costs and sales prices of their product quarterly, with the help of a standard costing system.

Standard Fixed overheads allocated to production are $62,500. Budgeted sales set for a quarter are 50,000 lamps.

Lumina gives out the following other standard data for a three month period.

|  | Per unit $ |
|---|---|
| 3.75 g glass tubing @ $1.70 per g | 6.375 |
| 2.25 g tungsten filament @ $1.20 g | 2.70 |
| 0.675 hrs semi skilled labour @ $6.00 per hr | 4.05 |
| Sales price per lamp | 18.00 |

Actual figures relating to costs and sales for the period of October to December are:

|  | $ |
|---|---|
| 182,926 g glass tubing | 300,000 |
| 100,800 g tungsten filament | 126,000 |
| 28,800 hrs semi skilled labour (hrs actually worked: 28,350) | 175,680 |
| Total Sales | 871,200 |
| Fixed overheads allocated to production | 64,000 |

The quantity actually sold during this quarter was 48,000 lamps.

**Required:**

(a) Calculate the following variances:

   (i) Sales volume contribution variance,
   (ii) Sales Price Variance,
   (iii) Material price, mix and yield variances for both raw materials,
   (iv) Labour rate, efficiency and idle time variances.

(8 marks)

(b) Reconcile the budgeted profit to the actual profit.

(5 marks)

(c) Explain the types of standard costs and its effects on employee motivation.

(7 marks)
**(20 marks)**

### 43. Variances - Nice-look Ltd

Nice-look Ltd manufactures and sells various cosmetic products in the European market. Nice-look's perfumes, namely Jasmine, Rose and Sandal, are famous amongst ladies of all the ages. The following information is related to the budgeted sales for quarter January – March 20X8.

| Product | Units | Contribution per unit $ | Total contribution $ |
|---|---|---|---|
| Jasmine | 750 | 12 | 9,000 |
| Rose | 800 | 13 | 10,400 |
| Sandal | 675 | 11 | 7,425 |
| Total | 2,225 |  | 26,825 |

The following is the actual result obtained for each product in the quarter:

| Product | Units | Contribution per unit $ | Total contribution $ |
|---|---|---|---|
| Jasmine | 700 | 14.40 | 10,080.00 |
| Rose | 900 | 12.50 | 11,250.00 |
| Sandal | 650 | 11.25 | 7,312.50 |
| Total | 2,250 |  | 28,642.50 |

The estimated total market for perfumes in a period of three months was 22,250 units. However, the actual total market for perfumes increased to 25,000 units for this quarter.

**Required:**

(a) Calculate the total market size variance and market share variance.

(5 marks)

**The following additional details related to the production of Jasmine are available.**

Actual material and labour hours used to produce 700 units of Jasmine are as follows:

|  | $ |
|---|---|
| 32,550 ml of material | 78,120 |
| 1,400 hours of direct labour | 14,700 |
| Selling price per unit | 147 |

Standard selling price and cost data for one unit of Jasmine is as follows:

| Direct material | 45ml at $2.50 per ml |
|---|---|
| Direct labour | 90 minutes at $14 per hour |
| Selling price | $145.50 |

(b) Calculate the following variances for the product Jasmine:

   (i) Sales variances,
   (ii) Material variances,
   (iii) Labour variances.

(9 marks)

(c) Explain the three key purposes of a budgeting system.

(6 marks)
**(20 marks)**

## 44. Planning and operational variances – Kid-world

Kid-world is a manufacturer and leading exporter of children's toys. The company operates a standard costing system to analyse and control manufacturing processes.

The standard cost and selling price during the period of three months is as follows:

|  | Per unit |
|---|---|
| Direct material | $38.14 |
| Direct material usage | 7.05 kg |
| Direct labour | $84.60 |
| Direct labour hours | 3 hrs |
| Selling price | $74 |

At the end of the three month period, the following rapid changes occurred in material and labour prices.

1. Direct material price is raised to $5.57 per kg.
2. Direct labour increased by $1.13 per hour.
3. It was decided to adopt a new production process which may lead to 5% saving in material usage and 10% reduction in labour hours.

In a Board meeting, Alex, the management accountant stated that "The company produces a range of standardised toys. It has been observed over the last six months that prices of our raw material and labour costs have suddenly changed. Due to such changes we have planned to implement a new process to allow for the cheapest production cost.

Therefore, our predetermined standard is not a realistic target in the current business conditions. The change in prices is an external, uncontrollable situation." Alex has suggested the revision of the standard in consideration of the change that has occurred.

Alex has also opposed using a traditional approach to variance analysis. He has recommended separating out total variances into planning and operational variances to overcome the problem.

The following actual result is obtained:

| Direct material per unit | 6.58 kg @ $5.78 per kg |
| Direct labour per unit | 3.05 hrs @ $29.60 per hr |
| Selling price per unit | $74.00 |
| Actual sales | 52,000 units |

**Required:**

(a) Calculate each planning and operational variance using the information provided.

(11 marks)

(b) Calculate direct material and labour variances based on the standard cost data.

(2 marks)

(c) Discuss the factors that should be considered while deciding whether a variance should be investigated.

(7 Marks)
**(20 marks)**

## 45. Reconciliation of budgeted and actual profit – Ash Plc

Ash Plc recorded the following actual results for Product RS8 for the last month:

| Product RS8 | 2,100 units produced and sold for $14·50 per unit |
| Direct material M3 | 1,050 kg costing $1,680 |
| Direct material M7 | 1,470 kg costing $2,793 |
| Direct labour | 525 hours costing $3,675 |
| Variable production overhead | $1,260 |
| Fixed production overhead | $4,725 |

Standard selling price and cost data for one unit of Product RS8 is as follows.

| Selling price | $15·00 |
| Direct material M3 | 0·6 kg at $1·55 per kg |
| Direct material M7 | 0·68 kg at $1·75 per kg |
| Direct labour | 14 minutes at $7·20 per direct labour hour |
| Variable production overhead | $2·10 per direct labour hour |
| Fixed production overhead | $9·00 per direct labour hour |

At the start of the last month, 497 standard labour hours were budgeted for production of Product RS8. No stocks of raw materials are held. All production of Product RS8 is sold immediately to a single customer under a just-in-time agreement.

**Required:**

(a) Prepare an operating statement that reconciles budgeted profit with actual profit for Product RS8 for the last month. You should calculate variances in as much detail as allowed by the information provided.

(14 marks)

(b) Discuss how the operating statement you have produced can assist managers in:
(i) controlling variable costs;
(ii) controlling fixed production overhead costs.

(6 marks)
**(20 marks)**
**(Adapted from 2.4 June 2006)**

## 46. Sales variances – Spike Co

Spike Co manufactures and sells good quality leather bound diaries. Each year it budgets for its profits, including detailed budgets for sales, materials and labour. If appropriate, the departmental managers are allowed to revise their budgets for planning errors.

In recent months, the managing director has become concerned about the frequency of budget revisions. At a recent board meeting he said 'There seems little point budgeting any more. Every time we have a problem the budgets are revised to leave me looking at a favourable operational variance report and at the same time a lot less profit than promised.'

Two specific situations have recently arisen, for which budget revisions were sought:

**Materials**

A local material supplier was forced into liquidation. Spike Co's buyer managed to find another supplier, 150 miles away at short notice. This second supplier charged more for the material and a supplementary delivery charge on top. The buyer agreed to both the price and the delivery charge without negotiation. 'I had no choice', the buyer said, 'the production manager was pushing me very hard to find any solution possible!' Two months later, another, more competitive, local supplier was found.

A budget revision is being sought for the two months where higher prices had to be paid.

**Labour**

During the early part of the year, problems had been experienced with the quality of work being produced by the support staff in the labour force. The departmental manager had complained in his board report that his team were 'unreliable, inflexible and just not up to the job'.

It was therefore decided, after discussion of the board report that something had to be done. The company changed its policy so as to recruit only top graduates from good quality universities. This has had the effect of pushing up the costs involved but increasing productivity in relation to that element of the labour force.

The support staff departmental manager has requested a budget revision to cover the extra costs involved following the change of policy.

**Required:**

(a) Discuss each request for a budget revision, putting what you see as both sides of the argument and reach a conclusion as to whether a budget revision should be allowed.

(8 marks)

The market for leather bound diaries has been shrinking as the electronic versions become more widely available and easier to use. Spike Co has produced the following data relating to leather bound diary sales for the year to date:

**Budget**

| Sales volume | 180,000 units |
| Sales price | $17·00 per unit |
| Standard contribution | $7·00 per unit |

The total market for diaries in this period was estimated in the budget to be 1·8m units. In fact, the actual total market shrank to 1·6m units for the period under review.

**Actual results for the same period**

| Sales volume | 176,000 units |
| Sales price | $16·40 per unit |

**Required:**

(b) Calculate the total sales price and total sales volume variance.

(4 marks)

(c) Analyse the total sales volume variance into components for market size and market share.

(4 marks)

(d) Comment on the sales performance of the business.

(4 marks)

**(20 marks)**
**(Adapted from December 2007)**

## QUESTION BANK

# SECTION E: PERFORMANCE MEASUREMENT AND CONTROL

### 47. Performance Evaluation - Serene Bay

Serene Bay is an uptown restaurant overlooking the ocean. It serves a variety of cuisines, including Italian and Continental. Most of the customers are wealthy businessmen and high profile executives, looking for a peaceful dining experience.

Since buying the restaurant two years ago, the sole owner, Robert Green has carefully recorded the non financial data in addition to the usual financial data. He oversees the preparations himself, and is very particular about the quality of the food served.

The following is the financial, as well as the non financial information, based on the balanced scorecard format.

|  | 20X8 | 20X7 |
|---|---|---|
| **Financial Information** |  |  |
| Total Turnover ($'000) | 945 | 900 |
| Turnover from special events ($'000) | 300 | 200 |
| Cost attributable to special events ($'000) | 230 | 120 |
| Total Profit ($'000) | 169 | 130 |
| **Internal Business Processes** |  |  |
| Average service delay at peak times (mins) | 25 | 15 |
| Idle time (mins) | 486 | 540 |
| Reported cases of food poisoning | 7 | 4 |
| **Customer Satisfaction** |  |  |
| Regular customers attending weekly | 15 | 9 |
| Complimentary letters from satisfied customers | 4 | 1 |
| Average expenditure per customer ($) | 51 | 30 |
| **Learning and Growth** |  |  |
| Special theme evenings introduced | 2 | - |
| New entrées in the menu introduced during the year | 2 | 4 |
| Total proposals submitted to cater for special events | 8 | 3 |

**Required:**

(a) Taking only the financial data into consideration, comment on the financial performance of the restaurant, and compare it with the previous year.

(8 marks)

(b) Taking the non financial data into consideration, give your comments on each perspective of the balanced scorecard (excluding financial performance) and also on the overall performance of the restaurant.

(12 marks)
**(20 marks)**

## 42: Performance Measurement and Control

### 48. Balanced scorecard and building block - Fresh Foods

Fresh Foods is a company engaged in the business of collecting agriculture produce from farmers, processing the produce, and distributing it to the malls. The following is the statistical information related to the company's performance evaluation.

|  | 20X8 | 20X7 | Target |
| --- | --- | --- | --- |
| Revenue growth | 5.5% | 4% | Up to 6% |
| Average selling price per product ($) | 235 | 220 |  |
| Industry average selling price ($) | 240 to 250 | 230 to 240 |  |
| Number of malls buying Fresh Foods' products | 25 | 20 | Increase by 10% |
| Client retention rate | 50% | 46% | Increase by 5% |
| Employee retention rate | 77.5% | 78% | 79% |
| Wastage of raw material | 5% | 3% | 2.5% |
| Industry average | 2.5% | 3% |  |
| New products launched | 4 | 4 | 6 |
| Average time taken to launch a new product | 3 months | 3 months | 2 months |

**Required:**

(a) Explain a balanced scorecard. Also explain the building blocks model.

(6 marks)

(b) Assess the performance of Fresh Foods using the balanced scorecard.

(12 marks)

(c) Suggest two ways to improve the performance measurement system in Fresh Foods.

(2 marks)
**(20 marks)**

### 49. Not-for profit organisations, behavioural issues - Osho Spiritual Centre

Osho Spiritual Centre (OSC) offers yoga classes to people of all ages. As the popularity of yoga is increasing day by day, OSC has expanded its operations in the form of an additional three branches in various parts of the country. The sole owner of OSC, Lily Geller, employs four branch managers to oversee the operations of the four branches.

Every year, Lily Geller announces targets for the year and bonus policy is based on the targets given. For the current year, the bonus policy is as follows:

➢ if 95% to 100% of the targeted revenue is earned – 5% of annual salary
➢ if 100% to 105% of the targeted revenue is earned – 10% of annual salary and
➢ if more than 105% of the targeted revenue is earned – 20% of annual salary

However the above policy is subject to the following:

➢ the profit should not be less than 95% of the targeted profit and;
➢ remuneration to trainers should not exceed $147 per working day and hire expenses of exercise room should not be more than $52.5

The following is information for the year for Riverdale branch, provided by the branch manager, Richard:

|  | Actual ($) | Targets ($) |
| --- | --- | --- |
| Revenue | 176,450 | 169,000 |
| Net Profit | 28,500 | 30,000 |
| Remuneration to Trainers | 54,000 | Max 140 per working day |
| Exercise room hire expense | 19,800 | Max 50 per working day |

Working days are 360 per year.

Richard gives preference to the quality of services offered, as he believes that this will lead to the growth of OSC in the long-term. However, he feels that emphasis on quality may affect the financial performance in short-term and consequently he may not get the bonus.

**Required:**

(a) Asses the financial performance of OSC, considering the targets.

(8 marks)

(b) Discuss the chances of Richard being eligible for the bonus, and, if eligible, calculate the percentage of bonus he will get. Also, comment on the behavioural issues arising from the bonus policy.

(4 marks)

Siddha Yoga Foundation (SYF) is a not for profit organisation conducting yoga classes at a nominal fee. The objectives of SYF are as follows;

- to spread awareness of the ancient practice,
- to serve maximum members of the society,
- to provide service at minimum fees.

The financial data for the year is given below:

|  | $ |
|---|---|
| Sales | 68,200 |
| **Less: Costs** | |
| Yoga Instructors | (35,000) |
| Exercise room hire expense | (17,500) |
| Props cost (such as floor exercise mats, foam blocks, etc.) | (500) |
| Other costs | (10,000) |
| **Surplus** | **5,200** |

The number of working days is the same as those of OSC.

**Required:**

(c) Comment on the problems of having non quantifiable objectives in not for profit organisations.

(4 marks)

(d) Comment, with reasons, whether the financial data of the two organisations can be compared.

(4 marks)
**(20 marks)**

### 50. Financial and non-financial performance indicators - Concept Academy

Concept Academy is a new business, which publishes professional books. Concept carries out all the work related to writing and printing the books, and sells them world wide. In the first year it published six books and started production on another set of five books.

The management is confident that even if there are two competitors, their business will be successful and will grow quickly.

The management knows that the business will not earn any profit for them in the first few years, and are prepared for it.

The management believes that through a forum, Concept can reach target customers, and use it to create new business. The forum will indirectly be used for advertisement. Therefore in the second year, Concept created a forum where it invested significant money for its development. All the development costs for the forum were written off as incurred.

## 44: Performance Measurement and Control

Significant expenditure on launch marketing was incurred in the first two quarters of the second year. It is not expected that marketing expenditure will continue to be as high in the future, as they are the launching costs.

The following is the information for the first two quarters of the second year when Concept actually sold the books (six books written and printed in the first year were sold in the second year. There was no sale in the first year.)

|  | Quarter 1 $'m |  | Quarter 2 $'m |  |
|---|---|---|---|---|
| Sales |  | 5.25 |  | 8.20 |
| **Less**: Cost of sales (see note) |  | (2.50) |  | (4.40) |
| Gross profit |  | 2.75 |  | 3.80 |
| Less: Expenses |  |  |  |  |
| Forum development | 1.50 |  | 1.30 |  |
| Administration | 1.20 |  | 1.70 |  |
| Distribution | 0.35 |  | 0.45 |  |
| Marketing | 0.75 |  | 0.60 |  |
| Total expenses |  | (3.80) |  | (4.05) |
| **Loss for quarter** |  | **(1.05)** |  | **(0.25)** |

**Note:** the company decided to amortise the cost incurred in writing the books over five years. Therefore, 1/20th of the writing cost is included in the cost of sales of each quarter. The writing costs related to the second set which is yet to be completed is not included in the cost of sales, as it will also be amortised over five years once the set is complete. The printing cost of the books sold is also included in the cost of sales, but not amortised. The printing is outsourced and only the number of books ordered is actually printed. Stock of the printed books is not maintained.

The management has identified some non-financial indicators. The following is the data related to non-financial indicators:

|  | Quarter 1 | Quarter 2 |
|---|---|---|
| Number of inquiries | 220,850 | 391,960 |
| Number of inquiries converted into actual sale | 125,830 | 189,450 |
| On-time delivery | 95% | 88% |
| Sales return | 2% | 3% |
| Customer complaints due to errors in the books | 5% | 15% |
| Proper handling of customer complaints | 90% | 85% |
| Forum visitors | 50,600 | 125,000 |

The following is data related to a close competitor:

Ability to convert inquiry into an actual sale is 45%. The customer complaint rate is 7%.

**Required:**

(a) Using the financial data given above, assess the financial performance of Concept Academy during its first two quarters.

(10 marks)

(b) Comment on the performance of Concept Academy using the non-financial data given above (use competitor's data where available).

(6 marks)

(c) Discuss the importance of non-financial indicators in performance management.

(4 marks)
**(20 marks)**

## 51. Divisional performance assessment and ROI - Mystique Ltd

Mystique Ltd is an electronics store that has a number of stores across London. The manager of the company is an ambitious person, and is looking to expand his activities, by continuously adding the number of stores.

Mystique assesses the performance of each of their stores individually. The expected return on investment (ROI) of Mystique is 10%. Some of the stores have been able to achieve an ROI above this target.

The market for Mystique is rapidly increasing. The stores of the company, at an average, have a gross profit ratio of around 40%.

Below is financial data given for two of Mystique Ltd's stores for the last year: Store A, Trafalgar Square and Store B, Oxford Street

|  | Store A ($'000) | Store B ($'000) |
| --- | --- | --- |
| Sales | 860 | 675 |
| Gross profit | 362 | 285 |
| Net profit | 75 | 50 |
| Assets employed (investment) | 585 | 360 |

**Required:**

(a) Discuss the past financial performance of store A and B using ROI and any other measure you feel appropriate from the given data. Using your findings discuss whether each of the measures you used correctly reflects the stores' actual performance.

(13 marks)

(b) Discuss the disadvantages of comparing divisional performance.

(7 marks)
**(20 marks)**

## 52. Transfer pricing and external considerations in performance measurement – Elegant Ltd

Elegant Ltd has three divisions, Graceful, Stylish and Classy. The Graceful division is operating at full capacity (12,500 hours). There is sufficient demand for Graceful's product.

**Direct costs of the product are:**

|  | $ |
| --- | --- |
| Direct materials | 44 |
| Direct wages (1 production hour) | 15 |

Graceful division's overheads are $195,000 per annum of which $125,000 is variable.

The selling price of the product is $95 per unit.

It is Elegant's policy to make inter divisional transfers, at a 25% mark-up on the transferor division's total costs.

Stylish has a capacity of 14,000 units. Stylish produces 10,000 units. The remaining capacity for 4,000 units can be utilised for further processing on Graceful's product. The product can then be sold at $120 per unit. The cost of further processing for Stylish is $21 per unit.

## 46: Performance Measurement and Control

According to company policy, if the net profit exceeds the target, a bonus will be given to the manager. The target profit for the Graceful division is $250,000.

**Required:**

(a) State whether it is advisable to sell 4,000 units internally, considering the overall objective of Elegant to maximise profit. Discuss the behavioural issues that would arise if the internal transfer is made, considering the bonus policy.

(12 marks)

Both Stylish and Classy divisions of Elegant produce the same product but work in two different countries. Elegant's management is of the opinion that the performance of the two divisions should be assessed in relation to each other. This is because it believes that interdivisional comparison is the technique by which performances, efficiencies, costs, and profits of the divisions can be studied in a better way.

Roger, a new management accountant, is of the opinion that the performance of an organisation cannot be measured effectively based on internal parameters in isolation. Therefore, he suggests that while assessing the performance of Elegant's divisions, allowance should be made for external considerations.

(b) Discuss the need to allow for external considerations in performance management.

(8 marks)
**(20 marks)**

### 53. Return on investment – Smart Mart

Smart Mart is a company owned by Neil, which deals in clothes. Smart Mart has 10 divisions all over the country. Neil is interested in opening one more division in a developing city. However, according to the policy of the company, he opens a store only if the average expected ROI, gross profit and net profit of the first four years is more than the following:

|  | $ |
|---|---|
| Gross profit | 3 m |
| Net profit | 0.40 m |
| ROI | 15% |

Neil has estimated the following for the new division:

**Sales volume:** in the year one, sales volume will be 30,000 units. It will decrease by 5% in year two. In the year three, the sales volume will be equal to that of year two. In the fourth year, it will decrease by a further 5%.

**Sales price:** in the year one, the sales price will be $30. The price will be increased by 10% in year two. In the year three, it will reduce by 5%. Sales price in the year four will be the same as that of year three.

**Gross profit:** in the first year will be 40% and then will vary with the change in the sales price (as the direct cost per unit will remain constant over the period).

**Indirect expenses (excluding depreciation):** $150,000 for the first year will increase to $200,000 in years two, three and four.

**Initial investment:** $600,000 to be depreciated over four years.

**Required:**

(a) Calculate the average gross profit, net profit and ROI of the new division for the first four years, and comment on whether to open the new division, considering the above three criteria.

(12 marks)

(b) Explain the advantages and disadvantages of using ROI.

(8 marks)
**(20 marks)**

## 54. Performance management - Lavender

The following is information for Lavender, a motor bike manufacturing company, for 20X8.

|  | Actual | Target |
|---|---|---|
| Sales volume (units) | 145,000 | 150,000 |
|  | $'m | $'m |
| Sales (a) | 130.50 | 135.00 |
| **Variable costs** |  |  |
| Material and labour | 46.40 | 47.50 |
| Assembly | 14.60 | 15.00 |
| Distribution | 4.90 | 5.00 |
| Total variable costs (b) | 65.90 | 67.50 |
| **Fixed costs** |  |  |
| Assembly | 41.00 | 41.00 |
| Distribution | 11.00 | 11.00 |
| Administration | 1.00 | 1.00 |
| Total fixed costs (c) | 53.00 | 53.00 |
| Total cost (c) i.e. (a + b) | 118.90 | 120.50 |
| Profit (a- c) | 11.60 | 14.50 |

The company's current estimates in 20X9 are as follows:

| Sales volume | 150,000 units |
|---|---|
| Selling price | $900 per unit |
| Increase in material and labour rate | 5% over the rate in 20X8 |
| Increase in administration cost by | 0.10 m over the cost in 20X8 |

There is no change in the per unit variable distribution and assembly costs over 20X8 actuals.

In order to improve the performance of the company, Lavender's management has undertaken a strategic review and developed the following strategies:

### Strategy 1

Reduce the selling price by 5% of the estimated price. This will result in increasing the sales volume by 7% over the estimated sales volume.

### Strategy 2

Add a feature in the bike to increase its sales appeal. As a result the selling price per bike can be increased to $950. The additional cost for this will be as follows:

- Design cost (fixed $20 m amortised over four years)
- Material and labour cost will increase by 2% over the rate forecasted for 20X9 (i.e. over and above the general material and labour rate increase as stated above)

## 48: Performance Measurement and Control

**Strategy 3**

Obtain a cost-reduction technique from a Japanese company for $50 million. The cost is to be amortised over five years. As a result, variable costs will reduce by 15% compared to the initial forecast.

**Required:**

(a) Assess the financial performance of Lavender for 20X8.

(6 marks)

(b) Calculate the estimated profit for 20X9 using:
- Initial forecast
- Strategy 1
- Strategy 2
- Strategy 3

In addition, discuss the implications of the strategies in the long-run.

(14 marks)
**(20 marks)**

### 55. Performance measurement – Pace Co

Pace Company (PC) runs a large number of wholesale stores and is increasing the number of these stores all the time. It measures the performance of each store on the basis of a target return on investment (ROI) of 15%. Store managers get a bonus of 10% of their salary if their store's annual ROI exceeds the target each year. Once a store is built there is very little further capital expenditure until a full four years have passed.

PC has a store (store W) in the west of the country. Store W has historic financial data as follows over the past four years:

|  | 2005 | 2006 | 2007 | 2008 |
|---|---|---|---|---|
| Sales ($'000) | 200 | 200 | 180 | 170 |
| Gross profit ($'000) | 80 | 70 | 63 | 51 |
| Net profit ($'000) | 13 | 14 | 10 | 8 |
| Net assets at start of year ($'000) | 100 | 80 | 60 | 40 |

The market in which PC operates has been growing steadily. Typically, PC's stores generate a 40% gross profit margin.

**Required:**

(a) Discuss the past financial performance of store W using ROI and any other measure you feel appropriate and, using your findings, discuss whether the ROI correctly reflects Store W's actual performance.

(9 marks)

PC has another store (store S) about to open in the south of the country. It has asked you for help in calculating the gross profit, net profit and ROI it can expect over each of the next four years. The following information is provided:

Sales volume in the first year will be 18,000 units. Sales volume will grow at the rate of 10% for years two and three but no further growth is expected in year 4. Sales price will start at $12 per unit for the first two years but then reduce by 5% per annum for each of the next two years.

Gross profit will start at 40% but will reduce as the sales price reduces. All purchase prices on goods for resale will remain constant for the four years.

Overheads, including depreciation, will be $70,000 for the first two years rising to $80,000 in years three and four.

Store S requires an investment of $100,000 at the start of its first year of trading.

PC depreciates non-current assets at the rate of 25% of cost. No residual value is expected on these assets.

**Required:**

(b) Calculate (in columnar form) the revenue, gross profit, net profit and ROI of store S over each of its first four years.

(8 marks)

(c) Calculate the minimum sales volume required in year 4 (assuming all other variables remain unchanged) to earn the manager of S a bonus in that year.

(3 marks)
**(20 marks)**
**(Adapted from December 2008)**

### 56. Non-financial performance indicators – Ties Only

Ties Only is a new business, selling high quality imported men's ties via the internet. The managers, who also own the company, are young and inexperienced but they are prepared to take risks. They are confident that importing quality ties and selling via a website will be successful and that the business will grow quickly. This is despite the well recognised fact that selling clothing is a very competitive business.

They were prepared for a loss-making start and decided to pay themselves modest salaries (included in administration expenses in table 1 below) and pay no dividends for the foreseeable future.

The owners are so convinced that growth will quickly follow that they have invested enough money in website server development to ensure that the server can handle the very high levels of predicted growth. All website development costs were written off as incurred in the internal management accounts that are shown below in table 1.

Significant expenditure on marketing was incurred in the first two quarters to launch both the website and new products. It is not expected that marketing expenditure will continue to be as high in the future.

Customers can buy a variety of styles, patterns and colours of ties at different prices.

The business's trading results for the first two quarters of trade are shown below in table 1.

**Table 1**

|  | Quarter 1 |  | Quarter 2 |  |
|---|---|---|---|---|
|  | $ | $ | $ | $ |
| Sales |  | 420,000 |  | 680,000 |
| **Less:** Cost of Sales |  | (201,600) |  | (340,680) |
| Gross Profit |  | 218,400 |  | 339,320 |
| **Less:** Expenses |  |  |  |  |
| Website development | 120,000 |  | 90,000 |  |
| Administration | 100,500 |  | 150,640 |  |
| Distribution | 20,763 |  | 33,320 |  |
| Launch marketing | 60,000 |  | 40,800 |  |
| Other variable expenses | 50,000 |  | 80,000 |  |
| Total expenses |  | (351,263) |  | (394,760) |
| Loss for quarter |  | (132,863) |  | (55,440) |

**Required:**

(a) Assess the financial performance of the business during its first two quarters using only the data in table 1 above.

(12 marks)

The owners are well aware of the importance of non-financial indicators of success and therefore have identified a small number of measures to focus on. These are measured monthly and then combined to produce a quarterly management report.

The data for the first two quarters management reports is shown below:

**Table 2**

|  | Quarter 1 | Quarter 2 |
|---|---|---|
| Website hits* | 690,789 | 863,492 |
| Number of ties sold | 27,631 | 38,857 |
| On time delivery | 95% | 89% |
| Sales returns | 12% | 18% |
| System downtime | 2% | 4% |

* A website hit is automatically counted each time a visitor to the website opens the home page of Ties Only.

The industry average conversion rate for website hits to number of ties sold is 3.2%. The industry average sales return rate for internet-based clothing sales is 13%.

**Required:**

(b) Comment on each of the non-financial data in table 2 above taking into account, where appropriate, the industry averages provided, providing your assessment of the performance of the business.

(8 marks)
**(20 marks)**
**(Adapted from December 2007)**

# SOLUTION BANK

GTG
ACCA
ACCA
GTGA
ACCA
ACCA
GTG
ACCA
ACCA
ACCA
GTG
ACCA
ACCA
ACCA
ACCA
GTG
ACCA
GTG

**SOLUTION BANK**

# SECTION A: SPECIALIST COST AND MANAGEMENT ACCOUNTING TECHNIQUES

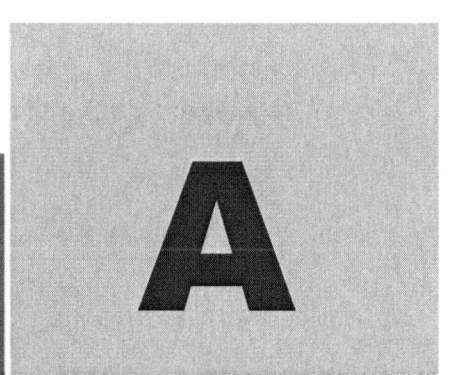

## 1. Traditional method and activity based costing - Egale Ltd

### Strategy

This question requires students to calculate the prices under both the traditional method and the activity based costing system. It also asks you to compare the results obtained under both methods.

- Don't forget to add a 10% mark up on cost while calculating the prices under both methods.
- In part (b), explain how cost, prices, revenue etc would be affected by the use of an ABC system.
- Calculate cost driver rate for each activity and allocate the fixed overheads to each system.

### (a) Calculation of the prices for mist cooling and water mist system

|  | Mist cooling $ | Water mist $ |
| --- | --- | --- |
| Variable costs | 1,450 | 1,254 |
| Add: Absorbed fixed overhead (W1) | 4,500 | 5,400 |
|  | 5,950 | 6,654 |
| Add: 10% mark-up | 595 | 665.4 |
| **Price** | **6,545** | **7,319** |

2 marks

**Working**

**W1**

Total machine hours are calculated as under
Machine hours = (996 units x 3 hrs) + (1,270 units x 3.6 hrs) = 7,560 hrs

1 mark

Fixed overheads are calculated as under:

|  | $ | $ |
| --- | --- | --- |
| Total costs |  | 14,376,780 |
| Less: Variable costs |  |  |
| Mist cooling ($1,450 x 996 units) | 1,444,200 |  |
| Water mist ($1,254 x 1,270 units) | 1,592,580 |  |
| Total variable costs |  | (3,036,780) |
| **Fixed overheads** |  | **11,340,000** |

1 mark

Under the traditional system, the overhead cost is allocated on machine hour basis. Therefore, overhead absorption rate per hour = Total fixed cost / total machine hours
= $11,340,000 / 7,560 hours
= $1,500

Mist cooling system = 3 hours x $1,500 = $4,500
Water mist system = 3.6 hours x $1,500 = $5,400

1.5 marks
**Maximum marks 4**

**(b)** Activity-based costing is an approach to costing that identifies individual activities as fundamental cost objects. It uses the costs of these activities as the basis for assigning costs to ultimate cost objects such as products or services.

*1 mark*

**The following are the benefits that may arise for Egale from the introduction of the ABC:**

- While allocating the overheads under activity based costing, activity consumed by each product is taken into consideration. A one-to-one relationship is identified between the cost and cost drivers. Therefore, the origin of the costs could be identified more clearly. All relevant cost drivers are provided by Egale.

  *1 mark*

- Activity-based costing also reveals the appropriate cost of each activity consumed in the organisation. Activity-based costing can help Egale to control costs by giving importance to the activities that generate them. For example, set up costs are the most important cost and are higher than other overheads. Proper training could be given to the staff to reduce the set up costs. Therefore, activity based costing is a means of cost control.

  *1 mark*

- Activity-based costing calculates the costs of each activity and assigns the activity cost to products on the basis of activity consumption. It encourages optimum pricing. Therefore, it is more useful in determining the minimum price that Egale would have charged for each system.

  *1 mark*

- Under activity-based costing, the overheads are allocated to the products on the basis of the activity consumption (cost driver). This means that all cost is considered and assigned on a more realistic basis. Therefore, it helps when deciding the more profitable product or services.

  *1 mark*

- Activity-based costing also provides accurate information about costs to help with decision-making. This would further help the managers to make correct decisions in key areas such as product pricing and cost control.

  *1 mark*
  **Maximum marks 6**

**(c) Calculation of the prices of each system under an activity based costing**

|  | Mist cooling $ | Water mist $ | Marks |
|---|---|---|---|
| Total overhead cost (W1) (a) | 6,283,100 | 5,056,900 | 0.5 |
| No. of systems (b) | 996 | 1,270 | 0.5 |
| Overhead per system (a / b) | 6,308.33 | 3,981.81 | 0.5 |
| Variable cost | 1,450.00 | 1,254.00 | 0.5 |
| Total cost per system | 7,758.33 | 5,235.81 | 0.5 |
| Add: 10% mark up | 775.83 | 523.58 | 1 |
| Price | 8,534.16 | 5,759.39 | 0.5 |

*3 marks*

**Workings**

**W1 Overhead allocation to the operation on the basis of ABC**

| Activity | Cost driver | Total overheads $ | Total activity consumption | Cost/driver $ | Total overhead (W2) $ Mist cooling | Total overhead (W2) $ Water mist |
|---|---|---|---|---|---|---|
| Set ups | Number of set ups | 8,780,000 | 5,000 | 1,756.00 | 5,268,000 | 3,512,000 |
| Materials handling | Number of movements of materials | 1,500,400 | 12,400 | 121.00 | 750,200 | 750,200 |
| Inspection costs | Number of inspections | 1,059,600 | 31,440 | 33.70 | 264,900 | 794,700 |
| **Total overheads** |  | **11,340,000** |  |  | **6,283,100** | **5,056,900** |

It is a total of activities consumed by each of the systems e.g. total movements of material = 6,200 + 6,200 = 12,400

*3 marks*

**W2 Total overhead consumed by each system**

**Set up costs**

Mist cooling = Cost per driver x activity consumption
= $1,756 x 3,000
= $5,268,000
Water mist = $1,756 x 2,000
= $3,512,000

*1 mark*

**Materials handling costs**

Mist cooling = Cost per driver x activity consumption
= $121 x 6,200 = $750,200
Water mist = $121 x 6,200 = $750,200

*1 mark*

**Inspection costs**

Mist cooling = Cost per driver x activity consumption
= $33.70 x 7,860 = $264,900
Water mist = $33.70 x 23,580 = $794,700

*1 mark*
**Maximum marks 7**

(d) The traditional pricing method that is based on machine hours does not take into consideration the activities that drive costs. The cost drivers are identified from activity based information. The cost of manufacturing the mist cooling system has risen to $7,758.33 under ABC whereas the cost of the water mist system has fallen to $5,235.81 per system.

*1 mark*

The price of $7,319 charged for a water mist system under the traditional method exceeds the costs of $5,235.81 calculated using ABC. In fact, it is possible that the company is losing sales opportunities for the water mist system, as their prices are very high compared to the prices calculated using ABC, and are therefore uncompetitive. The company needs to take into consideration the prices that are charged by the competitors before making a final decision on pricing. On the basis of the information currently available, the company should decrease the price of their water mist system and increase the price of the mist cooling system.

*2 marks*
**Maximum marks 3**

2. **Traditional method and activity based costing – Northern High-Tech Inc**

**Strategy**

The question requires you to calculate the unit cost of product using two important methods
(i) Traditional absorption costing
(ii) Activity based costing.

This question is relatively simple to answer.

**Key points**

➢ Part (a) of this question is very basic and requires allocating overheads on the basis of labour hours. Calculate the overhead absorption rate considering total direct labour hours for the period.
➢ In part (b), be careful while calculating the cost driver rate for each activity.
➢ In part (c), calculating the variations between the overheads allocated under both the methods will help you to comment on which method is appropriate to use.

(a) **Cost per unit for each product under the Traditional Method**

|  | Deluxe model $ | Regular model $ |
|---|---|---|
| Direct material | 120 | 48 |
| Labour | 80 | 32 |
| Factory overhead (W1) | 100 | 100 |
| **Total cost per unit** | **300** | **180** |

84657159

*1.5 marks*

## Workings

### W1 Calculation of overheads per unit using the traditional method

In the traditional costing approach, the factory overhead is allocated on the basis of direct labour hours (DLH).

$$\text{Absorption rate for factory overhead} = \frac{\text{Total factory overhead cost}}{\text{Total direct labour hour}}$$

$$= \frac{\$2,000,000}{(25,000 \text{ hrs} + 75,000 \text{ hrs})} = \$20 \text{ per hour}$$

1.5 marks

**Calculation of overhead cost per unit**

|  | Deluxe model $ | Regular model $ | Marks |
|---|---|---|---|
| **Overhead cost** |  |  | 1 |
| (25,000 DLH x $20 per DLH) | 500,000 |  |  |
| (75,000 DLH x $20 per DLH) |  | 1,500,000 |  |
| **Overhead cost per unit** |  |  | 1 |
| ($500,000 / 5,000 units) | 100 |  |  |
| ($1,500,000 / 15,000 units) |  | 100 |  |

Maximum marks 4

### (b) Cost per unit for each product under activity based costing (ABC) method

The cost driver rate for each activity is calculated as follows:

| Activity (i) | Activity Driver | Budgeted cost pool (ii) $ | Activity consumption (iii) | Activity Rate (ii / iii) = (iv) $ | Marks |
|---|---|---|---|---|---|
| Engineering | Engineering hours | 125,000 | 12,500 hrs | 10 | 1 |
| Setups | Number of setups | 300,000 | 300 setups | 1,000 | 1 |
| Machine running | Machine-hours | 1,500,000 | 150,000 hrs | 10 | 1 |
| Packing | Number of packaging orders | 75,000 | 15,000 orders | 5 | 1 |

Factory overhead costs are assigned to both products, as shown by these calculations.

**Deluxe printer**

| Activity (i) | Activity Rate (ii) $ | Activity consumption (iii) | Total overhead (ii x iii) = (iv) $ | Unit overhead (iv / 5,000 units) = (v) $ | Marks |
|---|---|---|---|---|---|
| Engineering | 10 | 5,000 hrs. | 50,000 | 10 | 1 |
| Setups | 1,000 | 200 setups | 200,000 | 40 | 1 |
| Machine running | 10 | 50,000 hrs. | 500,000 | 100 | 1 |
| Packaging orders | 5 | 5,000 orders | 25,000 | 5 | 1 |
| **Total** |  |  | **775,000** | **155** |  |

**Regular printer**

| Activity (i) | Activity Rate (ii) $ | Activity consumption (iii) | Total overhead (ii x iii) =(iv) $ | Unit overhead (iv /15,000 units) =(v) $ | Marks |
|---|---|---|---|---|---|
| Engineering | 10 | 7,500 hrs. | 75,000 | 5.00 | 1 |
| Setups | 1,000 | 100 setups | 100,000 | 6.67 | 1 |
| Machine running | 10 | 100,000 hrs. | 1,000,000 | 66.67 | 1 |
| Packaging orders | 5 | 10,000 orders | 50,000 | 3.33 | 1 |
| **Total** |  |  | **1,225,000** | **81.67** |  |

**Calculation of cost per unit under the activity based costing (ABC) system**

|  | Deluxe model | | Regular model | | Marks |
|---|---|---|---|---|---|
|  | $ | $ | $ | $ |  |
| Direct material |  | 120 |  | 48 | 0.5 |
| Labour |  | 80 |  | 32 | 0.5 |
| **Factory overhead** |  |  |  |  | 1 |
| Engineering | 10 |  | 5 |  |  |
| Setups | 40 |  | 6.67 |  |  |
| Machine running | 100 |  | 66.67 |  |  |
| Packing | 5 | 155 | 3.33 | 81.67 |  |
| **Total Cost per unit** |  | 355 |  | 161.67 | 0.5 |

**Maximum Marks 12**

### (c) Comparison of alternative costing approach

|  | Allocation method | | Variance | Marks |
|---|---|---|---|---|
|  | Traditional | ABC |  |  |
|  | $ | $ | $ |  |
| **Deluxe model** |  |  |  |  |
| Total overhead | 500,000 | 775,000 | (275,000) | 1 |
| Unit overhead cost | 100 | 155 | (55) |  |
| **Regular model** |  |  |  |  |
| Total overhead | 1,500,000 | 1,225,000 | 275,000 | 1 |
| Unit overhead cost | 100 | 81.67 | 18.33 |  |

*It is a difference between the overheads allocated under the traditional method and the ABC method.*

**Comment**

Even though both the models have widely different cost driven activities, the overhead cost per unit is the same for both models i.e. $100 according to the traditional method. This is because the overhead costs are allocated on the basis of labour hours and the activities which have a cause-effect relationship with the overheads are ignored. For example, the company recorded 200 setups for the Deluxe model and 100 setups for the regular model.

**1 mark**

As the ABC system used the cost of each activity as the basis for assigning costs to the model, the ABC system has come up with more realistic product costs. The overhead cost of the Deluxe model has gone up by $55 whereas the overhead cost of the regular model has fallen by $18.33. Therefore, it is appropriate to use the activity based costing method for allocating overhead costs to the products.

**1 mark**
**Maximum marks 4**

## 3. Cost drivers – Pearl

### Strategy

It is very easy to score marks in this question. The question tests the students' overall knowledge on the activity based costing system. Part (a) and (c) are based on the theory of the ABC system. However, part (b) involves calculation which requires the student to be well-versed in computation.

In part (a), establish a one-to-one relationship between cost and the cost driver for analysis of the given information on ABC. Therefore, ensure suitable cost drivers are provided for each overhead cost to adopt activity based costing.

In part (b), clear identification of cost drivers for each cost, will help you to calculate the cost driver rate for each activity. The answer of this part affects the decision which needs to be taken in part (c).

In order to make the correct decision in part (c), it is important to think clearly. State the affects of the decision on costs, profit and sales of the company.

**(a)** The basis of activity-based costing is to recognise activities that give rise to costs. In order to identify the relation between these costs and cost drivers, a comprehensive study of the various operations of the business needs to be carried out. Ideally a one-to-one relationship should exist between costs and cost drivers. If not, activity-based costing proves comparatively less useful for information on product cost and hence, cost control.

The management accountant believes that he can use the information provided to review the store's performance from an activity-based costing perspective. His only concern is that he has not been able to establish a clear relationship between the 'other costs' and the proposed cost drivers for the three-month period.

For example, few of the employees of Pearl, e.g. the office staff, would be receiving their pay as fixed basic salary. Hence, these wage costs cannot be linked to sales, purchase orders or consultations. If these wage costs are allocated to product costs, using the appropriate cost drivers, it is possible that better product cost information will arise. This is because it could prove more suitable to retailing than floor area.

Therefore, in order to use activity based costing, the management accountant needs information of the cost drivers for wage costs. Carrying out investigation of the costs can help the management accountant to establish and clarify the links between costs and activities.

*1 mark for each point discussed*
**Maximum marks 4**

**(b) Calculation of activity cost driver rate**

As sales staff collect the payment, it is reasonable to link sales staff wages to the items sold:

**Sales staff wages recovery rate** = $64,800/6,500 (W1) = $9·969 per item sold

E.g. Sales staff wages for Kitchen department = 1,000 items x $9.969 = $9,969

*1 mark*

It is reasonable to allocate consultation staff wages on the basis of the number of consultations.

**Consultation staff wages recovery rate** = $24,960/1,248 (W1) = $20·00 per consultation.

E.g. Consultation staff wages for Bathrooms department = 200 consultations x $20 = $4,000

*1 mark*

As customers collect their goods from the warehouse, warehouse staff need to handle each item. Therefore, these wages are linked to items sold:

**Warehouse staff wages recovery rate** = $30,240/6,500 (W1)= $4·652 per item sold.

E.g. Warehouse staff wages for Dining rooms department = 4,000 items x $4.652 = $18,610

*1 mark*

Administration staff process purchase orders, therefore their wages are allocated using purchase orders as a base.

**Administration staff wages recovery rate** = $30,624/4,400 (W1) = $6.96 per order.

E.g. Administration staff wages for Kitchen department = 1,000 orders x $6.96 = $6,960

*1 mark*

All other overheads except general overheads which are apportioned on a different basis are not space costs. Therefore, it seems that general overheads are related to floor space.

**General overheads absorption rate** = $175,000/40,000 (W1) = $4·375 per square metre.

E.g. General overheads for Bathrooms department = 10,000 Sq meters x $4.375 = $43,750

*1 mark*

**Possible activity-based costing profit statement**

| Department | Kitchen $ | Bathrooms $ | Dining rooms $ | Total $ |
|---|---|---|---|---|
| Sales | 210,000 | 112,500 | 440,000 | 762,500 |
| Less: | | | | |
| Cost of goods sold | (63,000) | (36,000) | (176,000) | (275,000) |
| **Contribution** | **147,000** | **76,500** | **264,000** | **487,500** |
| Less: Overhead costs | | | | |
| Sales staff wages | (9,969) | (14,954) | (39,877) | (64,800) |
| Consultation staff wages | (15,960) | (4,000) | (5,000) | (24,960) |
| Warehouse staff wages | (4,652) | (6,978) | (18,610) | (30,240) |
| Admin staff wages | (6,960) | (6,264) | (17,400) | (30,624) |
| General overheads | (70,000) | (43,750) | (61,250) | (175,000) |
| **Profit** | **39,459** | **554** | **121,863** | **161,876** |

*All these overhead costs are allocated using recovery rates, calculated in the working notes i.e. activity recovery rates × activity consumed by each department*

*5 marks*

**Working**

**W1 Proposed cost drivers**

| Total number of items sold | 1,000 + 1,500 + 4,000 | 6,500 |
|---|---|---|
| Total number of purchase orders | 1,000 + 900 + 2,500 | 4,400 |
| Total floor area | 16,000 + 10,000 + 14,000 | 40,000 |
| Total number of consultations | 798 + 200 + 250 | 1,248 |

*1 mark*
**Maximum marks 9**

**(c) Proposal to close down the Bathrooms department**

From the point of view of the absorption costing method, it is highlighted that the bathrooms department is making a loss. However it seems to be making a small profit under the activity-based costing system. The following are a few reasons that can be attributed to this:

➢ The variable contribution of the Bathrooms department towards overheads is $76,500. It is also making a profit before general overheads of $44,304 ($43,750 + $554). Hence, the suggestion of closing the department due to financial reasons will not hold true. The company, however, will need to investigate the reasons for low profitability of the department.

➢ The management of Pearl could also take up a detailed study of the bathrooms sales. This will help them to analyse the product types which are most preferred by customers or are most profitable, which move slowly and which can be discontinued in the future. This can help to prevent the closure of the department.

➢ Fixed overheads of $43,750 in each three month period are apportioned to the Bathrooms department. Fixed overheads are costs that are incurred on a continuous basis. If the Bathrooms department is closed down, the overall profit will reduce by the same amount. Apart from this, there could be other costs that have been allocated to the Bathrooms department, and would continue after its closure. The overall profit will again fall by this amount.

➢ Before closing down the Bathrooms department, the management needs to consider whether or not the space occupied by the Bathrooms department can be put to better use. The two options that could be considered are expanding the current ventures or using that space for an altogether new venture.

➢ Customers of Pearl might be patronising the store as they provide a wide variety of products for home furnishings. The closure of the Bathrooms department may redirect customers to a competitor's store. This could affect the sales of the other departments. Additionally, some customers might not visit the store as it could be perceived as no longer providing a sufficient range of products.

*1.5 marks for each point discussed*
**Maximum marks 7**

## 58: Specialist Cost and Management Accounting Techniques

### Score More

A common mistake that students make is selecting inappropriate cost drivers to allocate the overhead costs. For example, it is improper to allocate general overheads on the basis of the number of items sold, when a better cost driver (i.e. the floor area) is available.

Often, students use the number of employees as the cost driver for allocating the sales staff wages which is a wrong answer. You need to allocate the sales staff wages based on the number of items sold.

In Part (c), rather than merely evaluating whether to close the bathrooms department, you need to suggest hypothetical solutions to improve the performance of the department. This will fetch you higher marks.

### 4. Activity based costing – Matrix Ltd

### Strategy

Part (a) of the question is very simple. The only tricky area in this part is the allocation of overhead costs under ABC. You should calculate the cost per driver for each activity to allocate overhead costs to each model. The formula should be given in the solution.

Part (b) of this question requires you to comment on the statement made by managers in the meeting regarding the acceptance of the ABC system. Clear thinking will help you to justify each statement.

**(a) Calculation of the total profit using both traditional and ABC methods**

**(i) Traditional method (labour hours basis)**

|  | Model X | Model Y | Model Z | Total | Marks |
|---|---|---|---|---|---|
| Output (Units) | 800 | 1,500 | 2,500 | 4,800 |  |
|  | $ | $ | $ | $ |  |
| Sales (a) (Selling price per unit x output) | 4,680,000 | 12,000,000 | 12,500,000 | 29,180,000 | 1 |
| Less: Costs |  |  |  |  |  |
| Materials | 2,400,000 | 1,875,000 | 2,500,000 | 6,775,000 | 1 |
| Direct labour ($8 per hour) | 800,000 | 1,760,000 | 1,440,000 | 4,000,000 | 1 |
| Overheads (at $11.8) (W1) | 1,180,000 | 2,596,000 | 2,124,000 | 5,900,000 | 0.5 |
| Total Costs (b) | (4,380,000) | (6,231,000) | (6,064,000) | (16,675,000) | 0.5 |
| **Total Profit / (loss) (a – b)** | **300,000** | **5,769,000** | **6,436,000** | **12,505,000** | 0.5 |
| Profit / (loss) per unit | 375 | 3,846 | 2,574.40 |  | 0.5 |

> Profit per unit is calculated by dividing the total profit by the total output.

**Working**

**W1**

Total overhead cost = $5,900,000
Total labour hours = 100,000 + 220,000 + 180,000 = 500,000 hours
Overhead per labour hour = $5,900,000 / 500,000 hours = $11.8 per hour

Therefore, overheads absorbed by each model are:

Model X = 100,000 hours x $11.8 = $1,180,000
Model Y = 220,000 hours x $11.8 = $2,596,000
Model Z = 180,000 hours x $11.8 = $2,124,000

1.5 marks
**Maximum marks 5**

## (ii) Activity Based Costing

|  | Model X | Model Y | Model Z | Total | Marks |
|---|---|---|---|---|---|
| Output (Units) | 800 | 1,500 | 2500 | 4,800 | |
|  | $ | $ | $ | $ | |
| Sales (a) | | | | | 0.5 |
| (Selling price per unit x output) | 4,680,000 | 12,000,000 | 12,500,000 | 29,180,000 | |
| **Less:** costs | | | | | |
| Materials | 2,400,000 | 1,875,000 | 2,500,000 | 6,775,000 | 0.5 |
| Direct labour ($8 per hour) | 800,000 | 1,760,000 | 1,440,000 | 4,000,000 | 0.5 |
| **Overheads** | | | | | |
| Delivery costs at $5,000 (W1) | 750,000 | 500,000 | 1,000,000 | 2,250,000 | 0.5 |
| Set-up costs at $20,384.62 (W2) | 917,308 | 1,019,231 | 713,461 | 2,650,000 | 0.5 |
| Quality test costs at $5,128.21 (W3) | 205,128 | 333,333 | 461,539 | 1,000,000 | 0.5 |
| **Total cost (b)** | **(5,072,436)** | **(5,487,564)** | **(6,115,000)** | **(16,675,000)** | |
| **Total Profit / (loss) (a-b)** | **(392,436)** | **6,512,436** | **6,385,000** | **12,505,000** | 0.5 |
| Profit / (loss) per unit | (490.55) | 4341.62 | 2,554 | | 0.5 |

**Workings**

**W1   Absorption rate = Overhead cost / Cost driver**

$$\text{Deliveries to retailers cost per delivery} = \frac{\text{Overhead cost of deliveries to retailers}}{\text{Total number of deliveries}}$$

$$= \frac{\$2,250,000}{450} \quad (150 + 100 + 200)$$

$$= \$5,000$$

1.5 marks

**W2**

$$\text{Setups cost per setup} = \frac{\text{Setup overhead cost}}{\text{Total number of setups}}$$

$$= \frac{\$2,650,000}{130} \quad (45 + 50 + 35)$$

$$= \$20,384.62$$

1.5 marks

**W3**

$$\text{Quality test control costs per quality test} = \frac{\text{Quality control costs}}{\text{Total number of tests}}$$

$$= \frac{\$1,000,000}{195} \quad (40 + 65 + 90)$$

$$= \$5,128.21$$

1.5 marks
**Maximum marks 7**

### (b) Opinion on the comments made during the meeting

➢ The first concern raised in the meeting was that incremental costs cannot be calculated with the help of ABC costing. This information is needed to determine the break-even point of the product. Hence, optimal discounts can be given to huge contracts. The results of ABC costing will hugely depend on finding the right relationship between costs and cost drivers.

ABC costing might not help in this case. An incremental analysis will be required to find the correct pricing of the navigation system in huge contracts. There is a possibility that ABC might not give details about the interdependence of costs and revenues. This is because costs are linked to various activities and it is difficult to attribute them to a given activity.

Another drawback could be that ABC costing is based on historic events and hence, the data cannot be fully relied upon.

2 marks

## 60: Specialist Cost and Management Accounting Techniques

> The next concern raised was that ABC can only help to provide information about the use of labour hours in assessing the viability of each product. But it may not prove to be helpful to gain any further information. This is not true. As we can see, the case with Model X, though it shows that the product is making a profit of $300,000 under the traditional costing method, ABC has revealed that it is actually making a loss of $392,436. This is because of the difference in the level of costs allocated and profitability among the methods.

The main reason of this was that the overheads were allocated on labour hour basis. However, labour hours are not relevant. The overhead costs of the deliveries and set-up costs are not related to labour hours but to a different set of activities. This is highlighted by the loss shown for Model X under the ABC method.

The company needs to redesign its deliveries and set ups in order to reduce the costs of Model X and allow it to continue in the market. Apart from this, there could be other non-financial aspects favouring the continuation of the model in the market. For example, it portrays that the company has a good product base and caters to all the varied needs of its customers.

*2 marks*

> As labour repeats a process of production, they learn from it and eventually the labour hours required reduce. In ABC costing this learning curve is not considered. Under ABC it is assumed that the cost per activity remains constant as the number of times the activity is repeated, the cost increases. However, in practice, marginal costs reduce as the number of activities increases. The learning curve operates only in cases where the employee is inexperienced or the processes are new.

The managers' views are right that some costs do not change with either labour hours or any cost driver, and therefore do not fall easily under ABC. This is because there is no cause and effect relationship.

*2 marks*

> The view of the managers that any method of costing does not make a difference is true only partially. We observe that the overall profit of $12,505,000 under both the methods remained the same. However, ABC costing revealed that Model X made a loss of $490.55 per unit. The company needs to decide on the continuation of this product. Moreover, if the company had carried inventory, then the method of inventory valuation would have differed, thus affecting profit calculations.

*2 marks*
**Maximum marks 8**

### 5. Product life cycle – Target Inc

**Strategy**

Part a, b and d are theoretical questions and hence fairly simple to score full marks.

**Key points**

(a)
> Planning and design stage and its related costs
> Manufacturing and sales stage and its related costs
> Service and abandonment stage and its related costs
> Facilitate the use of cost analysis by pointing out the committed costs
> Related to life cycle costing

(b) Here you need to mention the relationship between the theory and the practical case study.
> Facilitate the evaluation of effectiveness of initial planning and design
> Facilitate evaluation of alternatives
> Identifies the area of cost reduction and input for other processes
> Use of committed costs
> Difference between the life cycle revenue and life cycle costs, and annual income and annual expenses

(a) The concept of the product life cycle indicates the phases/stages of the product. The product life cycle consists of planning and design, launch of the product, its growth and at last its abandonment.

*1 mark*

However the length of time a product will stay in any stage is not certain. One product may stay in a stage for longer than another. Stages of the product are closely related to the business functions, such as research and development, design, production, marketing, distribution and customer service. The stages of a life-cycle are:

**(i) The planning and design stage:** business functions and related costs included in this stage are as follows:

> Research and Development- research and development expenditure
> Design- cost of product design

*1 mark*

**(ii) The manufacturing and sales stage:** business functions and related costs included in this stage are as follows:

- Production : production or manufacturing costs
- Marketing: marketing costs
- Distribution: distribution costs

1 mark

**(iii) The service and abandonment stage:** business functions and related costs included in this stage are as follows:

- After sales service: cost of after sale services, including provision for spare parts and expert services.
- Disposal of production facility; cost of abandonment and disposal of the product.

1 mark

The product life cycle shows the costs that will be incurred at the each stage of the production process. Committed costs are the costs that will be incurred in the future, on the basis of decisions that have already been taken in the past. Studies show that 80% of the budgeted total costs are committed at the planning and design stage. Hence, it is a useful tool to evaluate the alternative decisions at the design and development stage.

1 mark

Life-cycle costing which is based on the product's life cycle refers to the system that tracks and accumulates every individual cost which is incurred during the whole life cycle of a product, starting from its initial planning stage to the post sales service and abandonment stage.

1 mark

Therefore the concept of product life cycle is closely related to the concept of life cycle costing.

**Maximum marks 3**

**(b)** By implementing life cycle costing principles, Target can evaluate the effectiveness of its initial planning, and cost data to clarify the economic impact of alternatives chosen in the design, engineering phase etc.

Life-cycle costing will help the management of Target to understand the cost consequences of developing and making a product, and to identify areas in which cost reduction efforts are likely to be most effective. It provides premises for decision-making regarding product introduction, product mix and regarding discontinuing certain products.

1 mark

Life-cycle analysis indicates the committed costs of a product; hence Target can reduce product cost during its life cycle by emphasising on product planning, product design and development. Life-cycle costing forms an input to the evaluation processes such as value management, economic appraisal and financial appraisal.

Life-cycle costs also provide useful information for strategically evaluating pricing decisions.

While calculating life-cycle revenue and life-cycle costs, it may be noted that the calculation of annual revenue or annual costs is meaningless. The revenue and the costs for the entire life-cycle of the product will have to be considered.

1 mark

Again, in annual accounts, the non-production costs such as research and development and design are normally considered as deferred cost, and are amortised during the useful life of the product. But, in order to know the life-cycle revenue and costs of the product, one needs to consider revenue and costs for the entire life-cycle.

1 mark

Therefore by implementing life-cycle costing Target can evaluate the long-term picture of product profitability.

1 mark

**Maximum marks 2**

## 62: Specialist Cost and Management Accounting Techniques

**(c)**

### Strategy

Again this is a simple problem, but it is based on a case study. Read it carefully. Do not confuse it with reasonable profit and reasonable contribution and actual profit and actual contribution.

First find out the fixed cost for each year and then calculate the annual contribution.

**Key points**

- Find out the variable cost by comparing the costs at two activity levels.
- Find out the fixed cost by subtracting variable cost from the total costs
- Remember to include design costs while calculating total costs.
- Calculate reasonable profit as a percentage of revenue and reasonable contribution and compare it with the actual amounts.
- Comment on your findings.

**Product life cycle income statement**

|  | $ | $ | Marks |
|---|---|---|---|
| Revenue (W1) |  | 2,295,000 | 2 |
| Less: |  |  | 2 |
| variable costs (W1) | 1,020,000 |  | 4 |
| fixed costs (W1) | 290,000 |  | 2 |
| marketing costs (W1) | 170,000 |  | 2 |
| design costs (W1) | 325,000 | (1,805,000) | 1 |
| Profit (W1) |  | 490,000 |  |

**Workings**

**W1 Annual profitability statement**

|  | Year 1 | Year 2 | Year 3 | Year 4 | Year 5 | Total |
|---|---|---|---|---|---|---|
| Budgeted units | 8,000 | 12,000 | 15,000 | 10,000 | 6,000 | 51,000 |
|  | $ | $ | $ | $ | $ | $ |
| Selling price per unit | 45 | 45 | 45 | 45 | 45 | 45 |
| Revenue | 360,000 | 540,000 | 675,000 | 450,000 | 270,000 | 2,295,000 |
| Less: variable costs (@ 20 per unit) | (160,000) | (240,000) | (300,000) | (200,000) | (120,000) | (1,020,000) |
| Fixed costs (W2) | (50,000) | (70,000) | (70,000) | (50,000) | (50,000) | (290,000) |
| Marketing costs |  | (70,000) | (60,000) | (40,000) |  | (170,000) |
| Design and development costs |  |  |  |  |  | (325,000) |
| Net profit | 150,000 | 160,000 | 245,000 | 160,000 | 100,000 | 490,000 |
| Profit considered reasonable (revenue *.3) |  |  |  |  |  | 459,000 |
| Actual contribution (marketing and design costs are considered as fixed costs) |  |  |  |  |  | 1,275,000 |
| Contribution considered reasonable (60%* revenue) |  |  |  |  |  | 1,377,000 |

*Marketing and design and development costs are not included in the fixed costs as given in the question.*

**Note:** Marketing and design costs are considered as fixed costs.

## W2 Calculation of fixed costs

|  | $ |
|---|---|
| Expected cost at an activity level of 5,000 units | 150,000 |
| Expected cost at an activity level of 9,000 units | 230,000 |
| So variable costs per unit = difference in total cost/ difference in total units. ( 80,000/4,000) | 20 |
| Variable costs at an activity level of 5,000 units | 100,000 |
| Fixed costs( total cost - variable cost) | 50,000 |
| so fixed costs above the activity level of 10,000 units will be | 70,000 |

### Assessment

(i) The net profit of $490,000 is slightly more than the reasonable profit of $459, 000, hence Target can go ahead with the production of the stated monitor.

*1 mark*

(ii) Contribution of $1,275,000 is a little lower than the reasonable contribution of $1,377,000. Hence, Target needs to implement strict cost control and has to monitor its variable costs.

*1 mark*

(iii) Profit is dependant on the budgeted sales. A slight reduction in the budgeted sales could make the whole product unprofitable. Target needs to evaluate its market forecasts very carefully, and accordingly determine the product price and design.

*1 mark*
**Maximum marks 15**

## 6. Product life cycle - Santa's workshop Plc

**Strategy**

This is a simple question, although it involves a lot of calculations. If you have understood the concept of product life cycle costs, you can score high marks on these types of questions.

### Key points

**Part (a)**
- Prepare a statement showing product life cycle budget by calculating each element of cost.

**Part (b)**
- Calculate the percentage of research and development costs with respect to total costs.
- Design developed at the research and development stage controls the subsequent costs.

**Part (c)**
- Calculate the forecasted sales in terms of units according to the marketing department's proposal.
- Calculate the revised batch sizes.
- Prepare a product life cycle budget the same way it is prepared under part (a).

### (a) Budgeted Life-Cycle Operating Income Statement for the new toy

|  | $ | $ | $ |
|---|---|---|---|
| A. Sales (W1) |  |  | 35,000,000 |
| B. Life-cycle costs: |  |  |  |
| i. R & D and design costs | 8,000,000 | 8,000,000 |  |
| ii. Manufacturing cost: |  |  |  |
| Variable cost of toys (W2) | 17,500,000 |  |  |
| Variable cost of batches (W4) | 525,000 |  |  |
| Fixed costs | 900,000 | 18,925,000 |  |
| iii. Marketing cost: |  |  |  |
| Variable cost of toys (W5) | 3,500,000 |  |  |
| Fixed costs | 200,000 | 3,700,000 |  |
| iv. Distribution costs: |  |  |  |
| Variable cost of batch (W7) | 140,000 |  |  |
| Fixed cost | 320,000 | 460,000 |  |
| v. Customer-service cost of toys (W8) | 700,000 | 700,000 |  |
| Total life-cycle costs (I + II + III + IV + V) |  |  | (31,785,000) |
| C. Life-cycle operating income (A - B) |  |  | 3,215,000 |

*Remember you are calculating variable cost of batches. So do not multiply the variable cost with the total number of units.*

*1 mark for each cost element and one for total*

## 64: Specialist Cost and Management Accounting Techniques

**Workings**

**W1**

Sales = 350,000 Toys x $100 per Toy = $35,000,000

**W2**

In the manufacturing activity,

$$\text{Variable cost of toy} = \frac{350,000 \text{ Toys}}{\$50 \text{ per toy}}$$

$$= \$17,500,000$$

**W3**

In the manufacturing activity,

$$\text{Number of batches} = \frac{350,000 \text{ Toys}}{100 \text{ Toys per batch}}$$

$$= 3,500$$

**W4**

In the manufacturing activity,
Variable cost of batch = 3,500 batches x $150 per batch

$$= \$525,000$$

**W5**

In the marketing activity,
Variable cost of toys = 3,500 toys x $10 per toy

$$= \$3,500,000$$

**W6**

In the distribution activity,

$$\text{Number of batches} = \frac{\text{Number of toys}}{\text{Number toys per batch}}$$

$$\text{Number of batches} = \frac{350,000 \text{ Toys}}{200 \text{ Toys per batch}}$$

$$= 1,750$$

**W7**

In the distribution activity,
Variable cost of batch = 1,750 batches x $80 per batch

$$= \$140,000$$

**W8**

In the customer-services activity,
Variable cost of toys = 350,000 toys x $2 per toy

$$= \$700,000$$

*0.5 marks for each working*
**Maximum marks 4**

**(b) Total costs during the product's life cycle: 31,785,000**

Costs after the research and development stage: 8,000,000
Percentage of the total product life-cycle costs will be incurred by the end of the R & D and design stages

$$= \frac{100}{31,785,000} \times 8,000,000$$

$$= 25.17\%$$

**1 mark**

Therefore committed cost at this stage = 74.83% (i.e. 100% - 25.17%)

According to the analyst, committed costs at the R & D and design stage for the new toy will be 80% of the total budgeted costs. This means that the R & D and design stage itself determines what the manufacturing cost of the product will be. It also indicates that by an appropriate product design with the use of value engineering the actual costs in the subsequent stages of the product life-cycle can be greatly reduced. In the case of Santa's workshop, the cost planned to be incurred is relatively low. (i.e. 74.83%)

2 marks

Nevertheless, Santa's workshop needs to identify

- the product features which are non value added and accordingly curtail those features
- add those features which children love in the design stage itself

Only then Santa's workshop can effectively control manufacturing, marketing and distribution costs.

1 mark
**Maximum marks 2**

**(c)**

| Sales | 350,000 units x 120% = | 420,000 units |
| Selling price per Toy | $100-$10 | $90 |
| Toys per batch (Manufacturing activity) | 100 x 120% = | 120 units |
| Toys per batch (Distribution activity) | 200 x 120% = | 240 units |

> Be careful, here you might make a mistake. The batch size of the distribution department is different.

4 marks

**Budgeted Life-Cycle Operating Income for the new toy**

|  | $ | $ | $ | Marks |
|---|---|---|---|---|
| A. Sales (W1) |  |  | 37,800,000 | 1 |
| B. Life-cycle costs: |  |  |  |  |
| I. R & D and design costs | 8,000,000 | 8,000,000 |  | 1 |
| II. Manufacturing cost: |  |  |  |  |
|   Variable cost of toy (W2) | 21,000,000 |  |  |  |
|   Variable cost of batch (W4) | 525,000 |  |  |  |
|   Fixed costs | 900,000 | 22,425,000 |  | 2 |
| III. Marketing cost: |  |  |  |  |
|   Variable cost of watch (W5) | 4,200,000 |  |  |  |
|   Fixed costs | 200,000 | 4,400,000 |  | 1 |
| IV. Distribution costs: |  |  |  |  |
|   Variable cost of batch (W7) | 140,000 |  |  |  |
|   Fixed costs | 320,000 | 460,000 |  | 2 |
| V. Customer-service cost of toys (W8) | 840,000 | 840,000 |  | 1 |
| Total life-cycle costs (I + II + III + IV + V) |  |  | (36,125,000) |  |
| C. Life-cycle operating income (A - B) |  |  | 1,675,000 |  |

**Workings**

**W1**

Sales = 420,000 toys x $80 per toys

= $37,800,000

**W2**

In the manufacturing activity,
Variable cost of batch = 420,000 toys x $50 per toys

= $21,000,000

**W3**

In the manufacturing activity,

Number of batches = $\dfrac{420,000 \text{ toys}}{120 \text{ toys per batch}}$

= 3,500

## W4

In the manufacturing activity,
Variable cost of batch = 3,500 batches x $150 per toys

= $525,000

## W5

In the marketing activity,

Variable cost of toy = $\dfrac{420,000 \text{ toys}}{120 \text{ toys per batch}}$

= 3,500

## W6

In the distribution activity,

Number of batches = $\dfrac{\text{Number of toys}}{\text{Number of toys per batch}}$

= $\dfrac{420,000 \text{ toys}}{240 \text{ toys per batch}}$

= 1,750 batches

## W7

In the distribution activity,
Variable cost of batch = 1,750 batches x $80 per toys

= $140,000

## W8

In the customer-services activity,
Variable cost of toys = 420,000 toys x $2 per toys

= $840,000

The new toy has a relatively lower fixed cost and a higher variable cost. Therefore the profits calculated for the toy's life cycle according to the market research department's proposal are much lower than the original plan. Hence Brian should not accept the marketing department's proposal.

**Maximum marks 12**

(d) Target selling price of 350,000 units = 350,000 x 80
= 28,000,000

Expected profit: 20% of sales = 20% of 28,000,000
= 5,600,000

Target cost = Target price – Expected profit
= 28,000,000 - 5,600,000
= 22,400,000

1 mark

Actual cost of producing 350,000 toys (as per part a) = 31,785,000

Cost gap (31,785,000- 22,400,000) = 9,385,000

1 mark

This huge cost gap suggests that Santa's Workshop needs to apply cost reduction techniques such as value engineering. Such a gap could be reduced by changing the design and material requirements.

1 mark
**Maximum marks 2**

### Score More

It is essential to show all the workings while answering the problem. If you show your workings on paper and make a calculation mistake, you can still score some marks for showing these workings.

## 7. Target cost - Comfort Ltd

### Strategy

Part (a) and (b) are theoretical, hence you can score well. Part (c) is important and could appear in the examination as it relates to target costing processes.

### Key points

**Part (a)**
- Set target selling price
- Establish target profits
- Determine the target cost per unit
- Compare target cost with the current cost
- Cost reduction

**Part (b)**
- System for cost control and management of profit
- Increases cost consciousness and focuses on profit margins
- Keeps the costs to a minimum
- Comparison of standard costing with target costing as a cost reduction tool

---

**(a)** Comfort Plc will adopt the target costing approach to match its product costing with its marketing strategy. The target costing processes that Comfort could adopt are as follows:

(i) Set target selling price based on the customers' expectations and sales forecast: this involves extensive analysis of customers' expectations about the product features. Often the features which are valued by the customers are only included in the product design. This is followed by price determination which is based on the competitors' products and their prices and expected market conditions when the product will be launched.

*1 mark*

(ii) Establish target profit based on long term profit objectives and projected volumes: after ascertaining the price at which the product can be sold, the desired margin for the product is determined considering the long term profit objectives of the organisation and the expected demand at the ascertained price.

*1 mark*

(iii) Determine the target cost per unit: by deducting the expected profit margin from the target price, the cost target for the product is ascertained. The organisation has to manufacture products within the target cost, so that the desired profit can be earned.

*1 mark*

(iv) This target cost is then compared with the estimated current cost of the new product. The cost gap is then determined.

*1 mark*

(v) Targets for cost reduction for each component and production activity using value engineering and value analysis are determined in order to bridge the gap.

*1 mark*
**Maximum marks 4**

**(b)** The following are the implications of implementing target costing on cost control:

- Although target costing is not a costing system, it is considered as a comprehensive system for cost control, to manage profit over a product's life cycle. Implementation of target costing increases cost consciousness within the organisation and focuses on profit margins.

*1 mark*

- It does not aim to slash costs by trimming functions or closing departments. It is a continuous task to ensure that costs are always kept to a minimum.

*2 marks*

## 68: Specialist Cost and Management Accounting Techniques

> Implications of implementing target costing are different than the implications of implementing standard costing. Although both are cost reduction techniques, their implications differ from each other, as follows.

In the standard costing approach, actual costs of the product are compared with predetermined standard costs. Cost control is exercised through variance analysis. Its objective is to contain the actual costs within predetermined standard costs. In contrast, target costing as a cost control technique is used to keep costs at a minimum. Cost reduction is a continuous process in target costing, although it can be done most effectively in the design stage.

**1 mark**

> The target costing approach is a vital cost control tool because it is used basically at the product design stage. Research has shown that up to 90 per cent of costs are 'built in' at the product's design stage.

**1 mark**

Therefore by implementing target costing, Comfort can keep its cost at a minimum. Comfort can identify the cost reduction techniques and work on them to meet the target cost.

**Maximum marks 4**

### (c)

**Strategy**

This question involves a lot of calculations. If you have understood the concept of target costing clearly, then you have chance to score full marks here.

**Key points**

- First calculate the target cost.
- Then calculate each component cost.
- Idle time allowance: add it to the labour cost.
- Use the high and low point method to calculate variable and fixed overheads.
- Compare the target cost with the estimated cost to find out the cost gap.

**Cost per set of chairs**

|  | $ |
|---|---|
| Material (W2) | 470.00 |
| Labour (W3) | 283.15 |
| Overheads (W4) | 763.14 |
| Total cost | 1516.29 |
| Less: Target cost (W1) | (1500.00) |
| Cost Gap | 16.29 |

**4 marks**

**Workings**

**W1 Calculation of target cost**

|  | $ |
|---|---|
| Target selling price | 2000 |
| Less: expected margin (25% of sales) | (500) |
| Target cost | 1500 |

**1 mark**

**W2 Material cost**

| Material | Quantity | Price $ | Total $ |
|---|---|---|---|
| Wooden sheets | 10 | 20 | 200 |
| Polish | 10 | 15 | 150 |
| Other accessories | 10 | 12 | 120 |
| Total |  |  | 470 |

*Remember, you are calculating the costs for a complete set.*

**1 mark**

## W3 Labour cost

| Labour | Hours | Cost $ | Total $ |
|---|---|---|---|
| Carpentry department (5 hours x 10 chairs) | 50 | 5 | 250.00 |
| Idle time allowance (5/95*50)=2.63 hours) | 2.63 | 5 | 13.15 |
| Assembly workers ( 30/60 x10= 5 hours) | 5 | 4 | 20.00 |
| Total | | | 283.15 |

*Idle time adjustment is important. It should also be charged to the product costs.*

3 marks

## W4 Overhead cost

| Overhead costs | Hours | Cost $ | Total $ |
|---|---|---|---|
| Variable overheads ( W5) | 52.63 | 10 | 526.30 |
| Fixed overheads (W5) | 52.63 | 4.5 | 236.84 |
| Total | | | 763.14 |

*Overheads are absorbed on the basis of labour hours spent in the carpentry department i.e. 50 +2.63 = 52.63*

2 marks

## W5 Calculation of fixed overheads

$$\text{Variable overhead cost per hour} = \frac{\text{Difference in overhead costs at two volumes of production}}{\text{Difference in labour hours}}$$

$$= \frac{\$120{,}000 - \$80{,}000}{9000 - 5000}$$

$$= \frac{\$40{,}000}{4000}$$

$$= \$10 \text{ per hour}$$

Variable production overheads at 5000 labour hours:
5000 hours x $10 = $50,000

Fixed production overheads at 5000 labour hours would be total overheads minus variable overheads:
$80,000 – $50,000 = $30,000

Fixed production overheads for 12 months would be $30,000 x 12 = $360,000
Total labour hours in Carpentry department = 80,000

$$\text{Fixed production overhead absorption rate} = \frac{\text{Total fixed overheads}}{\text{Total hours}}$$

$$= \frac{\$3{,}60{,}000}{80{,}000}$$

$$= \$4.5 \text{ per hour}$$

3 marks
**Maximum marks 12**

### Score More

Show all the working notes. If you do any calculation mistake in the main answer, you will still get marks for preparing working notes and for giving the necessary explanations as given in note W5.

## 70: Specialist Cost and Management Accounting Techniques

### 8. Throughput accounting – Boots Footwear Ltd

**Strategy**

This is a tough question as it involves a lot of calculations. Read the question carefully, and ensure you do the calculations step by step. Before calculating the mix under marginal costing, identify the product mix, based on resource constraint.

**Key points**

➢ Hours available in the finishing department are a limiting factor in this question.

Part (b) relates to the calculation of throughput accounting ratios. This is simple, as you only have to calculate using the formula of the throughput accounting ratio.

**Key points**

➢ Throughput accounting ratio = return per factory hour / cost per factory hour
➢ Return per factory hour = Sales - material costs/usage of bottleneck resource
➢ Cost per factory hour = Total factory costs / Bottleneck resource hours available

Part (c) is also simple as you have to calculate the profitability using the profitable quantity mix. This is calculated by using the product mix derived in part (b).

Part (d) is a theoretical question. You should refer to the information given in the case study.

**Key points**

➢ Throughput accounting considers only material costs as variable costs. Other costs are considered as fixed costs.
➢ Marginal costing considers material, labour and variable overheads as variable costs.

---

**(a)**

|          |             | Hours  |
|----------|-------------|--------|
| Trainee  | 75,000/4    | 18,750 |
| Trekkers | 35,000/2.50 | 14,000 |
| Required |             | 32,750 |
| Available|             | 25,000 |
| Shortfall|             | 7,750  |

**Bottleneck resource**

Total 25,000 hours in a finishing department are less than the 32,750 hours required to produce 75,000 units of Trainers and 35,000 units of Trekkers. Therefore the expected demand for both products could not be satisfied. Hence, finishing hours are a limiting factor or bottleneck resource.

*1 mark*

**Calculation of net profit using marginal costing principles:**

|                                                                                                          | Trainers | Trekkers |
|----------------------------------------------------------------------------------------------------------|----------|----------|
| Selling price ($)                                                                                        | 100      | 150      |
| Variable costs(material + variable)                                                                      | 50       | 80       |
| Contribution                                                                                             | 50       | 70       |
| Hours required to produce one unit (units of limiting factor)                                            | 0.25     | 0.40     |
| contribution per hour of limiting factor (contribution per unit x number of units produced in one hour)  | 200      | 175      |
| Ranking                                                                                                  | I        | II       |

> One hour is required to produce 4 Trainers; based on this, the time required to produce one pair of shoes is calculated.

So BFL should first use the available hours to satisfy the expected demand of Trainers, then BFL can start the production of Trekkers.

*1 mark*

| Units | Type | Bottleneck resource Per unit (hours) | Bottleneck resource Consumed (hours) | Marks |
|---|---|---|---|---|
| 75,000 | Trainers | 0.25 | 18,750 | |
| 15,625 | Trekkers | 0.40 | 6,250 | 1 |

Total 25,000 hours are available, out of which 18,750 hours are required to produce Trainers. So in the remaining 6,250 hours, 15,625 units of Trekkers can be produced at the rate of 2.50 per hour.

**Profitability statement using the product mix of 75,000 units of Trainers and 15,625 units of Trekkers:**

| | Units | SP per unit ($) | $'000 | $'000 | Marks |
|---|---|---|---|---|---|
| **Sales revenue** | | | | | |
| Trainers | 75,000 | 100 | 7,500.00 | | |
| Trekkers | 15,625 | 150 | 2,343.75 | 9,843.75 | 1 |
| **Material cost** | | | | | |
| Trainers | 75,000 | 40 | 3,000.00 | | |
| Trekkers | 15,625 | 50 | 781.25 | (3,781.25) | 1 |
| **Variable production conversion costs** | | | | | |
| Trainers | 75,000 | 10 | 750.00 | | |
| Trekkers | 15,625 | 30 | 468.75 | (1,218.75) | 1 |
| **Contribution** | | | | | |
| Trainers (7,500-3,000-750) | | | 3,750.00 | | |
| Trekkers (2,343.75-781.25-468.75) | | | 1,093.75 | (4,843.75) | 1 |
| **Less:** Fixed production overheads | | | | (2,025.00) | 1 |
| **Net profit** | | | | 2,818.75 | 1 |

**Maximum marks 6**

(b) Throughput accounting ratio = $\dfrac{\text{Return per factory hour}}{\text{Cost per factory hour}}$

Return per factory hour = $\dfrac{\text{Sales - Material costs}}{\text{Usage of bottleneck resource}}$

Remember, here you have to consider the finishing department's time used to produce one unit.

1 mark

**Calculation of return per factory hour**

| | Trainers | | Trekkers | |
|---|---|---|---|---|
| | $ | Units | $ | Units |
| Sales | 100 | | 150 | |
| Materials/components costs | (40) | | (50) | |
| Return per unit (sales – material costs) | | 60 | | 100 |
| Bottleneck resource (units required) | | 0.25 | | 0·40 |
| Return per factory hour | 240 | | 250 | |

2 marks

Cost per factory hour = $\dfrac{\text{Total factory costs}}{\text{Bottleneck resource hours available}}$

Here the total time available in the finishing department is used.

1 mark

**Calculation of cost per factory hour:**

| Variable overhead costs (Fixed in short-term) | $ |
|---|---|
| Trainers (75,000 x $10) | 750,000 |
| Trekkers (15,625 x $30) | 468,750 |
| | 1,218,750 |
| Fixed production overheads | 2,025,000 |
| Total factory costs | 3,243,750 |
| Bottleneck resource hours available | 25,000 |
| Cost per factory hour | 129.75 |

2 marks

Calculation of throughput accounting ratio

|  | Trainers | Trekkers |
|---|---|---|
| Return per factory hour | $240.00 | $250.00 |
| Cost per factory hour | $129.75 | $129.75 |
| Throughput accounting ratio | 1.85 | 1.93 |

1 mark

In throughput accounting, if the return per factory hour is greater than the cost per factory hour, then the product is said to be worth producing. It is measured by using a throughput accounting ratio. In other words, if the throughput accounting ratio is more than one, the management can consider producing that product. Profit maximisation can be achieved by increasing the throughput accounting ratio.

**Maximum marks 5**

(c) Since Trekkers has a higher return per bottleneck hour than Trainers, BFL should manufacture Trekkers until it has satisfied the total demand for 35,000 units.

**Production mix of shoes based on the results of throughput accounting:**

| Type | Units manufactured | Shoes per hour of bottleneck resource | Total hours of bottleneck resource required |
|---|---|---|---|
| Trekkers | 35,000 | 2.50 | 14,000 |
| Trainers | 44,000 | 4.00 | 11,000 |

1 mark

Total 25,000 hours are available, out of which 14,000 hours (35000/2.50) are required to produce Trekkers. So in the remaining 11,000 hours, 44,000 units of Trainers can be produced at the rate of 4 per hour.

Projected Profit and Loss Account of BFL for the year ended 31 December 20X8.

(Based on the results of throughput accounting)

|  | Units | Selling price per unit ($) | $'000 | $'000 | Marks |
|---|---|---|---|---|---|
| Sales revenue |  |  |  |  |  |
| Trekkers | 35,000 | 150 | 5,250 |  |  |
| Trainers | 44,000 | 100 | 4,400 | 9,650.00 | 1 |
| (Minus) Material costs | Units | Material cost per unit |  |  |  |
| Trekkers | 35,000 | 50 | 1,750 |  |  |
| Trainers | 44,000 | 40 | 1,760 | (3,510.00) | 1 |
| Throughput return |  |  |  |  |  |
| Trekkers | 14,000 | 250 | 3,500 |  |  |
| Trainers | 11,000 | 240 | 2,640 | 6,140.00 | 1 |
| Less: |  |  |  |  |  |
| Variable overhead costs |  |  | 1,218.75 |  |  |
| Fixed costs (assumed fixed in short-term) |  |  | 2,025 | (3,243.75) | 1 |
| **Net Profit** |  |  |  | **2,896.25** | 1 |

(Total hours of bottleneck resource)

**Maximum marks 5**

(d) Both throughput accounting and marginal costing aim to identify the contribution per unit. The manner of calculating the contribution is the same under both methods except that the treatment given to a few costs is different.

Marginal costing considers material, labour and variable overheads as variable costs. Contribution is derived by subtracting the variable costs from the sales revenue.

2 marks

Throughput accounting considers only the material costs as variable costs. Labour and variable overheads are considered as fixed costs. Contribution is derived by subtracting the variable costs from the sales revenue.

*2 marks*

As labour and variable overheads are considered fixed costs, contribution will be higher according to throughput accounting.

*1 mark*

Marginal costing demands the correct categorisation of fixed and variable costs. The accuracy of decision making is dependent on this classification. For example, in part (b) the variable production conversion cost amounting to $1,218,750 is treated as a fixed cost. In part (a), this variable production conversion cost is treated as variable cost. If it is treated as fixed cost while solving part (a), then it will not affect the ranking of products within the company under either marginal costing or throughput principles.

*1 mark*

In both marginal costing and throughput accounting, the rate of contribution per unit of the bottleneck resource is calculated to find out the optimum product mix. However, rankings obtained under both methods may be different from each other.

**Maximum marks 4**

## 9. Activity based costing – Jola Publishing

### Strategy

The given question is related to activity based costing. Part (a) is worth 8 marks and asks you to point out the reasons for a change in the reallocation of overheads to the products CB and TJ, under ABC principles and traditional (absorption) costing methods. Your answer should focus on the role of cost drivers.

Parts (b) and (c) are very simple. They require calculations of cost per unit and margins for both the products under the traditional method as well as the ABC principles of absorption of overheads.

---

**(a)** The company used absorption costing based on machine hours for allocation of overheads. However, when the overheads were re-allocated under the ABC principles, the overhead allocation to the two products changed slightly.

The following are the main reasons for such a change:

➢ For example, CB has absorbed $0.05 overheads more than traditional costing. The main reason for such a small change is that the property costs cover a significant portion (75%) of the total overheads. The cost driver used to allocate the property costs is machine hours. Therefore, in this regard the cost will not be affected by the method used for the allocation of overheads.

➢ The allocation of the quality control overheads will be significantly affected by the method used. This is because the cost driver used under ABC is the number of inspections whereas the cost driver used under absorption costing is machine hours. There is a huge difference between the number of inspections made and machine hours used for each product. As CBs are very short books, their production takes less time as compared to TJ. Therefore, CBs will absorb a small amount of overheads under traditional costing based on machine hours.

On the other hand, CBs go through frequent government inspections and quality assurance checks. Therefore, they undergo more frequent inspections as compared to TJ. This will result in high amount of quality control overheads which will be allocated to CB under ABC costing.

➢ Although the production set-up overheads are only 2% of the total overheads, the method used will change the allocation of overheads. This is because there is a big difference in the production runs required for each book. CB is produced in only 4 production runs whereas TJ requires 12 runs. Therefore, CB will absorb a lower amount of production set-up costs under ABC than under absorption costing based on machine hours.

To conclude, switching to ABC will not make a lot of difference in the total cost as the property cost which is 75% of total overheads is allocated using the same cost driver under both the methods. However, it will greatly affect the cost allocation of quality control and production set up. Therefore, the company should use ABC for better overhead allocation – this will help in controlling the cost.

*2 marks for each point discussed*
**Maximum marks 8**

## 74: Specialist Cost and Management Accounting Techniques © GTG

### Score More

Don't misunderstand the requirement. If you provide Study Text explanations for the process involved in ABC, you might not gain the maximum marks.

**(b) Calculation of cost per unit using machine hours (traditional method) for overhead absorption**

|  | CB $ per unit | TJ $ per unit | Marks |
|---|---|---|---|
| Selling price | 9.30 | 14.00 | 0.5 |
| **Less:** Costs |  |  |  |
| Materials: |  |  |  |
| Paper (400g x $2/kg), (100g x $1/kg) | 0.80 | 0.10 | 1 |
| Printing ink (50ml x $30/ltr), (150ml x $30/ltr) | 1.50 | 4.50 | 1 |
| Machine cost ($12 per hour) | 1.20 | 2.00 | 1 |
| Overheads (at $24 per hour) (W1) | 2.40 | 4.00 | 0.5 |
| Total Costs (b) | (5.90) | (10.60) | 0.5 |
| Profit / (loss) per unit (a – b) | 3.40 | 3.40 | 0.5 |

**Workings**

**W1 Calculation of overhead rate per hour**

Total overhead cost = $2,880,000
Total machine hours = (1,000,000 x 6mins) + (120,000 x 10mins) = 120,000 hours
Overhead per machine hour = $2,880,000 / 120,000 hours = $24 per hour

Therefore, overheads absorbed by each book are:

CB = 6mins x $24 per hour = $2.40
TJ = 10mins x $24 per hour = $4

1.5 marks
**Maximum marks 4**

**(c) Calculation of cost per unit using activity based costing for overhead absorption**

|  | CB $ per unit | TJ $ per unit | Marks |
|---|---|---|---|
| Selling price | 9.30 | 14.00 | 1 |
| **Less: Costs** |  |  |  |
| Materials: |  |  |  |
| Paper (400g x $2/kg), (100g x $1/kg) | 0.80 | 0.10 | 1 |
| Printing ink (50ml x $30/ltr), (150ml x $30/ltr) | 1.50 | 4.50 | 1 |
| Machine cost ($12 per hour) | 1.20 | 2.00 | 1 |
| Overheads (at $24 per hr) (W2) | 2.41 | 3.88 | 0.5 |
| Total Costs (b) | (5.91) | (10.48) | 0.5 |
| Profit / (loss) per unit (a – b) | 3.39 | 3.52 | 0.5 |

**Workings**

**W1 Calculation of overhead absorption rate**

| Activity | Drivers | CB (a) | TJ (b) | Total (c) = a/b | Annual overheads (d) | Rate per driver (d)/(c) |
|---|---|---|---|---|---|---|
| Property costs | Machine hours | 100,000 | 20,000 | 120,000 | $2,160,000 | $18 |
| Quality control | No. of inspections | 180 | 20 | 200 | $668,000 | $3,340 |
| Production set up costs | No. of set ups | 4 | 12 | 16 | $52,000 | $3,250 |

2 marks

## W2 Allocation of annual overheads to both types of books

### For CB

| Activity | Activity consumption | Rate per driver (W1) | Overheads $ | Overhead per unit $ |
|---|---|---|---|---|
| Property costs | 100,000 | $18 | 1,800,000 | 1.80 |
| Quality control | 180 | $3,340 | 601,200 | 0.6012 |
| Production set up costs | 4 | $3,250 | 13,000 | 0.013 |
| **Total** | | | **2,414,200** | **2.41** |

2 marks

### For TJ

| Activity | Activity consumption | Rate per driver (W1) | Overheads $ | Overhead per unit $ |
|---|---|---|---|---|
| Property costs | 20,000 | $18 | 360,000 | 3 |
| Quality control | 20 | $3,340 | 66,800 | 0.56 |
| Production set up costs | 12 | $3,250 | 39,000 | 0.325 |
| **Total** | | | **465,800** | **3.88** |

2 marks
**Maximum marks 8**

## 10. Activity based costing – Triple Ltd

**Strategy**

This is a simple question requiring knowledge of activity based costing. In part (a), you need to derive the cost per unit for each of the three products, D, C and P using the traditional method.

In part (b) also, you need to derive the cost per unit, but using the ABC method. It is worth 12 marks; hence you need to show all your workings (up to two decimal points) as required by the question.

Part (c) tests your understanding of the difference between both the methods.

### (a) Cost per unit for each product under the traditional method

| | D | C | P |
|---|---|---|---|
| Direct material | 20 | 12 | 25 |
| Labour (W1) | 3 | 9 | 6 |
| Production overhead (W2) | 42 | 28 | 84 |
| **Total cost per unit** | **65** | **49** | **115** |

2 marks

### W1 Labour costs

Direct labour costs $6 per hour.
D = $6 x 0.5 hours = $3
C = $6 x 1.5 hours = $9
P = $6 x 1 hour = $6

1.5 marks

### W2 Production overheads

Production overheads are absorbed on a machine hour basis. The overhead absorption rate is $28 per machine hour.
D = $28 x 1.5 hours = $42
C = $28 x 1 hour = $28
P = $28 x 3 hours = $84

1.5 marks
**Maximum marks 3**

## (b) Cost per unit for each product under the ABC method

|  | D $ | C $ | P $ |
|---|---|---|---|
| Material | 20.00 | 12.00 | 25.00 |
| Labour | 3.00 | 9.00 | 6.00 |
| Production overheads (W1) | 94.95 | 79.07 | 69.21 |
| **Total cost per unit** | **117.95** | **100.07** | **100.21** |

2 marks

**Workings**

**W1 Calculation of overheads allocation**

**Product D**

| Activity (i) | Activity rate (W2) (ii) | Activity consumption (iii) | Total overhead (iv) |
|---|---|---|---|
| Set-ups | 341.90 | 75 | 25,643 |
| Machining | 5.60 | 1,125 | 6,300 |
| Materials handling | 818.13 | 12 | 9,817 |
| Inspection | 196.35 | 150 | 29,453 |
| **Total** |  |  | **71,213** |
| Production (in units) |  |  | 750 |
| Overhead per unit ($71,213/750 units) |  |  | **94.95** |

2 marks

**Product C**

| Activity (i) | Activity rate (W2) (ii) | Activity consumption (iii) | Total overhead (ii x iii) = (iv) |
|---|---|---|---|
| Set-ups | 341.90 | 115 | 39,319 |
| Machining | 5.60 | 1,250 | 7,000 |
| Materials handling | 818.13 | 21 | 17,181 |
| Inspection | 196.35 | 180 | 35,343 |
| **Total** |  |  | **98,843** |
| Production (in units) |  |  | 1,250 |
| Overhead per unit ($98,843/ 1,250 units) |  |  | **79.07** |

2 marks

**Product P**

| Activity (i) | Activity rate (W2) (ii) | Activity consumption (iii) | Total overhead (ii x iii) = (iv) |
|---|---|---|---|
| Set-ups | 341.90 | 480 | 164,113 |
| Machining | 5.60 | 21,000 | 117,600 |
| Materials handling | 818.13 | 87 | 71,177 |
| Inspection | 196.35 | 670 | 131,554 |
| **Total** |  |  | **484,444** |
| Production (in units) |  |  | 7,000 |
| Overhead per unit ($484,444/7,000 units) |  |  | **69.21** |

2 marks

## W2 Calculation of activity rate

The cost driver rate for each activity is calculated as follows:

*It is calculated as a percentage of total overheads - e.g. 20% of total overheads are assigned to machining. Therefore, machining cost is $130,900 (20% x $654500).*

| Activity (i) | Activity driver (ii) | % (iii) | Budgeted cost (W1) (iv) $ | Activity consumption (v) | Activity rate (iv/v) = (vi) |
|---|---|---|---|---|---|
| Set-ups | Number of set-ups | 35 | 229,075 | 670 | 341.90 |
| Machining | Machine hours | 20 | 130,900 | 23,375 (W3) | 5.60 |
| Materials handling | Material movements | 15 | 98,175 | 120 | 818.13 |
| Inspection | Number of inspections | 30 | 196,350 | 1,000 | 196.35 |
| Total | | 100 | 654,500 | | |

*4 marks*

### W3 Total machine hours

| | | |
|---|---|---|
| D | (1.5 hours x 750 units) | 1,125 hours |
| C | (1 hour x 1,250 units) | 1,250 hours |
| P | (3 hours x 7,000 units) | 21,000 hours |
| **Total hours** | | **23,375 hours** |

*1 mark*
**Maximum marks 12**

### (c) Comparison of alternative costing approach

| Product | Traditional Cost per unit $ | ABC Cost per unit $ | Variance $ |
|---|---|---|---|
| D | 42 | 95 | (53) |
| C | 28 | 79 | (51) |
| P | 84 | 69 | 15 |

*2 marks*

As the ABC system uses the cost of each activity as the basis for assigning costs to the product, the ABC system has come up with more realistic product costs. The overhead costs of products D and C have gone up by $53 and $51 respectively and the overhead cost of product P has fallen by $15.

*1 mark*

ABC reflects the efforts required to produce a product. Here, product P may require longer time than D and C which may be due to longer production lines.

*1 mark*

Comparison of the activity volume required by each product per 1,000 units

| Product | Set-ups | Materials movements | Inspections |
|---|---|---|---|
| D | 100 | 16 | 200 |
| C | 92 | 17 | 144 |
| P | 69 | 12 | 96 |

From the above table, we can conclude that:

➢ product P requires less number of set-ups, material movements and inspections than D and C. Due to this the overhead cost per unit for P has fallen.

➢ the machining overhead cost per unit for P is two times higher than D (i.e. 3/1.5 hours) and three times (i.e. 3/1 hour) higher than that of C. As the machine overheads are only 20% of the total overheads, this is a small effect.

*2 marks*
**Maximum marks 5**

## 11. Target cost – Edward Co

### Strategy

Target costing is one of the important areas of the syllabus. The given question requires an understanding of the process and benefits of target costing. It also requires an explanation of possible steps of how a cost gap might be closed by an organisation. Parts (a), (b) and (c) have theoretical answers. Hence, it is easy to score full marks.

Part (d) required candidates to be able to calculate the cost of a unit (in this case, a radio).

### (a) Target costing process

Target cost per unit is the estimated long-term cost per unit of a product or service that enables the manufacturer or service provider to achieve the desired profit per unit, when selling at the target price.

Target cost per unit = Target price per unit – Desired (target) profit per unit

**1 mark**

The determination of the target selling price will involve:

1. **Wide range of customer analysis**: it should consider which features of the product are valued by the customers and which are not. Those features that are valued by the customers will be included in the product design.
2. **External analysis**: this will take into account the competitor's products and the market conditions expected at the time the product will be launched. Hence, heavy emphasis is placed on external analysis before any consideration is made regarding the internal cost of the product.

**1 mark**

From the target selling price, the desired profit margin is deducted, which leaves the target cost. In order to meet the desired profit margin, an organisation will need to meet this target. The target cost is compared to the estimated cost to arrive at the target cost gap. Cost estimates are made based on the current standard of material, labour and overheads. In most of the instances, the target cost is lower than the estimated cost and the difference between the two is the 'target cost gap'.

**1 mark**
**Maximum marks 2**

### (c) Benefits of adopting target costing

#### (i) Cost control

In the traditional system, cost control procedures take place at the 'cost incurring' stage. This is often very late to make a substantial impact on a product that is too expensive to make.

However, in the case of target costing, it is easy to implement cost control procedures from the initial stages. If a cost gap exists at the design stage, more and better efforts can be put in by the design team to close the cost gap.

#### (ii) Enhanced profitability

In the traditional system, an organisation may not be fully aware of the constraints in the external environment until after the production has started. Cost reduction at the initial stage is much more difficult as many of the costs are 'designed into' the product.

Under target costing, costs per unit are often lower - this enhances the profitability. Target costing has been shown to reduce product cost by around 20% to 40%, depending upon the product and the existing market conditions.

#### (iii) Reduction in time taken

Under traditional practices, there are often prolonged intervals whilst a team goes 'back to the drawing board'.

It is often said that target costing reduces the time taken to get a product to the market because it has an early external focus, tends to help get things right the first time and therefore reduces the time to market.

### (iv) Features valued to customers

Only those features that are of value to customers will be included in the product design. Target costing at an early stage carefully considers the product that is intended. Features that are unlikely to be valued by the customers will be excluded.

This is often insufficiently considered in cost plus methods.

### (v) External focus to product development

Traditional approaches are internally driven as they calculate the selling price by calculating the cost and then adding a margin.

Under target costing, the organisation will have an early external focus for its product development. Businesses have to compete with others (competitors) and an early consideration of this will tend to make them more successful.

*1 mark for each correctly explained benefit*
**Maximum marks 4**

### (c) Steps to reduce a cost gap

To eliminate the 'gap', cost management accountants help the engineering planners and designers to decompose the target cost into each cost element, according to their detailed production functions. The production engineers determine standards for material and parts usage, labour consumption, etc.

| | |
|---|---|
| **Analysis of radio features** | ➢ Identifying improved radio designs that reduce the cost of radios without sacrificing functionality.<br>➢ Eliminating unnecessary functions that increase the costs of radios (functions which customers are not prepared to pay extra for).<br>➢ Changing material specifications without affecting the quality of the radio.<br><br>This can be referred to as value engineering or value analysis. |
| **Costs involved in the components of a radio** | Edward Limited should look at the significant costs involved in the components.<br>➢ New suppliers could be identified or different materials could be used to reduce cost.<br>➢ Attention would be needed not to damage the perceived value of the radio.<br>➢ Efficiency improvements should also be made by reducing waste or idle time that might exist. Standard parts should always be used in the design. |
| **ABC approach for overhead allocation** | Significant increase in the productivity will spread the fixed overheads over a greater number of radios. Similarly, Edward Limited should consider an activity based costing approach to its overhead allocation. It may disclose more favourable cost allocations for the digital radio or ideas for reducing costs in the business. |
| **Team approach** | Edward Limited should bring together members of the marketing, design, assembly and distribution teams to allow discussions and brainstorming sessions for methods to reduce costs. |
| **Association workers** | Productivity gains may be possible by changing working practices or by 'de-skilling' the process.<br><br>➢ Automation is increasingly common in assembly and manufacturing and Edward Limited should investigate what is possible here to reduce the costs.<br>➢ The learning curve may ultimately help close the cost gap by reducing labour costs per unit.<br>➢ Clearly reducing the percentage of idle time will reduce product costs.<br>➢ Better management, smoother work flow and staff incentives could all help here.<br>➢ Focusing on continuous improvement in production processes may help. |

*1 mark for each correctly explained idea*
**Maximum marks 4**

## (d) Calculation of expected cost per unit and cost gap

|  | $ | $ |
|---|---|---|
| Material costs |  |  |
| Component 1 - circuit board | 4.10 |  |
| Delivery cost ($2,400/4,000 bathces) | 0.60 | 4.70 |
| Component 2 - Wiring |  | 0.13 |
| ($0.50 per meter x 25/100 metre x 100/98) |  |  |
| Other materials |  | 8.10 |
|  |  | 12.93 |
| Labour costs |  | 7.00 |
| ($12.60/hour x 30/60 hours x 100/90) |  |  |
| Production overheads |  |  |
| Variable overheads ($20/hour x 30/60 hours) | 10.00 |  |
| Fixed overheads ($12/hour x 30/60 hours) | 6.00 | 16.00 |
| **Target cost** |  | **35.93** |
| Less: Desired cost ($44 x 0.80) |  | 35.20 |
| **Cost gap** |  | **0.73** |

**Maximum marks 10**

**Working**

### W1 Production overhead cost (using high low method)

| | |
|---|---|
| Extra overhead cost between month 1 and 2 | $80,000 |
| Extra assembly hours | 4,000 |
| Variable cost per hour | $20/hour |
| Monthly fixed production overhead ($700,000 – (23,000 x $20/hour)) | $240,000 |
| Annual fixed production overhead ($240,000 x 12) | $2,880,000 |
| Absorption rate of fixed overheads ($2,880,000/24,000 hours) | $12/hour |

**Score More**

The examiner has commented that most of the candidates lost marks in the calculation of production overhead cost using the high-low method. You should not add 10% to the cost (or time taken) as it is not the same as correctly adjusting by a factor of 100/90 (assuming a 10% loss for waste in this case).

## SOLUTION BANK

# SECTION B: DECISION-MAKING TECHNIQUES

## 12. Sensitivity analysis – Smart Kids Ltd

### Strategy

Part (a) (i) – simple calculations of existing cash flows and cash flows after changes in variables should be given with proper explanations and workings. Sensitivity in percentage terms should also be given. Explanation of sensitivity analysis should include both merits and demerits of the method as a project sustainability test.

Steps for calculations:

- Statement showing original profit / net cash flow.
- Separate statements showing change in cash-flows and percentage change in net cash flows due to change in overhead and labour cost and selling price.
- Explanation highlighting strengths and weaknesses of sensitivity analysis

Part (ii) – answer to this should include a point-by-point analysis of HOW uncertainty affects decision-making and WHAT SKL should consider while launching the new soft toy.

Part (b)- The answer to the question should be presented in a simple statement that will calculate the expected values. Do not forget to multiply the results of each event by the related probability to arrive at the final expected value of profit.

---

**(a)**
**(i) Calculation of project cash flows**

|                  | $   | $    |
|------------------|-----|------|
| Sales price      |     | 40   |
| Less: costs      |     |      |
| Direct material  | 7   |      |
| Direct labour    | 20  |      |
| Overhead costs   | 6   | (33) |
| **Profit**       |     | **7** |

1 mark

Cash flow from the product 'Bobby D' = $7 x 30,000 units = $210,000

**Sensitivity of net cash flow to increase in overhead costs**

|                         | $    | $       |
|-------------------------|------|---------|
| Sales price             |      | 40      |
| Less: costs             |      |         |
| Direct material         | 7    |         |
| Direct labour           | 20   |         |
| Overhead costs($6 + 2%) | 6.12 | (33.12) |
| **Profit**              |      | **6.88** |

1 mark

Cash flow from the product 'Bobby D' = $6.88 x 30,000 units = $206,400
Hence, the cash flow has decreased by $3,600 (210,000 – 206,400) or 1.71%    [(3,600/210,000) x 100]

0.5 marks

## Sensitivity of net cash flow to decrease in labour costs

|  | $ | $ |
|---|---|---|
| Sales price |  | 40 |
| Less: costs |  |  |
| Direct material | 7 |  |
| Direct labour (20 – 5%) | 19 |  |
| Overhead costs | 6 | (32) |
| **Profit** |  | **8** |

1 mark

Cash flow from the product 'Bobby D' = $8 x 30,000 units = $240,000  [(30,000/210,000) x 100]
Hence, the cash flow has increased by $30,000 (240,000 – 210,000) or 14.28%

0.5 marks

## Sensitivity of net cash flow to decrease in selling price and thereby an increase in sales

|  | $ | $ | Marks |
|---|---|---|---|
| Sales price(40 - 0.5) |  | 39.50 |  |
| Less: costs |  |  |  |
| Direct material | 7 |  |  |
| Direct labour | 20 |  |  |
| Overhead costs | 6 | (33.00) |  |
| **Profit** |  | **6.50** | 1 |

*Do not forget to add the increase in sales (4%)*

Cash flow from the product 'Bobby D' = $6.50 x (30,000 units + 4%) = $6.50 x 31,200
= $202,800

Hence, the cash flow has decreased by $7,200 (210,000 - 202,800) or 3.4%  [(7,200/210,000) x 100]

0.5 marks

Sensitivity analysis evaluates the effect of changes in project variables on project net cash flow. The objective is to determine those variables where the smallest change produces the biggest change in a project's cash flows, also known as the key or critical project variables. Therefore, sensitivity analysis is a "what if" technique that measures how the expected values in a decision model will be affected by changes in the critical data inputs.

1 mark

Sensitivity analysis provides decision-makers with information about the responsiveness of the project to the parameters. Once the crucial factors have been determined, the decision-makers can concentrate only on those crucial factors, and thereby ensure the sustainability of the project

1 mark

However, a sensitivity analysis is restricted. This is because in this analysis technique only one project variable at a time may be changed. In reality, however, several project variables may change simultaneously. For example, an increase in inflation could lead to increases in variable costs, fixed costs and sales price.

Sensitivity analysis, although it may identify the key or critical variables, is not a method of evaluating project risk since it cannot assess the likelihood of a change in these variables. This is because a sensitivity analysis does not assign probabilities to project variables. On the other hand, sensitivity analysis can be used to highlight those project variables that require close monitoring, if a particular investment project is to be successful. It can also bring to the management's attention the need to check the assumptions underlying the key or critical variables.

2 marks
**Maximum marks 8**

### Score More

A sensitivity analysis provides decision-makers with information about responsiveness of net cash flows to change in underlying parameters. Decision makers can concentrate only on the crucial factors once these are known and hence check the sustainability of the project.

Discussing the above alone will not complete the answer. Candidates must also discuss how a sensitivity analysis is restricted and reflects changes in response to a change in only one underlying parameter at a time. The weakness of sensitivity analysis that it does not assign probabilities to the project variables should also be explained.

**(ii)** Managers need to make decisions on whether to accept an investment project or not. Smart Kids launches a new soft toy character every year and as such the manager of Smart Kids faces this dilemma every year. SKL might need to consider the following in relation to uncertainty:

- Uncertainty about the acceptance of the new soft toy in the market.

> *It is important to relate the points to the scenario!*

- Although it may use its past experience to predict the outcome of the project, uncertainty will still prevail in the absence of any accurate data.

- Uncertainty increases with project life. SKL might face a lower uncertainty in this respect since the project life is only one year.

- Absence of historical data is obvious when a new product is launched. Therefore SKL will not be able to predict with certainty the behaviour of the factors affecting the decision and hence will be unable to assign any probability to the occurrence of a particular state of nature.

- Management judgement and experience and scenario analysis may, in certain cases, help associate probabilities to future cash flows.

*3 marks*

This assessment of project risk can help the manager to a great extent. It can also bring to management's attention to projects that might be rejected as being too risky, or projects that might be worthy of reconsideration if ways of reducing project risk could be found.

Information plays an important role in decision-making for investment projects. Hence, uncertainty about the future outcome can be reduced substantially by gathering related information and thereby knowledge about the environment. Accurate information would enable the decision-maker (manager) of SKL to prepare a reliable analytical model and to determine the outcomes of a particular course of action.

> *Say HOW the uncertainty may be reduced, as this will help the examiner know that you can apply the concepts to the scenario*

*2 marks*

Therefore, when a decision is required to be taken under uncertainty, the following techniques can be used by the manager to obtain information:

**Focus group**

A focus group is a qualitative technique in which a small group of people is selected for a free discussion about their opinion on and attitude towards a particular subject such as product, services, idea etc. This technique can prove to be a relatively inexpensive and easy way of getting feedback about likes, dislikes and perceptions regarding the new soft toy to be launched by SKL.

A focus group is a highly effective technique for reducing uncertainty for a new product launch in the market by finding out about customer opinions. This technique can also be used for existing products, to analyse the change in the needs and tastes of the customers. Hence, a focus group helps the management to understand the needs, sensitivity and expectations of its target group, with regard to a particular product.

**Market research**

Market research is a systematic and objective technique of gathering, recording and analysing information about customers, market, competitors, government regulations, economic trends, technological advances, and other factors / elements of the business environment.

This technique is commonly used in the development and marketing of a new product. Market research is a technique by which the customer's views, likes, dislikes etc. can be analysed by the company. By analysing the outcome of the market research, an organisation can learn more about its current and potential customers.

*2 marks*
**Maximum marks 7**

84: Decision-Making Techniques                                                                                      © GTG

### (b) Expected value of profit according to budget for 20X0

|  | Pessimistic | Most likely | Optimistic | Marks |
|---|---|---|---|---|
| Units | 8,000 | 10,000 | 15,000 | Most likely sales level is 2,000 + pessimistic i.e. 8,000 = 10,000 |
| Selling price per unit ($) | 19 | 20 | 20 | |
| Sales | 152,000 | 200,000 | 300,000 | |
| Variable cost (W1) | (100,000) | (120,000) | (165,000) | |
| Contribution | 52,000 | 80,000 | 135,000 | 1 |
| Fixed cost | (60,000) | (50,000) | (48,000) | |
| Profit (Loss) | (8,000) | 30,000 | 87,000 | 1 |
| Probability | 0.20 | 0.70 | 0.10 | |
| Expected value (profit x probability) | (1600) | 21,000 | 8,700 | 1 |
| **Total expected value** | | | **28,100** | 1 |

(-1,600 + 21,000 + 8,700)

**Working**

**W1 Variable cost**

For pessimistic, 8,000 units x $12.50 per unit ($9.5 + $2 + $1) = $100,000
For most likely, 10,000 units x $12.00 per unit ($8 + $3 + $1) = $120,000
For Optimistic, 15,000 units x $11.00 per unit ($7 + $3 + $1) = $165,000

2 marks
**Maximum marks 5**

## 13. Production planning and decision-making - Almora Engineers

**Strategy**

Part (a) (i) - The answer should be prepared in three separate statements which will highlight ranking, product mix and profit from the product mix arrived at on the basis of ranking. Remember that there is a minimum demand which HAS to be met and only any extra hours left after this can be used for excess production of the remaining higher ranked product.

Part (ii) – the answer should be calculated based on revised ranking since now the workers can work on any job. Extra units should be produced only for the top ranked product since no maximum limit is specified for demand.

Part (b) - The answer to the question should be simply presented in statements that will present the answer using both criteria. Confusion should be avoided while defining the acts and events since this can alter the answer completely.

### (a)
### (i) Statement showing contribution per labour hour and ranking of the products:

|  | WT4 | WT6 | PL1 | PL7 | Marks |
|---|---|---|---|---|---|
| Selling price per unit ($) | 86.4 | 90 | 138.6 | 124.2 | |
| Less: | | | | | |
| Direct material per unit($) | 32.4 | 39.6 | 57.6 | 79.2 | |
| Direct labour rate per hour ($) | 7.2 | 7.2 | 7.2 | 7.2 | |
| Variable overhead per unit ($) | 3.6 | 3.6 | 5.4 | 5.4 | |
| Total variable cost ($) | (43.2) | (50.4) | (70.2) | (91.8) | |
| Contribution per unit ($) | 43.2 | 39.6 | 68.4 | 32.4 | 1 |
| Hours per unit | 7.2 | 7.2 | 9 | 3.6 | |
| Contribution per labour hour ($) | 6 | 5.5 | 7.6 | 9 | 1 |
| **Ranking** | **1** | **2** | **2** | **1** | |
| Minimum demand to be met (units) | 3,600 | 4,500 | 3,240 | 3,960 | |
| Hours required | 25,920 | 32,400 | 29,160 | 14,256 | 1 |
| Total hours required for fulfilling the minimum demand | 58,320 | | 43,416 | | |
| Maximum hours available | 60,000 | | 45,000 | | |
| Balance hours in each department to be used for the product with a higher ranking | 1,680 hours for WT4 | | | 1,584 hours for PL7 | 1 |

Ranking for both the departments is independent

Therefore, the total hours to be used for WT4 will be 25,920 + 1,680 = 27,600 hours
Total hours to be used for PL7 will be 14,256 + 1,584 = 15,840

1 mark

**Statement showing maximum units of each product that can be manufactured**

|  | Units to be manufactured | Total hours | Marks |
|---|---|---|---|
| **Welding department – total hours** |  | 60,000 |  |
| Used for WT4 | 27,600/7.2 = 3,833 | 27,600 | 1 |
| Balance hours left |  | 32,400 |  |
|  |  |  |  |
| To be used for minimum demand of WT6 | 4,500 | 32,400 | 1 |
| Balance hours left |  | Nil |  |
|  |  |  |  |
| **Pressing department – total hours** |  | 45,000 |  |
| Used for PL7 | 15,840/3.6 = 4,400 | 15,840 | 1 |
| Balance hours left |  | 29,160 |  |
| To be used for production of PL1 | 3,240 | 29,160 | 1 |
| Balance hours left |  | Nil |  |

*The units for WT4 are manufactured more since it has a greater ranking than WT6. Refer above statement*

**Statement showing profitability on the basis of above production schedule**

| Product | Contribution per unit ($) | Units to be manufactured | Total contribution ($) | Marks |
|---|---|---|---|---|
| WT4 | 43.2 | 3,833 | 165,585.60 | 0.5 |
| WT6 | 39.6 | 4,500 | 178,200.00 | 0.5 |
| PL1 | 68.4 | 3,240 | 221,616.00 | 0.5 |
| PL7 | 32.4 | 4,400 | 142,560.00 | 0.5 |
| **Total contribution** |  |  | 707,961.60 |  |
| Less: fixed costs |  |  | (90,000) |  |
| **Profit** |  |  | 617,961.60 | 1 |

*Do not forget to deduct this since this is a profit statement not contribution statement*

*Exclude additional training cost here since this statement is before training.*

**Maximum marks 10**

**(ii)** If the workers are given special training the company will be able to use the workers in both departments and so the total hours available will be 60,000 + 45,000 = 105,000 hours

Hence the revised production schedule will be as follows:

|  | WT4 | WT6 | PL1 | PL7 |
|---|---|---|---|---|
| Maximum hours available (60,000 + 45,000) |  |  |  | 105,000 hrs |
| Hours required for minimum production | 25,920 | 32,400 | 29,160 | 14,256 hrs |
| **Total** |  |  |  | **101,736 hrs** |
| Balance hours left |  |  |  | 3,264 hrs |
| Contribution per hour ($) | 6 | 5.5 | 7.6 | 9 |
| Revised ranking based on contribution per hour | 3 | 4 | 2 | 1 |
| Production in balance hours for PL7 (3,264/3.6 = 906 units) |  |  |  |  |
| Revised product mix after training | 3,600 | 4,500 | 3,240 | 3,960 + 906 = 4,866 |

*Ranking has changed since workers can now work in any department*

*3,264/3.6*

1 mark

**Statement of profitability showing profitability after training**

| Product | Contribution per unit $ | Units to be manufactured | Total contribution $ |
|---|---|---|---|
| WT4 | 43.2 | 3,600 | 155,520.00 |
| WT6 | 39.6 | 4,500 | 178,200.00 |
| PL1 | 68.4 | 3,240 | 221,616.00 |
| PL7 | 32.4 | 4,866 | 157,658.40 |
| **Total contribution** |  |  | 712,994.40 |
| Less: fixed costs |  |  | (99,000) |
| **Profit** |  |  | 613,994.40 |

*Do not forget to add the additional fixed costs of $9,000*

1 mark

The above statement shows that the profit has reduced by $3,967.20 ($617,961.60 – $613,994.40), hence the manager's option should **not be implemented** since it reduces profit. This is because an additional expense of $9,000 being incurred against an increase in contribution of only $5032.80.

1 mark
**Maximum marks 4**

**(b) Maximin criteria**

The two possible **courses of action** open to the manufacturer are:

$A_1$ - Use of Chemical Y and Z
$A_2$ - Use chemical X.

And two possible **events** are:

$E_1$ - the price of chemical X increases,
$E_2$ - the price of chemical X does not change.

**Pay-off table**

| Event | Action ($) | |
|---|---|---|
| | $A_1$ | $A_2$ |
| $E_1$ | (3,000) | (4,000) |
| $E_2$ | (3,000) | (1,000) |

| Action | Minimum payoff for this action ($) | Maximum of these ($) |
|---|---|---|
| $A_1$ | (3,000) | (3,000) |
| $A_2$ | (4,000) | |

Therefore, applying the maximin criteria, Action $A_1$ should be taken. The manufacturer should use chemical Y and Z.

3 marks

**Minimax criteria**

Minimax minimises the maximum regret (or opportunity loss) incurred by taking a particular decision. Regret is the amount of pay-off lost by not taking the optimal action for any particular event. It can be defined as the difference between:

i. the maximum possible pay-off under the event, and
ii. the payoff resulting from the action concerned for the same event.

**Regret table**

| Event | Action $ | |
|---|---|---|
| | $A_1$ | $A_2$ |
| $E_1$ | -3,000 – (-3,000) = 0 | -3,000 – (-4,000) = 1,000 |
| $E_2$ | -1,000 – (-3,000) = 2,000 | -1,000 – (-1,000) = 0 |

*Figures are in the negative; hence the greater amount is -3,000 and not -4,000*

| Action | Maximum regret for this action $ | Minimum of these $ |
|---|---|---|
| $A_1$ | 2,000 | 1,000 |
| $A_2$ | 1,000 | |

Therefore, applying the minimax criteria, action $A_2$ should be taken. The manufacturer should use chemical X.

3 marks
**Maximum marks 6**

## 14. Marginal costing – Albion Plc

### Strategy

Part (a) of the question should be answered carefully since material R2 is scarce, contribution per kg of R2 should be calculated in order to decide the ranking of products for the purpose of manufacture. Contribution figure will be wrong if you deduct fixed costs per unit from the selling price, to arrive at contribution per unit.

Part (b) should also be carefully approached since we need to arrive at the maximum price that can be paid, without incurring a loss. This can be done by adding the contribution per limiting factor to the existing market price.

Part (c) while comparing costs for the make or buy decision, the variable costs excluding the fixed cost per unit should be compared with the cost of buying. The examiner would also expect the candidates to write the other non-financial factors like quality, reliability and delivery time when deciding upon the supplier.

Part (d) requires a simple analysis of how and why the exclusion of fixed costs make marginal costing a weak technique for decision-making. This can be explained easily by providing based examples of fixed costs that may change in the short run.

---

**(a)** The optimum production schedule is found using the limiting factor analysis.

In the given sum, although the final product is made up of material R1 and material R2 there is a scarcity for material R2. Hence, we will calculate the contribution per unit only for material R2. This is because the optimum utilisation of R2 will decide the maximum possible contribution from available resources.

**Statement showing contribution per unit of R2 and ranking for production**

|  | AR2 | GL3 | HT4 | Marks |
|---|---|---|---|---|
| Material R2 ($/unit) | 2.5 x 2 = 5.00 | 2.5 x 3 = 7.50 | 2.5 x 3 = 7.50 |  |
| Material R3 ($/unit) | 2 x 2 = 4.00 | 2 x 2.2 = 4.40 | 2 x 1.6 = 3.20 |  |
| Labour ($/unit) | 4 x 0.6 = 2.40 | 4 x 1.2 = 4.80 | 4 x 1.5 = 6.00 |  |
| Variable o/h ($/unit) | 1.10 | 1.30 | 1.10 |  |
| **Variable costs ($/unit)** | **12.50** | **18.00** | **17.80** |  |
| Selling price ($/unit) | 21.00 | 28.50 | 27.30 |  |
| **Contribution ($/unit)** | **8.50** | **10.50** | **9.50** | 2 |
| Material R2 (kg/unit) | 2.00 | 3.00 | 3.00 |  |
| Contribution ($/kg of R2) | 8.5/2 = 4.25 | 10.5/3 = 3.50 | 9.5/3 = 3.17 | 2 |
| Ranking | 1 | 2 | 3 |  |

| Product | Demand (units) | R2 used (kg) | Production (units) | Contribution per unit ($) | Contribution ($) (Units produced x contribution per unit |
|---|---|---|---|---|---|
| AR2 | 950 | 1,900 | 950 | 8.5 | 8,075 |
| GL3 | 1,000 | 3,000 | 1,000 | 10.5 | 10,500 |
| HT4 | 900 | 600 | 200 | 9.5 | 1,900 |
|  |  | 5,500 |  |  | 20,475 |

Balancing quantity of R2 used to produce 200 units of HT4

4 marks

The optimum production schedule is 950 units of Product AR2, 1,000 units of GL3 and 200 units of HT4, giving a total contribution of $20,475. The fixed production overheads are ignored in this analysis because they are assumed not to vary with changes in the level of production.

**Maximum marks 8**

**(b)** Further supplies of Material R2 will be used to produce additional units of Product HT4 since we have already produced the required quantities for the maximum demand of AR2 and GL3. The ruling market price for R2 is $2.50, and the contribution per kg of material R2 for Product HT4 is $3·17. In order to cover the costs the product should recover an amount equal to the additional costs incurred.

Hence if Albion pays $3·17 + $2·50 = $5·67 per kg for Material R2, the additional units of Product HT4 produced will make a zero contribution towards fixed costs. $5·67 is therefore the maximum price.

1 mark

This is because we increased the cost of material R2, to an extent that resulted in the total cost of the product HT4 being equal to its selling price.

The total cost when material R2 is purchased at $5.67 per kg.

|  | $ |
|---|---|
| Material R2 (3 x 5.67) | 17.01 |
| Material R3 (1.6 x 2) | 3.20 |
| Labour (4 x 1.5) | 6.00 |
| Variable overhead | 1.10 |
|  | **27.31** |
| Selling price | 27.30 |
| Hence Contribution | 00.00 |

(Difference due to rounding off of contribution in the first stage)

2 marks

Hence, we do not get any contribution from the additional units produced.

**Maximum marks 3**

**(c) The variable cost of Product XY5**

|  | $ per unit |
|---|---|
| Material R3: 3 x 2 = | 6.0 |
| Labour: 1·7 x 4 = | 6.8 |
| Variable overhead: | 1.4 |
|  | **14.2** |
| Price offered by Folam | (10.2) |
| **Saving per unit** | **4.0** |

1 mark

The substitute offered by Folam gives a saving of $4 per unit. However, Albion Plc would also pay an annual fee of $50,000 for the right to use the substitute. In order to make the buying option cheaper we need to manufacture as many numbers of units that will lead to the total buying cost (fixed fee $50,000 plus per unit cost $10.20) to be less than the existing in house manufacturing cost.

Minimum number of units to be manufactured so that in house costs and buying costs are the same:

| Annual fixed fee | $50,000 |
|---|---|
| Saving per unit by buying substitute | $4 |
| Units to be manufactured ($50,000/$4) units p.a. | 12,500 |
| Units to be manufactured per month (12,500/12) | 1,042 |

1 mark

The company would need to manufacture more than 12,500 units per year of Product XY5, or 1,042 units per month, in order for the offered substitute to be financially acceptable. If it needed less than 12,500 units of Product XY5 per year, it would be cheaper to manufacture the product in house. This evaluation is from a short-term perspective. In the long run, buying in may lead to fixed cost savings and lower investment, increasing the benefits of buying in and lowering the break-even point.

2 marks

There are certain other factors that Albion Plc would need to consider before accepting Folum Limited's offer. These are as follows:

➤ Quality of the substitute offered should match the quality standards of Albion Plc. A Low price might imply low quality.

1 mark

➤ The lead time for delivery also needs to be considered since Albion would require prompt deliveries, to ensure production is not delayed.

1 mark

➤ If Albion depends excessively on Folum for supplies of the substitute product, they might become vulnerable to their future price increases. The increases might reduce or even eliminate the cost saving of buying in.

1 mark
**Maximum marks 7**

**(d)** Under marginal costing (variable costing), the contribution made by the products towards fixed costs and profits is the basis for decision-making in the short term. Fixed costs are ignored in these calculations since they are considered period costs that do not change in the short-term. Therefore the difference between the selling price and variable cost is used as a basis for decision-making.

0.5 marks

Traditionally, marginal costing is used for short-term decisions such as whether to stop production of a product, whether to buy a product from a supplier or make it in-house, and how to allocate scarce resources in order to maximize contribution.

0.5 marks

The assumption that fixed costs never change in the short-term may turn out to be incorrect. Certain fixed costs may depict this pattern e.g. rent. Rental amounts may not undergo a change in the short-term. However, certain other fixed costs such as administrative costs might decrease if certain products are discontinued in the short-term. The same might also be the case with related marketing costs. This will lead to a subsequent decrease in the long term fixed costs.

1 mark
**Maximum marks 2**

## 15. Production planning and shadow pricing - Chivassa Ronald

### Strategy

The question is very basic and requires that you calculate the contribution and solve the linear programming through graphs. Although the iso-contribution approach is simpler we have explained the equation solving approach, since it is easy for students.

Students should be careful while calculating the shadow price and identify the correct resource as critical; otherwise they may unnecessarily lose marks.

**(a)** In order to form a linear programming problem we need to formulate an objective function first. In order to do this we need to calculate contribution.

**Calculation of contribution per box**

|  | Caramium $ |  | Corrum $ |  | Marks |
|---|---|---|---|---|---|
| Selling price |  | 61.500 |  | 103.500 | 1.5 |
| Less variable costs |  |  |  |  |  |
| Workmen cost | 20.25 (0.75 hrs x $27) |  | 30.375 (1.125 hrs x $27) |  | 1.5 |
| Mineral powder per box | 24.30 (405g/1,000g x $60) |  | 24.30 (405g/1,000g x $60) |  | 1.5 |
| Other variable costs | 1.80 |  | 7.05 |  |  |
| Total variable costs |  | (46.350) |  | (61.725) |  |
| **Contribution** |  | **15.150** |  | **41.775** | 1.5 |

Let C1 be boxes of caramium to be produced, and C2 be boxes of corrum to be produced.

The objective function will be:

C = 15.15C1 + 41.775C2

0.5 marks

**(i) Hours constraint**

The maximum hours available are given as 18,000 hours. Each box of caramium requires 0.75 hours and each box of corrum requires 1.125 hours. Hence the constraint can be written as:

0.75C1 + 1.125C2 ≤ 18,000

1.5 marks

**(ii) Mineral powder constraint**

The maximum availability is given as 8,100 kg. Each box of caramium requires 405 g of mineral powder and each box of corrum also requires 405 g. Hence the constraint can be written as:

0.405C1 + 0.405C2 ≤ 8,100

1.5 marks

We have limited demand this season. Hence CR can manufacture only 16,000 boxes of caramium and 12,000 boxes of corrum.

Therefore:

C1 ≤ 16,000
C2 ≤ 12,000

The linear programming problem can now be written as:

C = 15.15C1 + 41.775C2

**(iii) Subject to constraints**

0.75C1 + 1.125C2 ≤ 18,000
0.405C1 + 0.405C2 ≤ 8,100
C1 ≤ 16,000

0.5 marks

C2 ≤ 12,000

0.5 marks

Non-negativity constraints
C1, C2 ≥ 0  *(Do not forget to write this constraint)*

0.5 marks

From solving the equations for C1 and C2 we get the following coordinates:

0.75C1 + 1.125C2 = 18,000
Put C2 = 0 we get 0.75C1 = 18,000 C1 = 24,000 therefore (24,000, 0)
Put C1 = 0 we get 1.125C2 = 18,000 C2 = 16,000 therefore (0, 16,000)

0.405C1 + 0.405C2 = 8,100
Put C2 = 0 we get 0.405C1 = 8,100 C1 = 20,000 therefore (20,000, 0)
Put C1 = 0 we get 0.405C2 = 8,100 C2 = 20,000 therefore (0, 20,000)

0.5 marks

The graph will appear as follows:

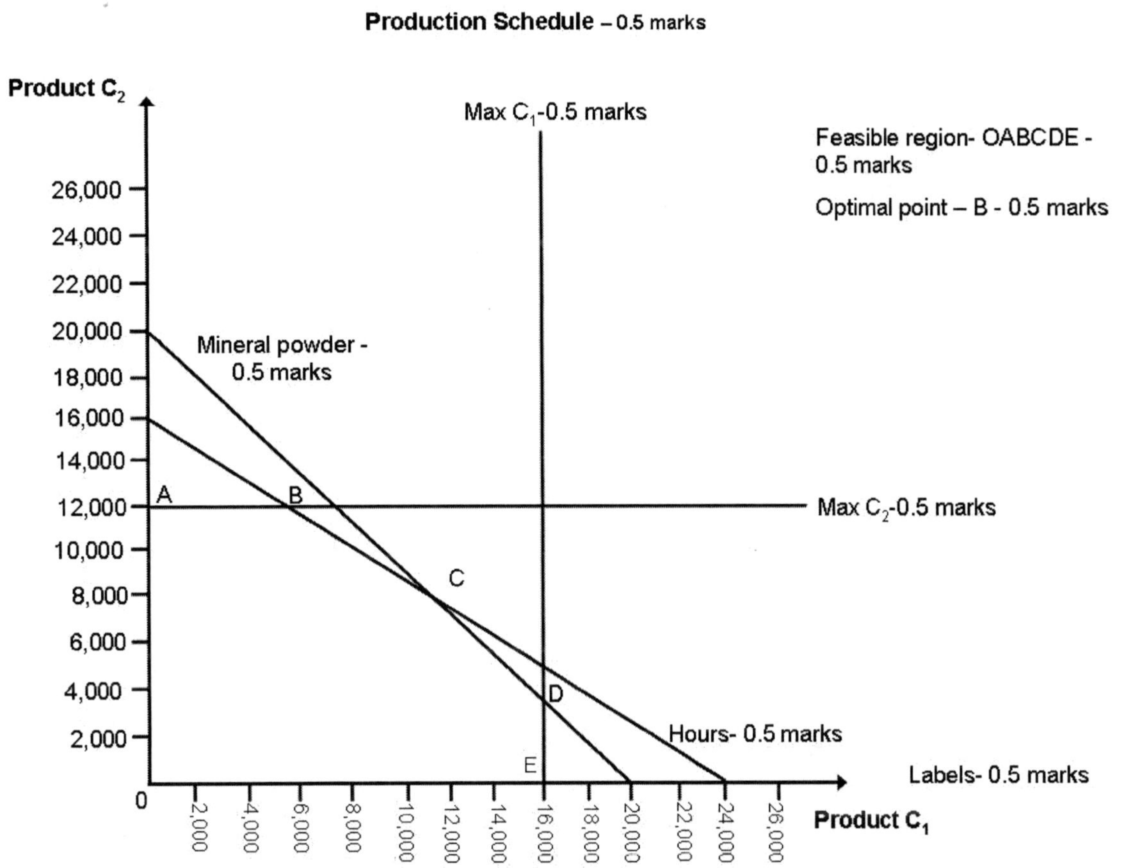
Production Schedule – 0.5 marks
Product $C_2$
Max $C_1$-0.5 marks
Feasible region- OABCDE - 0.5 marks
Optimal point – B - 0.5 marks
26,000
24,000
22,000
20,000
18,000
16,000
14,000
12,000
10,000
8,000
6,000
4,000
2,000
0
Mineral powder - 0.5 marks
A
B
C
D
E
Max $C_2$-0.5 marks
Hours- 0.5 marks
Labels- 0.5 marks
2,000
4,000
6,000
8,000
10,000
12,000
14,000
16,000
18,000
20,000
22,000
24,000
26,000
Product $C_1$

4 marks

The quadrilateral OABCDE is the feasible area according to the graph.

At point B the coordinates will be
C2 = 12,000 (1)
0.75C1 + 1.125C2 = 18,000 (2)

Substituting C2 = 12,000 in equation (2) we get C1 = 6,000

Hence, at point B the coordinates are (6,000, 12,000)

To find the co-ordinates of point C we will solve the two equations:

0.75C1 + 1.125C2 ≤ 18,000 (3)
0.405C1 + 0.405C2 ≤ 8,100 (4)

Multiply equation (3) by 0.54 and subtract equation (4) from it
We get C2 = 8,000 and hence substituting this value in equation (1) we get C1 = 12,000
Hence, the coordinates at point C are (12,000, 8,000)

At point D
C1 = 16,000 (5)
0.405C1 + 0.405C2 = 8,100 (6)

Substituting C1 = 16,000 in equation (6) we get C2 = 4,000
Hence, the coordinates at point D are (16,000, 4,000)

0.5 marks

## 92: Decision-Making Techniques

**We have the following possible production options:**

|   |   |   | Contribution $ |
|---|---|---|---|
| A | (0, 12,000) | 15.15(0) + 41.775(12,000) | 501,300 |
| B | (6,000, 12,000) | 15.15(6,000) + 41.775(12,000) | 592,200 |
| C | (12,000, 8,000) | 15.15(12,000) + 41.775(8,000) | 516,000 |
| D | (16,000, 4,000) | 15.15(16,000) + 41.775(4,000) | 409,500 |
| E | (16,000, 0) | 15.15(16,000) + 41.775(0) | 242,400 |

*2 marks*

The profit is maximum at point B where we manufacture 6,000 boxes of caramium and 12,000 boxes of corrum.

**Maximum marks 15**

**(b)**

### Strategy

In this answer it is very important to make the examiner aware that you understand shadow pricing. Explain the concept properly, and how it helps maximise profit / contribution. Calculation of shadow prices is yet another area where confusion can arise e.g. whether labour hours is a critical resource or mineral powder is a critical resource. So be careful!

A shadow price is an increase in value which would be created by having available one additional unit of a limiting resource at its original cost. This represents the opportunity cost of not having the use of the one extra unit.

The shadow price is the change in the objective value of the optimal solution of an optimisation problem obtained by relaxing the scarce resources by one unit. Each constraint in an optimisation problem has a shadow price or dual variable.

*Important to write the logic behind shadow price!*

A scarce resource only has a shadow price when it is binding. Where resources are not fully utilised (i.e., when the resources are in surplus) the shadow price is zero. This supports the logic that there can be no benefit in increasing the quantum of a resource of which there is already a surplus.

*2 marks*

In the above case we have the maximum contribution at point (6,000, 12,000).

Mineral powder in the above case is a non-critical resource since an increase in availability will not lead to higher profits. This means that we have spare material available and hence it is not scarce.

Labour in this case is a critical resource. If it is made available in more quantity it will increase our contribution. This can be observed by looking at the graph where the maximum contribution is earned at the intersection of the labour time line and the demand line.

*Clue to find critical resource*

*1 mark*

To find the shadow price we increase the labour time availability by 1 hour.
The revised equations will be
$C_2 = 12,000$
$0.75C_1 + 1.125C_2 = 18,001$
Hence we get $C_1 = 6,001$

The optimal solution will now be when we manufacture 6,001 boxes of caramium and 12,000 boxes of corrum

Contribution per extra unit of $C_1$ is $15.15. Hence we get an additional contribution of (15.15(1)) by manufacturing one extra box of caramium.

The shadow price is therefore as follows:
Caramium - $15.15
Corrum - Nil

*2 marks*
**Maximum marks 5**

## 16. Decision making – Spice Shock

### Strategy

The question deals with pricing decisions based on the incremental profit approach. Although part (a) seems easy it should be carefully answered highlighting cost and health concerns as well as the opportunity to earn revenue.

Part (b) seems to be an easy scorer since we just need to calculate the incremental profit / loss. However many would not give much importance to including the conclusion on whether Spice Shock will think of manufacturing the new product based on the calculations. Remember to include this. Remember to specify in your calculations the costs that are sunk costs. The examiner needs to know that you are aware of these.

Part (c) can be confusing since it tests mathematical knowledge along with logic. Remember that the incremental revenue should be $250,000 and hence accordingly calculate the price per kg.

---

**(a)** Various considerations while selecting the alternatives are those that are relevant to the manufacture of SM, which can be financial as well as non-financial. They may also include considerations of customer loyalty, reputation and possibility of action against the company by health organisations given the bad effects on health due to the flavour enhancer, MHA.

**Financial considerations**

**Image**

Spice Shock is a reputed brand which has an established image and any change in taste may not be popular with all customers. This may reduce the brand loyalty of customers.

1 mark

**Cost**

Spice magic requires shifting of existing labour resources from manufacture of original spice blend to SM. This will involve lost contribution from existing sales. The additional additive will also cost more to the company. However only incremental costs and lost contribution should be considered while arriving at a decision on whether to manufacture SM and sunk costs such as manger's salary, fixed overheads etc.

1 mark

**Revenue**

Additional revenue through the increased selling price is a definite encouragement to manufacture SM. The price should cover the additional costs in order to earn real profits.

1 mark

**Legal action**

Health organisations might take action against the company if they confirm the ill effects of MHA. This will act as a big blow to the reputation of Spice Shake which is known for quality.

1 mark
**Maximum marks 4**

**(b) Production cost for 1,000 kg of original spice mix**

|  | $ | Marks |
|---|---|---|
| Selling price per kg ($71.97 per 100g x 10) | 719.7 | |
| **Variable cost for 1,000 kg** | | |
| Base (980 kg x $36) | 35,280 | |
| Spices blend (20 kg x $20,000) | 400,000 | |
| **Total material cost** | 435,280 | |
| Add: Labour cost (2,000 hours x $27) | 54,000 | |
| **Total variable cost for 1,000 kg** | 489,280 | |
| | | |
| Cost per kg ($489,280/1,000 kg) | 489.28 | |
| Contribution per kg ($719.7 – $489.28) | 230.42 | 1 |
| Contribution per hour ($230.42 x 1000)/2000 hours) | 115.21 | 2 |

> Hours required per unit are not given, hence we calculate per hour contribution by dividing total contribution for 1,000 kg by total hours required to produce this output

**Statement showing costs for further processing**

| Cost | Relevance | $ | Marks |
|---|---|---|---|
| Additive cost | Additional cost of material (10 kg × 35,550) | 355,500 | 1 |
| Labour cost | This will contain two elements. Actual labour cost and lost contribution from existing sales<br>$27 × 1200 hours (actual labour cost)<br>$115.21 × 1200 hours (lost contribution) | <br><br>32,400<br>138,252 | 2 |
| Senior Manager's salary | Not relevant since it is a sunk cost | Nil | 1 |
| Overheads | Not relevant since it is a sunk cost | Nil | |
| Market survey cost | Sunk cost | Nil | 1 |
| Total incremental cost | | 526,152 | 2 |

*Separate marks are allotted for writing that these are sunk costs*

> **Tip**
> Remember that when spare labour capacity is not available the actual cost always includes the opportunity cost of contribution foregone. Hence the relevant cost is always actual cost plus profit / contribution foregone.

**Statement showing incremental revenues**

| | | Calculations | $ | Marks |
|---|---|---|---|---|
| Original spice mix | 1,000 kg | (1,000 kg × 719.7/kg) | 719,700 | |
| Spice magic | + 10 kg (additive) | (1,010 kg × 1345/kg) | 1,358,450 | |
| Incremental revenue | | | 638,750 | |
| Net profit / (loss) | | (638,750 – 526,512) | 112,598 | 2 |

*134. 5 per 100g × 10*

The extra profits are not big enough to make the management think about actually manufacturing Spice Magic. Total monthly contribution from existing Spice mix – $230.42 × 10,000 kg = $2,304,200

This is sizeable contribution and hence opting for a new spice mix by affecting the current sales is a risk. Given the ill effects of the additive MHA on health of consumers Spice Shock might not want to take the risk of putting its reputation at stake.

*Conclusion is important!*

2 marks
**Maximum marks 14**

**(c)** In order to earn an incremental profit of $250,000 the price should not only cover the incremental cost but also the original revenue earned. Remember that we need to earn incremental revenue of $250,000 i.e. additional $250,000 than what we presently earn.

Current earning = Current selling price × 1,000 kg = 719.7 × 1,000 kg = $719,700

Hence the price to earn a profit of $250,000 can be calculated as follows

$$= \frac{\text{Incremental cost} + \text{Required incremental profit} + \text{Existing revenue}}{\text{Number of unites of new product sold}}$$

$$= \frac{\$526,152 + \$719,700 + \$250,000}{1010} = \$1481.042$$

*Do not forget to include the incremental cost in the total since price should cover this in order to earn profit*

**Maximum marks 2**

## 17. Profit forecasting model

### Strategy

Part (a) of the question requires an analytical approach to the answer where students should not only write about cost but also revenue. The effect of the change in the model on cost as well as revenue should be explained so that the examiner knows that you can apply the concepts to a situation!

Part (b) divided in two parts, seeks to examine whether the student can think of various options for finding a solution to a pricing problem. In part (i) although the first method occurs easily, it is important to mention the second method to score full marks, where total costs are compared with total revenues. The answer to (b) (ii) should explain the benefits of the inclusion of managerial performance evaluation factors in the model.

Part (c) should include a detailed analysis of factors that will help profit forecasting model to be a more realistic measure of the future profits. Remember, only mentioning the factors that need to be considered in modelling will not show the examiner that you know the answer. Be sure that you provide reasons for HOW the factors help to make the model better.

---

(a) The cost model is a simple linear equation of the form y = a + bx. It denotes total cost as a function of the number of units manufactured, x. In the equation m is the marginal cost (i.e. variable cost per unit) and b is the fixed cost.

The fixed and the variable costs in the current and the revised model are:

| Costs | Revised ($) | Current ($) |
|---|---|---|
| Fixed | 4,750 | 5,000 |
| Variable | 0.6 | 0.8 |

As we can see although the fixed costs have fallen, the variable costs have risen. In comparison with the current model, the revised model generates lower cost estimates at lower output levels, but higher cost estimates at higher output levels. This is because since the variable cost multiple (0.8 which is multiplied by number of units of output) has increased, the cost model will lead to higher costs, as the output increases.

*2 marks*

The revenue function depicts the conventional non-linear downward sloping demand curve. The demand curve depicts that as the product is more and more available the price of the product falls. Applying this logic to the given case, if the company wants to sell more units, it has to lower the selling price of all of its units. Although the revision in the revenue function has created a lower initial price (from $20 to $19), it has also led to a slower decline in price as the units sold increase. The revision in the coefficient (which depicts price elasticity of demand) from 0·01 to 0·009 means that, a lower multiple will lead to a slower increase in revenue. Hence for any given reduction in units sold the price declines at a slower rate than before. Any price elasticity less than one depicts that the demand is not very responsive to any change in the price. In the revised revenue model the coefficient 0.009 is indicative of lower price elasticity. Therefore, compared to the current model, the revised model generates lower total revenue estimates at low unit sales, but greater total revenue estimates at high unit sales.

*Comment on price elasticity since it is a factor affecting the total revenue generated.*

*2 marks*
**Maximum marks 4**

(b)
(i) **Different methods of determining the optimal sales level are:**

➢ Using differential calculus to determine the marginal cost (MC) and marginal revenue (MR) functions and then solving the equation MR = MC (the point where optimal demand occurs). With an increase in production and sales volume, extra cost will be incurred and extra revenue earned. An increase in production, as well as sales, is profitable only until the point where marginal cost (i.e. the additional cost of producing one more unit) does not exceed the marginal revenue (i.e. the additional revenue earned if one additional unit is sold). The price at which profit can be maximised can be identified by equating the marginal cost and marginal revenue equations, and solving them for quantity produced and sold.

*1.5 marks*

# 96: Decision-Making Techniques

> Calculating the values of total revenue and total cost for all potential unit output levels and finding the point where revenues exceeded costs by the greatest absolute amount. Simply put we are comparing the profits at each level and choosing the output level where profit is the highest. This is yet another method of comparing the aggregate costs and revenues. This is a straight method where we take the absolute approach, instead of the incremental approach as in the differential calculus method.

*1.5 marks*

(ii) The current model includes variables for demand, cost and revenue. Hence it only quantifies the effects of these on the revenue. However, the efficient application of resources in the achievement of the optimum demand level should be quantified in the revised model. This will make the model a measure for efficient managerial performance. It will identify, quantify and respond to changing business variables due to a change in the management performance. The model must therefore be updated in order to incorporate the variables which reflect managerial performance (although it may not be possible to include all of these variables). This will provide the management with an overall performance evaluation when the model is applied to any given output and demand condition.

> Reason for WHY do we need to include managerial factors in the model?

*3 marks*
**Maximum marks 6**

### (c) The following points may be relevant while designing a good profit forecasting model:

**Historical information regarding future profit forecasts**

Historical information is often used as the source data for preparing the structures of cost and revenue models. Can the past accurately predict the future? In a dynamic market historical information can often be misleading since the underlying factors keep changing. Changes in technology and markets can have a strong influence on the relationship between cost and revenue. Since we are trying to predict future profits by using the profit forecasting model, it is necessary to consider the significance and impact of these issues on long-term forecasts. A possible solution may be to have a different forecasting model for long and short term. The accuracy requirements for data used for short term forecasts can be stricter.

*2 marks*

**Changes to unit variable costs**

It may not be realistic to assume that unit variable costs remain constant over all ranges of output in a cost model. Many factors affect the unit variable cost, like economies or diseconomies of scale. For example, as a result of bulk purchase discounts, unit variable costs will decrease as output increases. Depending on the purchase contract terms, these discounts may generate a downward step function in unit variable cost or even a smooth decreasing function (function whose graph appears to be a smooth decreasing curve).

*2 marks*

**Changing fixed costs during short term**

Similarly cost models assume a constant fixed cost over all ranges of output which may not be realistic. Step up in fixed costs within an activity range when a specific activity level is reached is a very common phenomenon, and hence should be incorporated in the cost model. It may also be possible to incorporate a sliding step cost to reflect the capacity being temporarily expanded, until the higher demand level is regarded as a permanent one.

> Do not forget to mention the stepped fixed cost effect on future profits

*2 marks*

**Inflation affecting future profit forecasts**

Many other factors affect profits in the long run. These include inflation which affects both costs and revenues. Depending on the time span covered by the forecast, these should be included in the models. Including inflation effect in the model will include application of an inflation factor, whether RPI or any other more specific inflator. They will depend on the industry for which forecasts are being made, since certain industry prices may decrease over time. They may once again adversely affect the profit forecasts.

> Inflation effect as well as deflation of price should be explained!

**Elasticity of demand**

Price elasticity of demand may also change over a period of time. Hence, this may also affect the profit forecasts. Including these effects in profit forecasting may however make the model more complex.

*2 marks*

**Other factors**

In a demand curve the defining factor for any change in the volume of sales is its price. However, there are many other factors that determine the price of a product other than volume. It could be tastes, customer income, competitors' price, population size and structure, advertising etc. These factors should also be included in the profit forecasting models to increase its validity.

2 marks
**Maximum marks 10**

## 18. Swot analysis, pricing strategies – Alocin Plc

**Strategy**

Part (a) – The equations should be framed properly since only proper variables and coefficients will provide correct answer for optimal sales level. While comparing the marginal revenue with marginal cost, remember that marginal cost means the variable cost of manufacture.

Part (b) – Both cost leadership and product differentiation should be explained first before these are applied to the given case. This will help display that the candidate is well aware of the concept as well as its APPLICATION.

Part (c) – The answer to this question should list the identification of the four factors of the SWOT analysis and also HOW Alocin can use its strengths and opportunities, and overcome its weaknesses and threats.

**(a)** Total fixed costs = $31,500,000

**Variable costs of producing a 'Cruiser'**

|  | $ |
|---|---|
| Materials (2 kilograms at $60 per kilogram) | 120 |
| Labour | 40 |
| Variable overheads | 20 |
| **Variable cost per unit / marginal cost of manufacturing 'Cruiser'** | **180** |

1 mark

Price function: $P_q = P_0 - bq$
The marketing director has predicted that at a sales price of $500, 500,000 units can be sold. Hence the equation may be written as follows:

$500 = P_0 - 20/25,000 (500,000)$  *(Price: demand relation is expressed as the sensitivity of demand to price)*
$500 = P_0 - 0.0008(500,000)$
$P_0 = 900$

1 mark

Therefore the price function can be expressed as $P_q = 900 - 0.0008q$

The total and marginal revenue functions may be expressed as follows from the above information.

Total Revenue = $900q - 0.0008q^2$

0.5 marks

According to given information
Marginal revenue (MR) function: $= P_0 - 2bq$
Hence substituting the values from above in the MR equation we have
Marginal Revenue = $900 - 0.0016q$

0.5 marks

According to the demand theory, profit is maximised at the point where Marginal Revenue (MR) = Marginal Cost (MC) (i.e. variable cost of manufacture). In the given case we have the marginal revenue and the marginal cost calculated above.

Therefore $900 - 0.0016q = \$180$  *(Marginal cost is calculated in the above statement)*
$q = 450,000$

1 mark

To find the selling price per unit (P) at which a quantity of 450,000 will be demanded we use the price function as previously calculated:
$P_q = \$900 - 0.0008q$ where $q = 450,000$
$P_q = \$540$

*1 mark*

The profit can be calculated as follows:

|  | $ |
| --- | --- |
| Sales revenue (450,000 units x $540) | 243,000,000 |
| Less: Variable costs (450,000 units x $180) | (81,000,000) |
| Contribution from sales of 'Cruiser' | 162,000,000 |
| Less: Fixed Costs | (31,500,000) |
| Profit from sale of 'Cruiser' | 130,500,000 |

*1 mark*
**Maximum marks 6**

**(b)**
**(i) Cost leadership**

Cost leadership is a strategy used to charge the least price for the products compared to competitors. This obviously gives the company cost leadership in an industry. This is especially important when the product price is elastic and hence customers react strongly to any change in the price of the product. The following factors may be important to achieve the desired cost leadership keeping customer preferences in mind.

➢ Higher management should understand the cost drivers for the product so that a price reduction can be achieved.

➢ Care must be exercised not to reduce the quality of the product since customer expectations for a quality product are also important. Accordingly the target price should be set at a level that will deliver high quality at a comparatively low price.

➢ Market sustainability should be aimed at by following the penetration pricing policy where low prices are offered for the initial period of the launch of the product. Although this means lower growth than the competitors it helps the companies survive longer.

*A point-by-point analysis helps make the answer clear.*

➢ A study of the market size for the product should be conducted so that the required target sales revenue and profit is generated.

➢ In the long term, the management should aim at earning customer and distributor loyalty in order to make the product demand less price elastic. This will keep the competitors at bay.

Alocin should be able to earn a sizeable market share by following the above steps since it already has an advantage by keeping the weight of Cruiser lower than half of the competitors' products. In such a scenario competitors will find it quite difficult to compete with Alocin.

*3 marks*

**(ii) Product differentiation**

Product differentiation involves promotion of multiple brands. This prevents competitors from entering the markets since they have to overcome brand loyalty for all products of the existing company by lowering prices of their own products.

A company must establish and identify some features of its product for which the customers are willing to pay a premium price. These may be a product's image, quality, durability, reliability, or the quality and availability of after sales support. Once these are established the company may invest in research that will result in a better product that contains one or all the above features, for which it may ask for a premium from the customer. Once the brand loyalty is established it is relatively easy to adopt a skimming pricing policy that aims to target the cream customers who have a high income. These customers are more likely to give a positive reaction to the price increase since they are loyal towards the brand and believe that they will receive a better product for a premium price.

*Make sure you explain the concept of price differentiation first. It will help score more!*

On the success of this pricing strategy the company may invest more in purchasing additional resources for large scale production which may generate economies of scale. This will in turn help to gradually reduce the price and change the marketing strategy to widen the customer base.

A skimming pricing policy succeeds only when the competitors cannot enter the market during the early days of the product launch. The main reasons for this are the advanced features of the new product which cannot be achieved so quickly and that too at a lower price.

In the current case, Alocin can easily use a skimming pricing policy since it is already an established brand. The added feature that Cruiser weighs less than half of the competitors' products is an advantage which will help earn the premium on the price from the existing customers who are loyal to Alocin brands.

> Remember to explain the applicability of the concept to the given case!

3 marks
**Maximum marks 6**

**(c)** SWOT analysis is an analysis of an organisation's strengths(S), weaknesses (W), opportunities (O) and threats (T). The analysis is basically aimed at assessing an organisation's capability to deal with the changing business environment. The four factors discussed above are analysed carefully to frame a better strategy for the company that will help in withstanding market pressures and changes. The results of the above analysis provide ways of exploiting an organisation's strengths and opportunities and overcome its weaknesses and threats. This leads to identification of both internal and external factors that affect an organisation. Hence this proves to be a tool for risk analysis.

2 marks

In the current situation the SWOT will be as follows
Strengths – Alocin is already an established brand
Weaknesses – Dependence on the supplier of CLO
Opportunities – To aim at manufacturing travel system for infants of low weight
Threats – Entry of competitors

> Explain each factor separately to enhance the quality of the answer

2 marks

The above will help analyse the likely reaction of competitors and also of customers to the launch of Cruiser. This will help decide the launch price of Cruiser. The threat of competitors may be overcome by setting up a strong control on the supply of CLO which the competitors may try to source, thereby controlling the price of Cruiser. This will also help in controlling the price of Cruiser.

2 marks

However, this SWOT analysis will not apply in every period and therefore it is necessary to continually analyse the opportunities and threats posed by the business environment in each period.

The strategic planning of Alocin should be based on SWOT analysis and hence it is essential that the management members should be aware of this technique. It is also essential that these people become aware of the entire organisation. The team should be chosen carefully. This is because there is always the risk that important factors may not be taken into account, due to the dynamic nature of the external business environment.

2 marks
**Maximum marks 8**

### 19. Shut down vs. continue and make vs. buy – Mariam Inc and Fast Pro

**Strategy**

Part (a) - The answer requires a thorough analysis of the options to close down any of the factories. It should include calculation of contribution lost as well as the effects of cost savings. Confusion should be avoided while calculating the transport costs.

Part (b) (i) – Although it is a make or buy decision, care should be exercised while calculating the lost contribution. It will be the difference between the current contribution and the revised contribution if we purchase product B outside. The final decision should be based on whether any additional contribution is generated by producing extra units of A, after accounting for the lost contribution per tonne.

Part (b) (ii) – Answer to this portion must be written step by step, calculating current contribution, contribution foregone and then the final gain / loss on subcontracting. Each statement should be prepared separately so that the examiner understands you are aware of the logical flow of the answer. Although the additional statements A and B are given in the answer, they need not be given in the actual exam answer.

**(a) Statement showing calculation of reduced demand for each city:**

| Previous year | New Jersey | Chicago | Dallas | Total |
|---|---|---|---|---|
| Units | (4,500,000/150) 30,000 | (1,800,0000/150) 120,000 | (9,000,000/150) 60,000 | 210,000 |
| Less:16.67% | (5,000) | (20,000) | (10,000) | (35,000) |
| | 25,000 | 100,000 | 50,000 | 175,000 |

1 mark

## 100: Decision-Making Techniques

**Budgeted production units**

The reduction of 35,000 can be effected by one of the following actions:
- close New Jersey and reduce Chicago by 5,000 units.
- close Chicago and increase New Jersey by 30,000 units and Dallas by 55,000 units.
- close Dallas and increase New Jersey by 25,000 units.

2 marks

In all of the above options the total production is equal to 175,000 which is the reduced output. There could be other combinations, but in order to arrive at the best combination we may consider the contribution analysis of the current situation, as follows:

|  | Contribution Analysis |  |  | Marks |
|---|---|---|---|---|
|  | **New Jersey** | **Chicago** | **Dallas** |  |
| Quantity | 30,000 | 120,000 | 60,000 |  |
|  | ($'000) | ($'000) | ($'000) |  |
| Sales | 4,500 | 18,000 | 9,000 |  |
| Less: Variable cost |  |  |  |  |
| Prime costs | 1,800 | 7,800 | 3,840 |  |
| Production overhead (variable) | 150 | 840 | 360 |  |
| Selling overhead (variable) | 300 | 1,440 | 480 |  |
|  | (2,250) | (10,080) | (4,680) | 1 |
| Contribution | 2,250 | 7,920 | 4,320 |  |
| **Contribution per unit** | **75** | **66** | **72** | 1 |
|  | (I) | (III) | (II) | 1 |

*Total contribution/ Units sold*

Chicago gives the least contribution and hence we should close it down. The production will be transferred to the other two depending on their capacity. Either of the factories can increase production up to double the current production capacity. However, the final decision will be based on the impact on the overall profitability of Mariam.

It would seem, from the above, that it would be preferable to choose option (ii), which is to close down the Chicago factory and correspondingly increase the production to the maximum amount(double) at New Jersey (i.e. 60,000 units) and the balance production transferred to Dallas. The position will be:

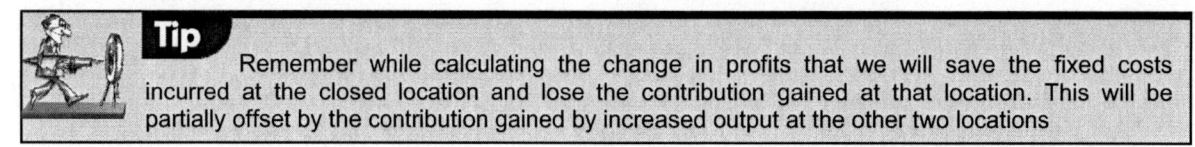

**Tip**: Remember while calculating the change in profits that we will save the fixed costs incurred at the closed location and lose the contribution gained at that location. This will be partially offset by the contribution gained by increased output at the other two locations

|  | $'000 |
|---|---|
| Contribution lost at Chicago | (7,920) |
| Fixed cost saved ($2,640 + $1,800 + $1,560) | 6,000 |
| Net loss | (1,920) |
| Contribution gain |  |
| (30,000 units x $75) | 2,250 |
| (55,000 units x $72) | 3,960 |
| Extra supervision (given) |  |
| New Jersey ($500,000) |  |
| Dallas ($700,000) | (1,200) |
| Additional transport (100,000 units x $15) | (1,500) |
| **Change in profit** | **1,590** |

*Head office costs are a cost allocation and hence will not be saved at branch level.*

*Additional contribution will be only on additional units manufactured since we are calculating the change in profits here!*

2 mark

**Tip**: Remember, 16.67% decrease in demand is for Mariam as a whole and not only for Chicago. Therefore the decrease should be spread evenly to all the three factories as calculated earlier. Considering this, demand from customers of Chicago will be 120,000 - 16.67% = 100,000. Therefore transport cost should be calculated on 120,000 units and not on 85,000 units.

**Note:** the following statement is not required to be included in the exam answer but it is methods that can be used as a means to cross verify that the decision is correct.

The profitability with the other options, rather than (i) and (ii) above, will be as follows:

|  | Close New Jersey and reduce Chicago $'000 | Close Dallas and increase New Jersey $'000 |  |
|---|---|---|---|
| Contribution lost | (2,250) | (4,320) | In case of Chicago we have reduced the output and hence the contribution is negative |
| Fixed cost saved: |  |  |  |
|   New Jersey ($750 + $300 + $450) | 1,500 |  |  |
|   Dallas ($1,200 + $840 + $1,080) |  | 3,120 |  |
| **Net loss:** | **(750)** | **(1,200)** |  |
| Contribution lost at Chicago (-5,000 x $66) | (330) |  |  |
| Contribution gained at New Jersey (25,000 x $75) |  | 1875 |  |
| Extra supervision- New Jersey | 30,000 - 16.67% | (500) |  |
| Additional transport: |  |  |  |
|   New Jersey (25,000 x $10) | (250) |  |  |
|   Dallas (50,000 x $12) |  | (600) |  |
| **Change in Profit** | **(1,330)** | **(425)** |  |

60,000 -16.67% of 60,000

It can be seen from the above that (ii), i.e. closure of the Chicago factory is preferable since it gives us a positive impact on profits, leading to an increase in the overall profit by $1,590,000.

**Maximum marks 8**

**(b)**
**(i)** Whether the offer of PQR Inc should be accepted

**Contribution foregone if offer is accepted:**

|  | Calculations | B $ |  |
|---|---|---|---|
| Present contribution (selling price – variable costs) | ($46,560 – $5,200 -$19,600 – $2,960) | 18,800 | $46,560 x 90% |
| Contribution on sub-contract (Buying price – Selling price) | ($46,560 – $41,904) | (4,656) |  |
| **Contribution forgone** |  | **14,144** |  |

1 mark

**Contribution from alternate use of production capacity**   Labour cost for product B

Capacity made available in terms of wages = 1,000 tonnes x $5,200 per tonne
= $5.2 million

0.5 marks

Direct wages per tonne of product A = $7,840 per tonne.
Number of tonnes of A that can be produced = $(5,200,000 / 7,840)
= 663 tonnes

0.5 marks

Increased contribution of product A = 663 tonnes x $27,520    Contribution from A
= $18,245,760                                                  $64,800 – ($7,480 +
= $18.246 million                                              $26,080 + $3,360)

1 mark

**Note:** availability of skilled labour is a limiting factor. Hence, wages are used to derive the capacity which would be made available by sub-contracting.

**Profitability on subcontracting**

|  | $'million |
|---|---|
| Increased contribution of product A | 18.246 |
| **Less:** Contribution forgone when sub-contracted @ $14,144 per tonne for 1,000 tonnes | (14.144) |
| **Profit** | **4.102** |

B should be subcontracted, and production of 663 tonnes of A should be taken up since we earn an additional profit of 4.102 million.

1 mark
**Maximum marks 4**

**(ii) Best combination of sub-contracting different products**

**A. Statement showing contribution per tonne**

|  | A | B | C |
|---|---|---|---|
| Selling price | 64,800 | 46,560 | 39,680 |
| Costs: |  |  |  |
| Direct wages | 7,840 | 5,200 | 3,960 |
| Direct materials | 26,080 | 19,600 | 16,400 |
| Direct packing | 3,360 | 2,960 | 2,240 |
| **Total variable costs** | **(37,280)** | **(27,760)** | **(22,600)** |
| **Contribution** | **27,520** | **18,800** | **17,080** |

**B.** Purchase price per product, per tonne is 90% of the existing selling price.

Purchase price per tonne for:

| A (64,800 x 90%) | $58,320 |
|---|---|
| B (from previous answer) | $41,904 |
| C ($39,680 x 90%) | $35,712 |

When one product is subcontracted it would release a capacity of 1,000 tonnes. The released capacity can be utilised for the production of other products.

1 mark

The following table shows the additional output of other products when one is sub-contracted. Additional output produced if the option of sub-contracting is undertaken, can be calculated as follows.

Output made available in terms of wages, equivalent to 1,000 tonnes

|  | Sub-contracting of product |  |  |
|---|---|---|---|
| **Additional output** | A | B | C |
| Wages ($'million) | 7.840 | 5.200 | 3.960 |
| **Product manufactured** | in tonnes |  |  |
| A (W1) | Nil | 663 | 505 |
| B (W2) | 1,508 (W1) | Nil | 762 |
| C (W3) | 1,980 | 1,313 | Nil |
| D (W4) | 1,153 | 765 | 582 |

Total released capacity = Direct wages of product sub-contracted x 1,000 tonnes

2 marks

**Workings**

Incremental output from the additional capacity made available can be calculated as follows:

= Additional capacity available / Direct wages of product manufactured using the released capacity

**W1 Units of A to be manufactured from:**

Additional capacity of B – 663 units (from previous statement)

Additional capacity of C – 3.960 / 7.840 = 505 units

**W2 Units of B to be manufactured from:**

Additional capacity of A – 7.840 / 5.200 = 1,508 units

Additional capacity of C – 3.960 / 5.200 = 762 units

**W3 Units of C to be manufactured from:**

Additional capacity of A – 7.840 / 3.960 = 1,980 units

Additional capacity of B – 5.200 / 3.960 = 1,313 units

**Contribution forgone on sub contracting**

Forgone contribution on sub-contracting different products is:

> For contribution per tonne refer to the statement A.

| Product | Present contribution ($ per tonne) refer A | Contribution on subcontracting ($ per tonne) refer B | Contribution forgone due to subcontracting ($ per tonne) | Total contribution forgone due to subcontracting ($ per tonne x 1000 units) ('000) |
|---------|---|---|---|---|
| A | 27,520 | 6,480 (64,800 - 58,320) | 21,040 | 21,040 |
| B | 18,800 | 4,656 (46,560 - 41,904) | 14,144 | 14,144 |
| C | 17,080 | 3,968 (39,680 – 35,712) | 13,112 | 13,112 |

*2 marks*

**Contribution gained on additional output manufactured (figure in millions)**

| Product sub-contracted | | A | B | C |
|---|---|---|---|---|
| Product produced | Existing contribution per tonne | Refer (i) (Units to be manufactured from additional capacity x contribution per unit) | | |
| A | 27,520 | Nil | 18,246 | 13,898 |
| B | 18,800 | 28,350 | Nil | 14,326 |
| C | 17,080 | 33,818 | 22,426 | Nil |

*2 marks*

**Net gain on subcontracting**

This can be calculated by the following formula:
Net contribution foregone for each product - additional contribution gained from each product

Net gain on subcontracting ($'000)

| Product sub-contracted | A | B | C |
|---|---|---|---|
| Product manufactured | | | |
| A | Nil | 4,102 | 786 |
| B | 731 | Nil | 1,214 |
| C | 12,778 | 8,282 | Nil |

*2 marks*

The highest additional contribution of $12,778,000 is achieved when we sub-contract A and produce additional quantities of C in the spare capacity. Hence, 1,000 tonnes of A may be subcontracted and additional production of C may be taken up.

*2 marks*
**Maximum marks 8**

## 20. Expected value – Shifters Haulage

**Strategy**

Part (a) is a theoretical question in which you are required to briefly explain the principles behind the given methods used to make decisions under uncertainty.

Part (b) has a computational requirement of six possible profits i.e. for small, medium and large van under both high and low demand. The examiner has commented that it is necessary to mention risk attitudes as 0.5 marks have been allotted for it.

Part (c) is a mixed question in which you need to take account of the various possible risk attitudes of the directors. Here, you need to apply your theoretical knowledge from part (a). It is expected that each potential risk attitude be taken in turn and appropriately applied to the figures to earn full marks.

## 104: Decision-Making Techniques

**(a) Maximax** is an optimistic approach to decision-making. Under this, the alternative which maximises the maximum outcome for every alternative strategy is selected. Therefore, investors who follow this approach select the alternative that could give them the best possible outcome. They will not consider all other possible outcomes and concentrate only on the alternative contributing the maximum outcome. Therefore, such investors are optimists or risk-takers.

*2 marks*

**Maximin** is a pessimistic approach to decision-making. Under this approach, the alternative that maximises the minimum outcome for every alternative strategy is selected. Investors following this approach will focus only on the potential minimum outcomes and select the alternative out of these that gives the maximum outcome. Therefore, such investors are said to be risk-avoiders and cautious or pessimistic in their outlook.

*2 marks*

**Expected value** is the weighted average of all possible returns. The investor assigns probabilities to all possible outcomes on the basis of their knowledge, experience etc. Then, different alternatives are evaluated in order to select the one which gives the maximum outcome.

For example, if an investor could expect $200 with a 0·4 probability and $100 with a 0.6 probability then on an average the return would be:

(0·4 x $200) + (0·6 x $100) = $140

This figure would then be used as a basis for the investment decision.

*2 marks*
**Maximum marks 5**

**(b) Statement showing the possible profit per period**

|  | Small van |  | Medium van |  | Large van |  | Marks |
|---|---|---|---|---|---|---|---|
| Demand | Low | High | Low | High | Low | High |  |
| Units sold (W1) | 100 | 100 | 120 | 150 | 120 | 190 | 1.5 |
|  | $ | $ | $ | $ | $ | $ |  |
| Sales | 1,000 | 1,000 | 1,200 | 1,500 | 1,200 | 1,900 | 1.5 |
| Less: |  |  |  |  |  |  |  |
| Variable costs | 400 | 400 | 480 | 600 | 480 | 760 | 1.5 |
| Goodwill | 100 | 100 |  | 100 |  |  | 1.5 |
| Variable cost adjustment (W2) |  |  | (48) |  | (48) | (76) | 1.5 |
| Depreciation | 200 | 200 | 300 | 300 | 400 | 400 | 1.5 |
| Total costs | (700) | (700) | (732) | (1,000) | (832) | (1,084) |  |
| Profit / loss | 300 | 300 | 468 | 500 | 368 | 816 | 1.5 |

**Workings**

*Don't forget to charge goodwill of $100 against profit if the demand for crates is greater than the capacity of the van.*

**W1 Units sold**

The number of crates sold can either be equal to the demand in the market or the capacity of van. If demand is greater than the capacity, the sales will be equal to the capacity of the van.

E.g. low demand for crates for a small van is 120 crates, whereas the capacity is limited to 100 crates. Therefore, sales will be only 100 (as 120 > 100).

However, if capacity exceeds demand, the sales will be equal to the number of crates demanded in the market. E.g. low demand for crates for medium van is 120 crates only but the capacity is more i.e. 150 crates. Therefore, the sales made during the period are only 120 crates (as 150 > 120).

*1 mark*

**W2 Variable cost adjustments**

If the capacity of the van is greater than the demand for crates, the variable cost will be lower by 10%.
E.g. in the case of a large van, its capacity is greater than the demand for crates in the market.

For low demand, variable cost adjustment will be
= 10% of $480 = $48

For high demand, variable cost adjustment will be
= 10% of $760 = $76

*1 mark*
**Maximum marks 9**

**Score More**

Avoid the following possible mistakes in part (b):
1. The capacity of the medium van is lower than the high demand. So, do not take 190 crates as sales; it should be 150 crates.
2. Do not forget to include goodwill adjustment in profit calculation. You might get marks even if you ignore this, but it is advisable to show it.
3. Don't calculate expected sales first and accordingly adjust other criteria.

---

(c) The decision of which type of van to buy depends upon the investor's risk attitude. If the investor is optimistic about the future, they will be ready to take high risk projects and challenges. Under an optimistic approach, the maximax criterion is adopted for decision-making where the alternative giving the maximum return is selected. Therefore, the investor will buy the large van because they are making the greatest profit of $816.

*2 marks*

When the investor is pessimistic about the future, a maximin criterion is useful for decision-making. As the investor is more cautious while accepting any kind of risk, they would concentrate only on the alternatives giving the minimum return and then select the best out of those.

Using this approach, the minimum payoff for each of the alternatives is identified. The minimum payoff for small, medium and large van is $300, $468 and $368 respectively. The higher of these payoffs, which is $468, is selected. Therefore, the investor would buy the medium van.

*2 marks*

Expected value is another method that can be applied to take decisions in situations involving risk. The expected value is calculated in the following way:

For small van = (0.4 x $300) + (0.6 x $300) = $300
For medium van = (0.4 x $468) + (0.6 x $500) = $487
For large van = (0.4 x $368) + (0.6 x $816) = $637

SH should buy large van, as their expected value, $637, is the highest amongst all other alternatives.

*2 marks*

The above analysis clearly shows that the company should only buy large van. However, the final decision depends upon the manager's attitude. Since it is given that he is more cautious while taking any decision, it would be wise to buy medium van. The small van would not be the correct choice.

*1 mark*
**Maximum marks 6**

## 21. Contribution - Higgins

**Strategy**

This is a direct linear programming question as indicated by an article written by **Geoff Cordwell**, the Paper F5 examiner. This article was published in the ACCA's Student Accountant Magazine, March 2008.

Parts (a) and (b) are based on Paper F2, Management Accounting, in which you are required to calculate contribution and determine the optimal production plan using the graphical method.

Part (c) requires you to explain the meaning and calculate the shadow price for materials and labour.

---

**Calculation of contribution per cue**

|  | Pool cue $ | Snooker cue $ | Marks |
|---|---|---|---|
| Selling price (a) | 41.00 | 69.00 | 0.5 |
| **Less: variable costs** | | | |
| Material cost (W1) | 10.80 | 10.80 | 0.5 |
| Craftsmen costs (W2) | 9.00 | 13.50 | 0.5 |
| Other variable cost | 1.20 | 4.70 | 0.5 |
| Total variable costs (b) | (21.00) | (29.00) | |
| **Contribution margin (a – b)** | **20.00** | **40.00** | 0.5 |

## Workings

### W1 Material cost

1 kilogram = 1,000 grams
Material cost for pool cues and snooker cues = 270 grams (0.27 kg) x $40 = $10.80

*0.5 marks*

### W2 Craftsmen cost

Pool cues = $18 x 0.50 hours = $9
Snooker cues = $18 x 0.75 hours = $13.50

*0.5 marks*
**Maximum marks 2**

### (b)

Let P be the number of pool cues and S be the snooker cues to be produced.
Let C be the contribution.

Higgins wants to maximise contribution.
Therefore the objective function is:
C = 20P + 40S

*0.5 marks*

### (i) Labour hour constraint

Craftsmen are able to work for 12,000 hours only for the given period. Each pool cue requires 0.5 hours and each snooker cue requires 0.75 hours. Hence the constraint can be written as:
0.5P + 0.75S ≤ 12,000

*1 mark*

### (ii) Material constraint

Each pool cue and snooker cue uses 270 grams of ash. The supply of ash is restricted to 5,400 kg per period. Therefore, the constraint can be written as
0.27P + 0.27S ≤ 5,400

*1 mark*

### (iii) Demand

The demand for the pool cues and snooker cues for the given period is 15,000 and 12,000 respectively.
Therefore:
P ≤ 15,000
S ≤ 12,000

*1 mark*

### (iv) Non negativity constraint

P, S ≥ 0

*0.5 marks*

Now, the linear programming problem (LPP) formulation will be:
Maximise contribution, C = 20P + 40S
Subject to constraints

0.5P + 0.75S ≤ 12,000
0.27P + 0.27S ≤ 5,400
P ≤ 15,000
S ≤ 12,000
P, S ≥ 0

*1 mark*

The first two constraints 0.5P + 0.75S ≤ 12,000 and 0.27P + 0.27S ≤ 5,400 represent the availability of craftsmen hours and material (ash) respectively. They are depicted by the straight lines to get the following coordinates.

Solving the equations for P and S we get the following coordinates:

0.50P + 0.75S = 12,000
Put S = 0 we get 0.50P = 12,000
P = 24,000
Put P = 0 we get 0.75S = 12,000
S = 16,000
Therefore, the coordinates are (24,000, 16,000)

*1 mark*

0.27P + 0.27S = 5,400
Put S = 0 we get 0.27P = 5,400
P = 20,000
Put P = 0 we get 0.27S = 5,400
S = 20,000
Therefore the coordinates are (20,000, 20,000)

1 mark

The graph will appear as follows.

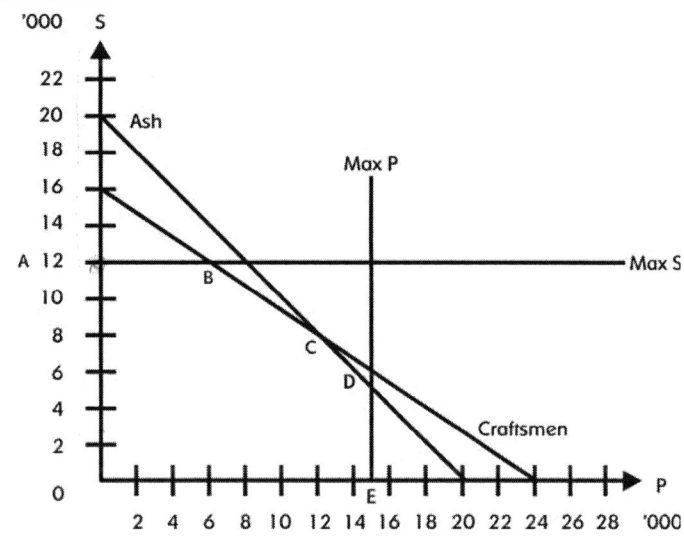

The quadrilateral OABCDE is the feasible area according to the graph.

4 marks

**At point O**, the coordinates will be (0, 0)

0.5 marks

**At point A**, the coordinates will be as follows:
To find out the points of intersection of the equation S ≤ 12,000, convert this inequality into the equation   S = 12,000.
As the equation is parallel to P, the co-ordinates of point A will be (0, 12,000).

0.5 marks

**At point B**
S = 12,000
Substituting S = 12,000 in equation (craftsmen hours) below
0.50P + 0.75(12,000) = 12,000
P = 6,000
Hence, at point B the coordinates are (6,000, 12,000).

1 mark

**At point C**
To find the coordinates of point C, we solve the two equations
0.50P + 0.75S = 12,000 (1)
0.27P + 0.27S = 5,400 (2)

Multiply equation (1) by 1.8 and (2) by 5 and subtract equation (1) from (2)
We get P = 12,000 and S = 8,000
Hence, the coordinates at point C are (12,000, 8,000).

1 mark

**At point D**
P = 15,000
Substituting P = 15,000 in the equation (craftsmen hours) below
0.5(15,000) + 0.75S = 12,000
S = 6,000
The coordinates at point D are (15,000, 6,000).

1 mark

**At point E,** the coordinates will be as follows:
To find out the points of intersection of the equation P ≤ 15,000 with the X-axis, convert this inequality into the equation   P = 15,000.
As the equation is parallel to S, the co-ordinates of point E are (15,000, 0).

0.5 marks

The optimum contribution can be determined by putting the value of the co-ordinates of all the corner points of the feasible region into the objective function C = 20P + 40S.

| Point | (P,S) | Calculation 20P + 40S | Contribution $ |
|---|---|---|---|
| A | (0, 12,000) | 20(0) + 40(12,000) | 480,000 |
| B | (6,000, 12,000) | 20(6,000) + 40(12,000) | 600,000 |
| C | (12,000, 8000) | 20(12,000) + 40(8,000) | 560,000 |
| D | (15,000, 6,000) | 20(15,000) + 40(6,000) | 540,000 |
| E | (15,000, 0) | 20(15,000) + 40(0) | 300,000 |

*2.5 marks*

The contribution is the maximum at point B. Therefore, Higgins should produce 6,000 pool cues and 12,000 snooker cues.

*0.5 marks*
**Maximum marks 13**

### (c) Shadow price

Shadow price is the increase in value that would be created by having available one additional unit of a limiting resource at its original cost. This represents the opportunity cost of not having the use of the one extra unit. Shadow price is a measure of how much the management is willing to pay to gain more units of a scarce resource. It represents the maximum amount they should pay for the scarce resource above the normal price.

*2 marks*

Each constraint in an optimisation problem has a shadow price or dual variable. A scarce resource only has a shadow price when it is binding. Where resources are not fully utilised (i.e. when the resources are in surplus) the shadow price is nil.

*1 mark*

The optimal production of P and S is 6,000 units and 12,000 units respectively. Therefore, at this production level, the required quantity of ash is:

(6,000 x 0.27 kg) + (12,000 x 0.27kg) = 4,860 kg

However, the supply is restricted to only 5,400 kg. This indicates that ash is a non-critical scarce resource and therefore it has a nil shadow price. Increase in availability of this material will not lead to higher profits. There is spare material in the case of ash, and hence we need not pay more to get it.

*2 marks*

Craftsmen hours are a critical resource. If more hours are made available, it will increase the contribution.
To find the shadow price we increase the craftsmen's available time by 1 hour.

*0.5 marks*

At point B,
S = 12,000
The equation for craftsmen hour constraint with an additional unit of scarce resource is
0.50P + 0.75S = 12,001

Substituting the value of S in the equation
0.50P + 0.75(12,000) = 12,001
P = 6,002

The optimal solution will now be for Higgins to produce 12,000 snooker cues and 6,002 pool cues.

*1 mark*

The contribution will increase by $40 ($20 x 2).

The shadow price is therefore:
ash: nil
craftsmen: $40 per extra hour

*1 mark*
**Maximum marks 5**

© GTG

Solution Bank: 109

## 22. Budgeted sales mix - Nerville

**Strategy**

Part (a) worth 12 marks requires calculation of break-even volume on the basis of a particular mix and per cent of margin of safety of budgeted sales revenue.

Part (b) worth 8 marks requires you to calculate the revised production schedule with a view to maximising profit for the next year based on the conditions / possible circumstances given.

**(a)**
**(i) Required number of units at break-even point**

$$\text{Breakeven point (in \$)} = \frac{\text{Fixed expenses}}{\text{Contribution to sales ratio}}$$

$$= \frac{\$1,507,968}{49.35\%}$$

$$= \$3,055,659 \text{ (approx)}$$

1 mark

**Break even volume**

$$\text{Break even volume} = \frac{\text{Break even revenue per product}}{\text{Selling price per unit of that product}}$$

E375: $\dfrac{\$1,191,755}{\$250}$ = 4,767 units

F294: $\dfrac{\$1,215,590}{\$300}$ = 4,052 units

E375: $\dfrac{\$648,314}{\$170}$ = 3,814 units

2 marks

Where,
Break even revenue per product = Total revenue x Proportion of that particular product in the total revenue

E375: $3,055,659 x $\dfrac{250}{641}$ = $1,191,755

F294: $3,055,659 x $\dfrac{255}{641}$ = $1,215,590

G142: $3,055,659 x $\dfrac{136}{641}$ = $648,314

Where,
Proportion of sales revenue = E375: F294: G142
= 5,000,000: 5,100,000: 2,720,000
= 250: 255: 136
= $\dfrac{250}{641} : \dfrac{255}{641} : \dfrac{136}{641}$

1 mark

**Workings**

**W1 Fixed expenses**

Required machine hour per one unit of E375 = $73.92/$52.80 = 1.4 hours
Required machine hour per one unit of F294 = $95.04/$52.80 = 1.8 hours
Required machine hour per one unit of G142 = $42.24/$52.80 = 0.8 hours

Hence,
Required machine hour for E375 = 1.4 hours x 20,000 units = 28,000 hours
Required machine hour for F294 = 1.8 hours x 17,000 units = 30,600 hours
Required machine hour for G142 = 0.8 hours x 16,000 units = 12,800 hours

Total required machine hours = 71,400 hours

Total production overheads = 71,400 hours x $52.80 = $3,769,920

Hence fixed overheads = $3,769,920 x 40% = **$1,507,968**

1 mark

1 mark

**W2 Contribution to sales ratio**

|  | E375 (20,000 units) || F294 (17,000 units) || G142 (16,000 units) || Total $ |
|---|---|---|---|---|---|---|---|
|  | Per unit $ | Total $ | Per unit $ | Total $ | Per unit $ | Total $ |  |
| Sales | 250·00 | 5,000,000 | 300·00 | 5,100,000 | 170·00 | 2,720,000 | 12,820,000 |
| Less: Variable costs |  |  |  |  |  |  |  |
| Direct materials | (47·50) | (950,000) | (52·75) | (896,750) | (38·30) | (612,800) | (2,459,550) |
| Direct labour | (28·88) | (577,600) | (32·80) | (557,600) | (21·32) | (341,120) | (1,476,320) |
| Royalties | (5·00) | (100,000) | (7·00) | (119,000) | (4·80) | (76,800) | (295,800) |
| Production overheads (Total overheads given x 60% variable) | (44·35) | (887,000) | (57·02) | (969,340) | (25·34) | (405,440) | (2,261,780) |
| **Contribution** | **124.27** | **2,485,400** | **150.43** | **2,557,310** | **80.24** | **1,283,840** | **6,326,550** |

Contribution to sales ratio = $\dfrac{\text{Contribution}}{\text{Sales}}$ x 100

= $\dfrac{\$6,326,550}{\$12,820,000}$ x 100

= 49.35% (approx)

5 marks
**Maximum marks 10**

**(ii) Margin of safety in % of budgeted sales**

Margin of safety = $\dfrac{\text{Budgeted sales revenue - Sales revenue at BEP}}{\text{Budgeted sales revenue}}$ x 100

= $\dfrac{\$12,820,000 - \$3,055,659}{\$12,820,000}$ x 100

= $\dfrac{\$9,764,341}{\$12,820,000}$ x 100

= 76.16%

2 marks
**Maximum marks 2**

(b)

| Product | E375 | F294 | G142 | Marks |
|---|---|---|---|---|
| Original contribution per unit | $124.27 | $150.43 | $80.24 |  |
| Change in contribution |  |  |  |  |
| Increase in production cost per unit | ($8.00) | ($8.00) | ($8.00) | 0.5 |
| Change in selling price per unit |  |  | $2.00 | 0.5 |
| **Revised contribution per unit (A)** | **$116·27** | **$142·43** | **$74·24** |  |
| Original machine hours per unit | 1·4 | 1·8 | 0·8 |  |
| Change in requirement of machine hours | x 1.05 | x 1.05 | x 1.05 |  |
| **Revised machine hours per unit (B)** | **1.47** | **1.89** | **0.84** | 1 |
| **Revised contribution per machine hours (A)/(B)** | **$79.09** | **$75.36** | **$88.38** | 1 |

| Product | E375 | F294 | G142 | Total |
|---|---|---|---|---|
| Volume (units) | 20,000 | 17,000 | 16,000 | |
| Original machine hours required (Units x Original machine hours per unit) | 28,000 | 30,600 | 12,800 | 71,400 |
| Revised required machine hours (Units x Revised machine hours per unit) | 29,400 | 32,130 | 13,440 | 74,970 |
| Total available hours | | | | 73,000 |
| **Deficit of hours** | | | | **1,970** |

2 marks

Due to the deficiency of machine hours, the production of the product that gives the least contribution per machine hour (limiting factor) needs to be compromised. Here, the product F294 provides the lowest contribution per unit of limiting factor (machine hour); the reduction in capacity should be reflected in production of that product before the other products.

In 1,970 machine hours, 1,042 units of the product F294 can be produced (i.e. 1,970 machine hours/1.89 machine hours per unit)

Hence, revised production of products can be as follows:

E375: 20,000 units
F294: 17,000 units – 1,042 units = 15,958 units
G142: 16,000 units

3 marks
**Maximum marks 8**

### Score More

If you misinterpret part (b) as a carried forward version of part (a) and do not take account of the fact that this is a separate requirement, you might lose marks. Even if you re-calculate the break even volume based on the revised costs, it will not fulfil the exact requirement of this question, and hence such answers are not awarded marks.

## 23. Contribution per limiting factor – Bookem Co

### Strategy

This question focuses on the kind of decision-making situations that managers might face in practice. Part (a) worth 10 marks is divided into two questions in which you need to calculate different requirements based on contribution per limiting factor i.e. processing hours. The number of processing hours could fairly easily be derived from the allocation of central costs at a fixed rate, based on processing hours.

In part (b), contribution per processing hour and the product mix will remain the same as calculated in part (a).

Part (c) provides you an opportunity to challenge the basis of the decision by critically examining the assumptions provided in the question. It is worth 4 marks so if you provide only two to three limitations, it would be good enough.

**(a)**
**(i)  Calculation of profitability of each line of business, based on the contribution per processing hour**

| | Holidays $000 | Tickets $000 | Flights $000 | Total $000 |
|---|---|---|---|---|
| Sales revenue | 7,685.00 | 3,770.00 | 3,045.00 | 14,500.00 |
| Less: Variable costs (W1) | (4,103.79) | (1,896.31) | (1,827.00) | (7,827.10) |
| Contribution | **3,581.21** | **1,873.69** | **1,218.00** | **6,672.90** |
| Contribution per processing hours | 201.19 | 144.13 | 103.22 | |
| **C/S ratio** | 46.60 | 49.70 | 40.00 | 46.02 |

## Workings

### W1 Variable costs

Variable costs = Direct costs − Advertising costs

|  | Holidays $000 | Tickets $000 | Flights $000 | Total $000 |
|---|---|---|---|---|
| Direct costs | 5,870·00 | 2,670·00 | 2,260·00 | 10,800·00 |
| Less: Advertising costs | 1,766·21 | 773·69 | 433·00 | 2,972·90 |
| Variable costs | 4,103·79 | 1,896·31 | 1,827·00 | 7,827·10 |

### W2 Processing hours = $\dfrac{\text{Central costs}}{\$65 \text{ per processing hour}}$

Processing hours for holiday packages = $\dfrac{\$1,157,000}{\$65 \text{ per processing hour}}$ = 17.8 hours

Processing hours for tickets = $\dfrac{\$845,000}{\$65 \text{ per processing hour}}$ = 13 hours

Processing hours for holiday packages = $\dfrac{\$767,000}{\$65 \text{ per processing hour}}$ = 11.8 hours

### (ii) Required sales to earn 10% profit more

Required sales ($000) = $\dfrac{\text{Fixed expenses + Target Profit}}{\text{Contribution to sales ratio}}$

= $\dfrac{\$6479.90 + \$1,024.10}{46.02\%}$

= $16,305.95

### W3 Fixed expenses

|  | $000 | $000 |
|---|---|---|
| Advertising costs |  |  |
| Earlier | 2,972.90 |  |
| Increase | 250.00 | 3,222.90 |
| Central costs |  |  |
| Holidays | 1,157.00 |  |
| Tickets | 845.00 |  |
| Flights | 767.00 |  |
|  | 2,769.00 |  |
| Increase | 215.00 | 2,984.00 |
| System upgradation |  | 273.00 |
| Estimated Fixed costs |  | 6,479.90 |

### W4 Target profit

Target profit = Current profit + 10% Increase
= $(658,000 + 255,000 + 18,000) + 10%
= $931,000 + $93,100
= $1,024,100

### W5 Contribution to sales ratio

C/S ratio = $\dfrac{\text{Contribution}}{\text{Sales}} \times 100$

= $\dfrac{\$6672.90}{\$14,500} \times 100$

= 46.02%

**(b) Opinion on upgraded system - whether it will provide sufficient processing hours to generate the revenue required to achieve the target profit of $1,024,100**

**W6 Percentage of current sales revenue in each service**

|  | Holidays $000 | Tickets $000 | Flights $000 | Total $000 |
| --- | --- | --- | --- | --- |
| Current revenue | 7,685·00 | 3,770·00 | 3,045·00 | 14,500·00 |
| % of total revenue $14,500 | 53 | 26 | 21 | 100 |

Target revenue to achieve the target profit of $1,024.10 = $16,305.95
Hence, target sales for each service can be calculated as follows:
Holidays = $16,305.95 x 53% = $8,642.15
Tickets = $16,305.95 x 26% = $4,239.55
Flights = $16,305.95 x 21% = $3,424.25

**Contribution on the sales of $16,305.95 = $16,305.95 x 46.02% = $7,504**

**Surplus hours can be calculated as follows:**

|  | Holidays $000 | Tickets $000 | Flights $000 | Total $000 |
| --- | --- | --- | --- | --- |
| C/S ratio | 46.60 | 49.70 | 40.00 | 46.02 |
| Sales revenue | 8642.16 | 4239.55 | 3424.25 | 16305.95 |
| Contribution | 4,027.25 | 2,107.06 | 1,369.70 | 7,504.00 |
| Contribution per hour | 201.19 | 144.13 | 103.22 |  |
| Required processing hours (Contribution/Contribution per hour x 1000) | 20,017 | 14,619 | 13,270 | **47,906** |

| Total available hours before upgrade |  |  |  | 42,600 |
| --- | --- | --- | --- | --- |
| Add: 13% increase |  |  |  | 5,538 |
| After upgrade, available hours |  |  |  | **48,138** |

| Surplus hours (Available hours - Required hours) |  |  |  | 232 |
| --- | --- | --- | --- | --- |

**Score More**

Normally, consideration is derived by deducting direct expenses from revenue. However, here it has been specifically mentioned that direct expenses include fixed elements. Hence, don't deduct direct expenses from revenue.

**(c) Limitations of the assumptions made in the sales mix**

In this example, it has been assumed that the sales mix will not change. This assumption may not be justified.

This is because:

(i) In practice, businesses usually generate different contribution per processing hour as any shift in the sales activities (from holidays to flight bookings) will have a negative effect on profitability.
(ii) If the cost classification between fixed and variable elements has been done incorrectly, the analysis will not be accurate.
(iii) The accuracy of the directors' estimates on fixed costs will have an impact upon the accuracy of the cost estimates.

2 marks per each correctly explained limitation
**Maximum marks 4**

## 24. Profit forecasting - Recco

**Strategy**

This question is entirely computational, except for two marks of theory. Here, you need to calculate benefits obtained under each of the three options using the same core information. You need to apply marginal costing and derive contribution first. In part (b), your answer should explain what action the directors should take to halt the decline in profitability.

## 114: Decision-Making Techniques

**(a) Option 1 - Increase production capacity**

| | Robin $ | Eagle $ | Hawk $ | Total $ | Marks |
|---|---|---|---|---|---|
| Selling price (per unit) | 400.00 | 470.00 | 320.00 | | |
| Less: Variable costs (per unit) | | | | | |
|     Material | 92.60 | 83.20 | 57.90 | | 1.5 |
|     Labour (labour hour per unit x $54.50/hour) | 65.40 | 49.05 | 76.30 | | 1.5 |
|     Overheads (machine hour per unit x $34.70/hour) | 138.80 | 190.85 | 86.75 | | 1.5 |
| Total variable costs | 296.80 | 323.10 | 220.95 | | |
| Contribution (per unit) | 103.20 | 146.90 | 99.05 | | 1.5 |
| Sales volume (p.a.) | 5,200 | 3,100 | 6,700 | | |
| Contribution (p.a.) | 536,640 | 455,390 | 663,635 | 1,655,665 | |
| Total contribution for three years | | | | 4,966,995 | 1 |
| Less: Fixed costs ($680,000 x 3 years) | | | | (20,40,000) | 1 |
|     Incremental costs | | | | (1,400,000) | 1 |
| Profit | | | | 1,526,995 | |

**Maximum marks 6**

**Option 2 - Improve product quality**

| | Robin $ | Eagle $ | Hawk $ | Total $ | Marks |
|---|---|---|---|---|---|
| Selling price (per unit) (original +5% increase) | 420.00 | 493.50 | 336.00 | | 1.5 |
| Less: Variable costs (per unit) | | | | | |
| Material | 92.60 | 83.20 | 57.90 | | |
| Labour (labour hour per unit x $54.50/hour) | 65.40 | 49.05 | 76.30 | | |
| Overheads (machine hour per unit x $34.70/hour) | 138.80 | 190.85 | 86.75 | | |
| Total variable costs | (296.80) | (323.10) | (220.95) | | |
| Increase in variable costs | (6.94) | (10.41) | (3.47) | | 1.5 |
| Contribution (per unit) | 116.26 | 159.99 | 111.58 | | |
| Anticipated Sales volume (p.a.) | 5,800 | 4,400 | 7,900 | | |
| Contribution (p.a.) | 674,308.00 | 703,956.00 | 881,482.00 | 2,259,746.00 | 1 |
| Total contribution for three years | | | | 6,779,238.00 | 1 |
| Less: Fixed costs ($680,000 x 3 years) | | | | (2,040,000.00) | 1 |
| Incremental costs | | | | | |
| Year 1 | | | 875,000.00 | | |
| Year 2 | | | 640,000.00 | | |
| Year 3 | | | 640,000.00 | (2,155,000.00) | 1 |
| Profit | | | | 2,584,238.00 | 1 |

**Maximum marks 6**

**Working**

**W1 Increase in variable costs**

Robin: $34.70 per hour x 0.2 hours = $6.94
Eagle: $34.70 per hour x 0.3 hours = $10.41
Hawk: $34.70 per hour x 0.1 hours = $3.47

**Option 3 - Preferred supplier status**

| | Robin | Eagle | Hawk | Marks |
|---|---|---|---|---|
| Contribution per unit | $103.20 | $146.90 | $99.05 | |
| Machine hour per unit | 4 | 5.5 | 2.5 | |
| Contribution per machine hour | $25.80 | $26.71 | $39.62 | 1.5 |
| Rank (priority) | 3 | 2 | 1 | 1.5 |

As mentioned in the example, Eagle must be produced using 28,600 hours (5,200 units) and from the rest of the available hours; either Hawk or Robin can be produced. According to the contribution per limiting factor of machine hours, first production priority should be given to Hawk.

| Total hours | 44000 |
|---|---|
| **Less:** Required hours for Eagle (5,200 units x 5.5 hours) | 28,600 |
| Available hours for Hawk | 15,400 |

*Due to shortage of hours, production of the rest of 540 units of Hawk and any units of Robin will not be possible*

Possible production of Hawk = 15,400hours/2.5 hours per unit = 6,160 units

**3 marks**

**Profit statement**

|  | $ |
|---|---|
| Contribution |  |
| Eagle (5,200 units x $146.90) | 763,880 |
| Hawk (6,160 units x $89.05) | 610,148 |
|  | 1,374,028 |
| Contribution for three years | 4,122,084 |
| **Less:** Fixed costs | (2,040,000) |
| Profit | 2,082,084 |

**2 marks**
**Maximum marks 7**

**(b)** Based on the calculations above, the best option from the given three is to improve the quality of the products, as this will maximise the profit.

However, the possibility that additional contribution can be generated by increasing the production capacity should also be considered, as these options are mutually exclusive.

**2 marks**
**Maximum marks 2**

## 25. Relevant cost – PF201

**Strategy**

The classification of costs for decision making is the subject of this question. In part (a), you need to define the types of costs in regards to the given scenario. In part (b), you need to prepare the revised assessment of Project PF201 for the short-term decision of whether or not the project should be continued.

**(a)**

|  | Definition | Example |
|---|---|---|
| Sunk cost | A cost which has already been incurred, and cannot be recovered. Therefore it has no impact on the decision and should not be considered when choosing between alternatives | Development costs incurred to date |
| Opportunity cost | The cost of foregoing an alternative course of action, or the benefit which has been given up by foregoing a possible course of action. | The contribution on the three years' sales which will be lost due to the delay in completing project BR156 |
| Relevant cost | A cost which will be incurred or can be avoided, subject to a decision which is yet to be taken | The variable cost of manufacturing the product once the project has been completed |

3 marks for sunk cost
2 marks for opportunity costs
2 marks for relevant cost
**Maximum marks 7**

# 116: Decision-Making Techniques

**(b)**

|  | PF201 ($m) | BR156 ($m) | Marks |
|---|---|---|---|
| Selling price per unit | 1.43 | 2.86 | |
| Less: Variable cost per unit | (1.12) | (1.96) | |
| Contribution per unit | 0.31 | 0.90 | 2 |

|  | |  Marks |
|---|---|---|
| Sales volume for first three years (40 + 55 + 50) | 145.00 | |
| Total contribution (Units x Contribution per unit) | **44.95** | 1 |
| Less: Development costs | | |
| Costs to date | | |
| Costs to complete | (31.14) | 1 |
| Additional development costs | (2.40) | 1 |
| Transfer of engineering team | (0.45) | 1 |
| Less: Opportunity costs of using engineering team on project PF201 (0.90 x 3 units) | (2.70) | 1 |
| Contribution earned | 8.26 | 1 |
| Less: Fixed costs | | |
| 700 hours x 145 units at $100 per hour | (10.15) | 2 |
| Profit / (Loss) | **(1.89)** | 1 |

Maximum marks 13

### Score More

The examiner has commented that the candidates who did not include fixed costs were awarded the relevant marks if they justified the exclusion on the basis that the fixed costs were unavoidable. Those who simply included fixed costs without any description were awarded one mark only, with the second mark awarded for a reference to the need to consider whether such costs were relevant.

Presentation of the answer should be fair and the calculations should be correct in order to gain full marks for such kind of questions.

## 26. Make or buy – Culum Ltd

### Strategy

In part (a), you need to evaluate the probable profit from different markets. In the export market, don't forget to consider the probabilities for the calculation of expected profits.

In part (b) your answer should be in a report form describing the options that are available to the company and significant issues for arriving at the final decision.

**(a) Calculations of profit**

**Profit in the domestic market**

|  | Standard | Premium | Deluxe | Total | Marks |
|---|---|---|---|---|---|
| Sales (in units) | **1,200** | **700** | **500** | | |
| Selling price per unit | 400 | 700 | 900 | | 1.5 |
| Less: Variable cost per unit | | | | | |
| Material | (102) | (165) | (180) | | |
| Labour ($50 x hours) | (90) | (130) | (160) | | |
| Variable overhead ($40 x hours) | (72) | (104) | (128) | | |
| Total variable cost per unit | (264) | (399) | (468) | | |
| Contribution per unit | 136 | 301 | 432 | | 1.5 |
| Contribution ($) (Sales units x Contribution per unit) | 163,200 | 210,700 | 216,000 | 589,900 | |
| Less: Fixed Costs | | | | (120,000) | 1.5 |
| Profit | | | | **469,900** | 1.5 |

Maximum marks 5

**Profit in the export market**

|  | Standard | Premium | Deluxe | Total | Marks |
|---|---|---|---|---|---|
| Contribution per unit ($) | 136 | 301 | 432 |  |  |
|  |  |  |  |  |  |
| **Units** | High | Medium | Low |  |  |
| Standard | 1,300 | 1,100 | 900 |  |  |
| Premium | 800 | 600 | 500 |  |  |
| Deluxe | 600 | 550 | 400 |  | 1.5 |
| **Export Contribution (units x contribution per unit)** | High | Medium | Low | Total |  |
| Standard | 176,800 | 149,600 | 122,400 | 448,800 |  |
| Premium | 240,800 | 180,600 | 150,500 | 571,900 |  |
| Deluxe | 259,200 | 237,600 | 172,800 | 669,600 |  |
|  | 676,800 | 567,800 | 445,700 | 1,690,300 | 2 |
| **Less:** Fixed costs |  |  |  |  |  |
| Fixed expenses | (120,000) | (120,000) | (120,000) | (360,000) | 1 |
| Marketing expenses | (60,000) | (40,000) | (20,000) | (120,000) | 1 |
|  |  |  |  |  |  |
| Profit | 496,800 | 407,800 | 305,700 | 1,210,300 | 1 |
| Probability | 0.55 | 0.35 | 0.10 |  |  |
| Expected profit | 273,240 | 142,730 | 30,570 | 446,540 | 1 |

**Maximum marks 7**

**(b) Report to management**

From,
Project team of Culum Ltd
1 December 2003

To,
The Managing Director of Culum Ltd

Subject: Sales market

Based on the given information, probable profits from the two options are as follows:

1. If we choose to service our domestic market – the profit will be $469,900.
2. If we decide to enter the export market, the result is a bit uncertain – the profit will be $446,540 (this has been derived using the expected value technique).

Looking only at these two figures, this appears unattractive, representing a fall of almost 5%.

However, there are several factors which need to be considered before arriving at a final decision. They are listed below:

1. Availability of production capacity to meet the demand: if volumes are constrained by production capacity, the assessment of potential profit will be adversely affected.

2. Period on which decision is to be based: the demand in the domestic market is stable. So if we choose to enter the export market, although the expected profit is less by 5%, this will be more profitable in long-term, provided there are growth opportunities in the export market. If so, the forecasts for the long-term ought to be researched.

3. The market research shows that the level of demand can be influenced by marketing activity. Accordingly, an assessment of the impact on additional marketing expenditure should be considered. Such additional marketing activity could lead to demand above the levels currently under consideration. Or such expenditure could ensure that low level of demand does not occur.

4. It has been assumed that the provided data, especially the sales volume, cost of marketing and probabilities, are accurate. Any inaccuracy in any or all of these can influence the final decision.

5. The applied method of expected value is based on the application of probabilities. Hence, the amount of $446,540 is an approximation. There are 55% chances of generating $496,800 profits, 35% chances of generating $407,800 profits and 10% chances of generating $305,700 profits. The final decision will therefore be influenced by the overall attitude to risk. If we wish to avoid the risk of a reduction in profit, we would either continue to service the domestic market, or take action to ensure that the low level of market demand does not occur. One possibility is increasing the marketing expenditure to further stimulate demand.

*1 mark for each correctly explained point*

**Conclusion**

Although the data available gives the impression of certainty, there are a number of factors to be considered before any decision is made.

For clear presentation of report, up to a maximum of 3
**Maximum marks 8**

## SOLUTION BANK

# SECTION C: BUDGETING

### 27. Zero-based budgeting – NN Ltd

**Strategy**

A fairly simple question as there is no calculation involved. You should be aware of the problems and benefits of zero based budgeting.

**(a) Memorandum**

To: The members of the senior management
From: Finance Director
Date: 03 February 2009

Re: The adoption of zero-base budgeting within NN Ltd.

This year, the traditional approach of incremental budgeting has been applied in NN Ltd. According to this approach, the previous year's budget has been used as a baseline. Amounts from last year's budget have been adjusted by adding or subtracting the change. These changes to the base budget have been made in order to reflect expectations for the current budget period.

*1 mark*

However, the inefficiency of the last budget period may be carried forward to the next year. As a result, the budget has been made without justifying the total expenditure. In the absence of this justification, inefficiencies may take place in the current budget too.

*1 mark*

These problems can be taken care of by implementing zero-based budgeting. Our managers and employees will benefit from the implementation of zero-based budgeting as follows:

- Zero-based budgeting helps in establishing policies based on an organisation's mission and goals. These policies provide directions to the managers and employees while working in the organisation.
- It helps them in selecting the desirable decision package and identifying the resources required to achieve the objectives of that decision package.
- Managers could allocate the appropriate level of resources within the organisation. This will ensure the optimum use of those resources.
- Managers can appraise themselves by evaluating each budget during and at the end of its implementation. Based on the variances, corrective actions can be initiated.
- The zero-based budgeting approach helps in eliminating the overestimation of costs or underestimation of revenue i.e. budget slack.
- It facilitates accurate performance evaluation as budget slacks are eliminated in the budgets. This will facilitate fair distribution of bonuses.

*3 marks*

However following are the consequences of implementing zero-based budgeting.

- This might be thought of as a cost-cutting affair by many. As a result, they may not like it. It is also a new concept, so many will like to stay away from it.
- The preparation of zero-based budgets is a time consuming affair. Hence it will need support from the top management.
- It requires detailed data and its processing. It also requires continuous updating of systems.
- While collecting the data for preparing the budgets, subordinates may cut short term costs in order to impress their superiors. Hence it may lead to long term losses.
- Lack of negotiation skills of the managers can result in not justifying a genuine/ actual expenditure needs to the senior management.

*5 marks*

Under zero-based budgeting, each manager has to start from scratch. Hence there will not be any base for preparing budgets. Managers have to ascertain the actual expenditure needs and then pile up the amount of expenditure required under different expenditure heads. Then to get the expenditure approved in the budget, each manager needs to justify his expenditure needs for the value additions.

1 mark

This does not mean that past budget targets will not be reviewed or re-evaluated. Zero-based budgeting is a cost analysis tool which, along with reviewing and re-evaluating past budgets, evaluates how each element of cost will contribute to the achievements of the company's objectives and goals.

1 mark

Zero-based budgeting could be called a complex system which requires major planning, and analytical and decision-making processes. Only the costs which are essential for the achievement of the ultimate goals of the company shall be identified and allowed in the zero-based budgeting.

Costs at different alternative decisions are identified. These costs and their associated objectives are then reviewed by the senior managers. Each activity along with its alternatives is assessed before justifying its inclusion in the budget. This can be done by identifying the following:
- The degree and extent of support that the proposed activity will contribute to the goals of the organisation.
- The likely impact that the organisation would have to face if a particular activity is not carried out.
- The effectiveness and efficiencies of the activities in achieving their designed objectives.

3 marks

In zero-based budgeting, activities are carried out in the following order.
- First activities are ranked
- This is followed by cost–benefit analysis
- Alternatives having the maximum possibility of achieving its designed objectives are selected

Therefore, prioritising or ranking the activities is the fundamental step in zero-based budgeting.

- The required resources to meet these budget targets are identified
- This is followed by the review of the proposed budget by the senior management
- Budgets are modified according to the instructions of the senior management
- Approved functional budgets are then consolidated into a master budget
- Finally these budgets are implemented
- Implementation is followed by monitoring and evaluation

Monitoring and evaluation in turn give the managers a chance to appraise themselves. This may initiate certain adjustments in order to achieve the objectives of the decision package.

2 marks

The implementation of any new system has problems and zero-based budgeting is not an exception to this. As the future development and ranking of the activities are dependent on initial planning, it requires efforts from all the personnel in the organisation to make it successful.

However, it will benefit the organisation in the following ways:
- Budgeting helps in envisaging the uncertainties of the future and in turn helps to prepare for it.
- Corporate planning and decision-making functions can get their inputs from Zero based budgeting.
- It helps in identifying and selecting the activities and in allocating resources to them. Therefore it helps in achieving established goals.
- It facilities the optimum use of resources.

3 marks

Although the preparation of zero-based budgets requires more human hours than the current conventional system, the benefits received from it are far more than the costs required for implementing it. Therefore we should adopt Zero based budgeting in NN Ltd. Instead of implementing the whole system we could introduce it on a piecemeal basis.

However, managers may show resistance to sparing the time required for such an in depth examination every year. This could be taken care of by introducing a policy which will require reviewing all the activities at least once during a three year period. Training seminars on the implementation of zero-based budgeting could be organised to educate employees and make all the employees comfortable with it.

2 marks

Thanks,

Yours sincerely,

(-------------------)
Finance Director

**Maximum marks 16**

© GTG

Solution Bank: 121

(b) Non-profit businesses have some special features which are different from manufacturing organisations. Most of the costs of non-profit organisations are discretionary costs. These costs do not have any direct input-output relationship which is seen in manufacturing companies like NN Ltd. Therefore, the budgeted costs of non-profit organisations might get inflated by adding a budget slack to it. As zero-based budgeting eliminates the budget slacks, it is more suitable for non-profit organisations than for manufacturing organisations.

2 marks

NN Ltd is a manufacturer of electronic office equipment in which most of the costs are production costs. As such they have a direct input-output relationship. The existence of such a relationship discourages budget slacks; hence traditional budgeting methods are more appropriate to NN Ltd

1 mark

Zero-based budgeting is more suitable to service organisations such as non-profit health organisations where most of the costs are discretionary costs. Additionally, zero-based budgeting helps non–profit organisations in determining their priorities and evaluating different decision packages, as lot of alternatives are available to achieve the organisation's objectives.

2 marks
**Maximum marks 4**

## 28. Budget preparation - Sine Ltd

### Strategy

A simple question, although it involves a lot of calculation. Follow a step by step approach and you can earn full marks here.

**Key points - Part (a)**
- First calculate the closing stock for each month
- Then calculate the production units for each month
- Then calculate the raw material requirement
- Then prepare the statement showing the budgeted costs
- Calculate the cost per unit of production for each month. This is required for answering part b.

**Key points - Part (b)**
- Calculate the value of closing stock by using the FIFO valuation method
- The value of opening stock + cost of production – value of closing stock = cost of sales

(a)
(i) **Production budgets (Finished products in Units)**

| Month | July | August | September | Total |
|---|---|---|---|---|
| Sales (units) | 30,000 | 35,000 | 60,000 | 125,000 |
| Closing stock (units)W1 | 7,000 | 12,000 | 2,000 | 21,000 |
|  | 37,000 | 47,000 | 62,000 | 146,000 |
| Opening stock (units) | (4,000) | (7,000) | (12,000) | (23,000) |
| Production (units) | 33,000 | 40,000 | 50,000 | 123,000 |

2 marks

(ii) **Material Usage budget (Raw material requirement in Units)**

| Month | July | August | September | Total |
|---|---|---|---|---|
| Material X (kg) (production x 1.5 kg per unit ) | 49,500 | 60,000 | 75,000 | 184,500 |
| Material P (kg) (production x 2 kg per unit) | 66,000 | 80,000 | 100,000 | 246,000 |

2 marks

(iii) **Production budget (money terms)**

|  | $ | $ | $ | Total $ |
|---|---|---|---|---|
| Material X (W2) | 179,100 | 228,000 | 285,000 | 692,100 |
| Material P (W3) | 304,680 | 384,000 | 480,000 | 1,168,680 |
| Labour(W4) | 52,800 | 64,000 | 88,000 | 204,800 |
| Variable production overhead ( $1 per unit) | 33,000 | 40,000 | 50,000 | 123,000 |
| Fixed production overhead ( $0.60 per unit) | 19,800 | 24,000 | 30,000 | 73,800 |
|  | 589,380 | 740,000 | 933,000 | 2,262,380 |
| Cost per unit | 17.86 | 18.50 | 18.66 |  |

2 marks

## 122: Budgeting

**Note:** As the information about the total fixed production overheads is not given in the question, fixed production overheads are absorbed on the basis of labour hours worked and hence would be similar in nature to the variable costs.

**Workings**

### W1 Calculation of closing stock units

It is given that the closing stock for July and August is 20% of the coming month's sales and closing stock of September is 10% of October's sales. So,
Closing stock of July = 20% of August's sales i.e. 20% of 35000 units = 7,000 units
Closing stock of August = 20% of September's sales i.e. 20% of 60,000 units = 12,000 units
Closing stock of September = 10% of October's sales i.e. 10% of 20,000 units = 2,000 units

*2 marks*

### W2

Material X used in July = (30,000 x 3·50) opening stock + (19,500 x 3·80) new purchases = $179,100
Material X used in August = 60,000 x 3·80 = $228,000
Material X used in September = 75,000 x 3·80 = $285,000

> Material other than the opening stock is valued at $3.80per kg.

*2 marks*

### W3

Material P used in July = (40,400 x 4·50) opening stock + (25,600 x 4·80) new purchases = $304,680
Material P used in August = 80,000 x 4·80 = $384,000
Material P used in September = 100,000 x 4·80 = $480,000

> Material other than opening stock is valued at $4.80 per kg

*2 marks*

### W4

Labour paid in July = 33,000 x (12/60) = 6,600 x 8·00 = $52,800
Labour paid in August = 40,000 x (12/60) = 8,000 x 8·00 = $64,000
Labour hours in September = 50,000 x (12/60) = 10,000 hours
Labour paid in September = (8,000 x 8·00) + (2,000 x 12·00) overtime hours = $88,000

*2 marks*
**Maximum marks 10**

**(b)** Opening stock of finished goods = $69,800  *1 mark*

Closing stock of finished goods = 2,000 x 18·66 = $37,320  *1 mark*

Cost of sales for three-month period = 69,800 + 2,262,380 - 37,320 = $2,294,860  *2 marks*

**Note:** As Sine Ltd follows the FIFO method for inventory valuation, the closing stock of September will represent the units produced in September. So Unit cost of production of September,$18.66 is used to value the closing stock.

*1 mark*
**Maximum marks 4**

**(c)**

### Strategy

This question is simple as it is a theory question.

**Key points**
- Evaluating activities that lead to costs
- Ensuring the supply of resources to perform those activities
- Resistance to accept, absence of required information, suitability of the approach

Activity based budgeting (ABB) is an approach to budgeting in which, instead of evaluating the cost elements, the activities causing costs are evaluated. This helps to ascertain whether they are essential for the budgeted production and sales volume. The attempt of an activity-based budget is to make certain that only those resources that are needed to perform activities required to meet the budgeted production and sales are made available.

*2 marks*

Hence, in this type of a budget, the targets are determined and only then the activities necessary to meet these targets are identified. The employees responsible for meeting a particular budget target need to have control over the events that affect the performance under their jurisdiction.

1 mark

However, this budgeting system has a few limitations:

(i) Activity based budgeting is an expensive and time-consuming system of budget preparation.

(ii) ABB is expected to produce initial errors, as it is a relatively new system. Additionally, the employees might not be ready to accept the activity based budgeting as they would not be familiar with this new system. This problem can be avoided with the help of an orientation programme and the involvement of top management, in order to motivate the personnel.

(iii) Activity based budgeting is suitable to only those organisations that use activity based costing. Under the ABC system, the cost of individual activities is calculated and assigned to cost objects on the basis of the activities needed to produce each product or service. Without this information it is not possible to evaluate the activities. In an ABC system, these activity centres are identified.

(iv) Due to short-term fluctuations, an activity-based approach may not always be suitable for month-to-month monitoring of actual performance. However, if the increase in activity lasts for a long period, it is likely that the organisation will need more resources and incur greater costs. The inevitable variability in the cost per activity focuses attention to whether resources are being used effectively or not and the levels that may be required in the future.

1 mark for each point
**Maximum marks 6**

## 29. Sales forecasting – Storrs Plc

**Strategy**

If the concept of moving average is clear to you, you can score full marks. Part (b) and part (c) are theoretical questions, hence they are fairly simple.

### Key points

**Part (a)**
- Prepare a table showing a seasonal variation each quarter.
- Adjust the residual error term.
- Find out the average trend of the centered moving average.
- Calculate the actual trend and forecasted sales for the quarters.

**Part (b)**
- Trend and seasonal variations are independent of each other.
- Repetition of pervious trends and seasonal variances –may not be true in all the cases.
- Opinion of the sales staff –important for preparing a successful budget.
- Relationship between reliability of data and quantity and accuracy.

**Part (c)**
- Top down approach:
  - Budgets are prepared by top management.
  - aligned to strategic objectives,
  - demotivates the persons responsible for budgets,
  - staff initiative and innovative ideas,
  - possibility of unsuccessful budgets

- Bottom up approach:
  - budgets are prepared by lower level management and reviewed by the superiors
  - time consuming,
  - demotivates,
  - detailed planning and coordination.

# 124: Budgeting

**(a)** The seasonal variations in sales can be calculated by comparing the central moving averages with the actual sales of each quarter.

| Quarter | Actual sales $000 | Centred moving average $000 | Seasonal variation $000 |
|---|---|---|---|
| 2007-08 | | | |
| 3 | 3,400 | 3,200 | 200 |
| 4 | 3,000 | 3,300 | (300) |
| 2008-09 | | | |
| 1 | 3,100 | 3,375 | (275) |
| 2 | 3,900 | 3,450 | 450 |
| 3 | 3,600 | 3562.50 | 37.5 |
| 4 | 3,400 | 3687.50 | (287.50) |

*As the centred moving averages are given from the second quarter of 07-08, data for first and second quarter of 07-08 has not been taken.*

*Seasonal variation is the difference between actual sales and the respective centered moving averages*

**3 marks**

The average seasonal variations and the residual error term will now be identified:

| Year | Quarter 1 $000 | Quarter 2 $000 | Quarter 3 $000 | Quarter 4 $000 | Total $000 |
|---|---|---|---|---|---|
| 2007-08 | | | 200 | (300) | |
| 2008-09 | (275) | 450 | 37.50 | (287.50) | |
| Average | (275) | 450 | 118.75 | (293.75) | Nil |

The sum of the average variations due to seasonal factors is nil. So, we don't need to adjust any residual error term against the average seasonal variations.

**2 marks**

The average trend of the centred moving averages during the period of observation is

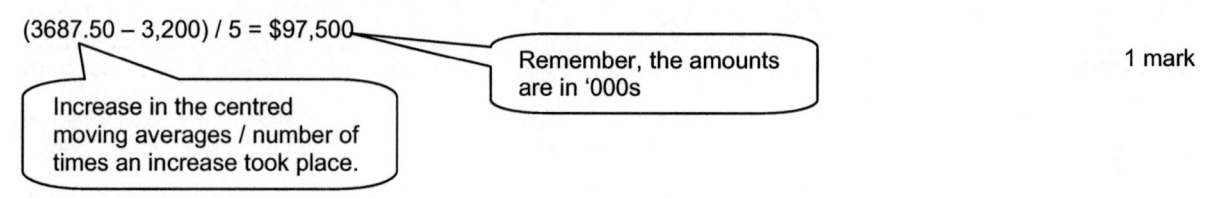

(3687.50 – 3,200) / 5 = $97,500

*Increase in the centred moving averages / number of times an increase took place.*

*Remember, the amounts are in '000s*

**1 mark**

**Actual trend**

| Quarters | 20X9 - 2010 | |
|---|---|---|
| | 3 $'000 | 4 $'000 |
| Base trend (central moving average for fourth quarter, 2008-09) | 3687.50 | 3687.50 |
| Add: Quarterly increasing trend | 292.50 (97.5 x 3) | 390 (97.5 x 4) |
| Forecasted adjusted trend | 3,980 | 4077.50 |
| Add: average seasonal trend | 118.75 | (293.75) |
| Forecasted sales for the quarter | 4098.75 | 3783.75 |

*Don't forget to add the average seasonal trend to the forecasted adjusted trend. Many students make a mistake here.*

**3 marks**

The management accountant has forecasted the sales of quarter 3 and 4 to be $4,098,750 and $3,783,750 respectively. These are higher than the amounts $ 3,800,000 and $ 3,600,000 forecasted by the sales director for the third and forth quarter.

**1 mark**

This can be due to the fact that the sales director had not calculated his data using the time series analysis. Hence, there are differences between the two forecasts.

**Maximum marks 8**

**(b)** The time series analysis used for forecasting the sales in part (a) is one of the techniques mentioned in the additive model used for forecasting. The additive model assumes that trends and seasonal variations are independent of each other, and do not have an impact on each other. Hence, an increasing trend is not linked to increasing seasonal variations.

*1 mark*

The model uses past data to reach conclusions. Hence, the underlying concept is that the previous trends and seasonal variations will repeat themselves in the future. This may not be the case at all times. There could be certain unexpected events taking place, a change in tastes and preferences of the consumers, a change in the economy etc.

*2 marks*

It is recommended that the opinion of the sales department is taken into consideration before finalising the budget. This is because the sales staff is more experienced and they know the market trends.

*1 mark*

Under the additive model, the reliability of the forecast depends on the quantity and accuracy of the data analysed. In the case of Airxpress, only the data of the last two years has been used to analyse future trends, hence the data cannot be fully relied upon. The reliability of data will also decrease as the period for which forecasts have been made increases.

*2 marks*
**Maximum marks 5**

**(c) Top-down approach and bottom-up approach**

**Top-down approach**

Under the top-down approach the budgets are prepared by the top management in line with the strategic objectives of the organisation. These budgets are then communicated to various departments or lower levels of management. Hence, on this basis the divisional budgets are prepared. The lower level management does not play a role in the process of the budget preparation.

*1 mark*

Since the top management prepares the budgets, they might build a higher level of expected performance, in order to motivate the employees to chase the targets. However, the employees will get the full support from the management .Moreover, the targets of various departments in the organisation would be synchronised.

*1 mark*

However, this approach is more suitable in small organisations where the top management is fully aware of the various aspects of the organisation. It is also suitable for organisations that do not want to utilise more resources for planning.

*1 mark*

**Limitations of this method are:**

- This approach does not consider the views of persons responsible for implementing and achieving the budgets, hence demotivates them.
- The approach does not encourage staff to take initiative or come up with innovative ideas.
- Under this approach, the top management must be aware of the hurdles that could be encountered while chasing targets. Employees need to communicate these obstacles, to ensure the successful implementation of the budget. This is especially important when the top management is not aware of all the aspects of the business.

*2 marks*

**Bottom–up approach**

The bottom up approach is the opposite of the top-down approach. The budgets and targets are prepared by lower level management, and are then passed on to the higher authorities for review and approval. All the divisional budgets are combined, to prepare the organisational budget. In this system all the levels of management are involved in the budget making process. Innovative ideas can be implemented from lower levels of management.

*2 marks*

This approach is more suitable for large organisations as each department is aware of the problems it will face, and hence can prepare more realistic budgets.

**Limitations of this method are:**

- Preparing the budget is time consuming, as it involves many people.
- It may demotivate those who prepared the original budget, if during the review the budgeted targets are modified substantially by the senior management.
- There is a greater need for detailed planning and coordination.

*2 marks*

A combination of the two approaches is preferable in the real world, as participation from all levels of management is required to make budgets successful.

**Maximum marks 7**

## 126: Budgeting

### 30. Learning rate - Sole Ltd

**(a) The projected cash flow from Marigold High School project**

|  | Units | Marks |
|---|---|---|
| Sales | 18,000 |  |
|  | $ |  |
| Sales revenue (W1) | 360,000 | 1 |
| **Costs** |  |  |
| Direct materials (W2) | 140,812.50 | 3 |
| Direct labour (W3) | 83,983.086 | 6 |
| Variable overheads (W4) | 45,000 | 1 |
| Rent (W5) | 60,000 | 1 |
| **Net cash flow** | **30,204.414** |  |

Soles Ltd is expecting a cash flow of $43,000 from the project. The above figure of the net cash flow i.e. 30,204.414 is much lower than the expected level. This proves that the project will not generate the expected cash flow.

1 mark

**Workings**

**W1 Sales revenue**

Sales revenue = $30,000 x 12
= $360,000

**W2 Direct materials**

Cost for the first batch = $12,500

|  |  | $ | Marks |
|---|---|---|---|
| Cost for first three batches | (3 x 12,500) | 37,500 | 1 |
| Cost of next three batches | (3 x (95% x 12,500)) | 35,625 | 1 |
| Cost of remaining six batches | (6 x (95% x 11,875)) | 67,687.50 | 1 |
| **Total cost** |  | **140,812.50** |  |

**W3**

Direct labour cost per batch for the first seven batches can be determined with the help of the learning curve equation.

$Y = a x^b$

Where,

Y = cumulative average time
a = labour cost of the first batch
x = number of batches
b = learning curve factor

$Y = 10,000 \times 7^{-0.1520}$
  = 10,000 x 0.7439523
  = 7439.523

2 marks

The cumulative average cost of the seven batches is $7,439.523

Labour cost for the first 7 batches is = $7,439.523 x 7
= $52,076.661

The rest of the batches will have a labour cost equal to the cost of the 7$^{th}$ batch. In order to find out the cost of the 7$^{th}$ batch, we need to deduct the cost of the first 6 batches from the cost of the 7 batches.

© GTG

This could be calculated using the learning curve equation.

$Y = a x^b$

$Y = 10,000 \times 6^{-0.1520}$
  $= 10,000 \times 0.7615896$
  $= 7,615.896$

*2 marks*

Average labour cost for the first 6 batches is $7,615.896.

Labour cost for the first 6 batches = 7,615.896 × 6
                                    = $45,695.376

Cost of the 7$^{th}$ batch = Cost of the first 7 batches – cost of the first 6 batches
              = 52,076.661 – 45,695.376
              = $6,381.285

*1 mark*

Total cost for 12 batches:
First 7 batches = $52,076.661
Next 5 batches = $31,906.425
(5 × 6,381.285)
Total cost = $83,983.086

*1 mark*

**W4**

Variable overhead = $1.75 × 18,000
                  = $31,500

*0.5 marks*

**W5**

Yearly rent = 5,000 × 12
            = $60,000

*0.5 marks*
**Maximum marks 12**

**(b)** Soles Ltd. could accept the project as it has a positive net cash flow. The company can also take a few steps to increase the cash flow of the product, to make it more feasible.

➢ One major step Soles Ltd. could take is to convince Marigold High School to pay a higher price for the shoes. If the company is able to increase their selling price, then their cash flow will increase considerably.

*1 mark*

➢ Soles Ltd. can look for alternative suppliers who can supply them raw-materials at lower costs. This would help them reduce costs, and thus increase cash flow.

*1 mark*

➢ Another alternative could be to look for cheaper material without compromising on the quality of the product.

*1 mark*

➢ Reduction in the variable overheads such as electricity can also help to improve the scenario.

*1 mark*

➢ The company can consider training its employees and also improve the quality of people hired. This can prove to be time consuming and expensive in the short run but will pay off in the long run.

*1 mark*

➢ Soles Ltd. could try to negotiate a reduction in the rent. They could also look for alternatives to avoid additional rental.

*1 mark*

➢ The company can take steps to reduce the labour costs. This can be done by re-engineering the work process, or by simplifying the product design without changing its features to a great extent.

*1 mark*
**Maximum marks 5**

## 128: Budgeting

(c) The learning curve phenomenon is an important tool for forecasting costs. It can also be used in budgeting. It illustrates the effect of learning / experience on labour time and cost, over a period. To calculate its effect on labour time, we will need to calculate the time taken by the first batch (1,000 hours) and the time taken by the second batch.

**At 80%**

| Labour time for first batch | 1,000 |
|---|---|
| Average time for two batches @ 80%= (1,000 x 0.8) | 800 |
| Total time for two batches (800 x 2) | 1,600 |
| Time taken for second batch (1,600 - 1,000) | 600 |

*1.5 marks*

**At 70%**

| Labour time for first batch | 1,000 |
|---|---|
| Average time for two batches @ 80% (1,000 x 0.7) | 700 |
| Total time for two batches (700 x 2) | 1,400 |
| Time taken for second batch (1,400 - 1,000) | 400 |

*1.5 marks*

From the above figures we can see that a 70% learning rate lowers the time taken by two successive batches by a larger degree. Hence, the learning rate of 70% is a faster rate as compared to the learning rate of 80%.

Note: Learning rate can be easily measured when the production doubles between the first and the second batch. Hence by applying the learning rate for the time taken by the first batch, cumulative average time taken by the first two batches can be ascertained.

*1 mark*
**Maximum marks 3**

### 31. Learning curve concept - Labnew Ltd

**Strategy**

Part (a) and Part (b) are theoretical questions and hence you can score good marks.

**Key points**

**Part (a)**
- Reduction of labour time per unit.
- Consequent reduction in labour cost.
- Helps in budgeting, and in fixing a selling price.
- Also helps in planning, controlling and reducing material waste

**Part (b)**
- Used only in case of complex and labour intensive procedures.
- Labour rate may not remain constant over a certain period.
- Repetition of jobs/procedure.
- Not applicable for experienced jobs
- Rate of reduction is constant- not true

**Part (c)**

This problem has complex mathematical calculations. Understand the logic behind the calculations.

**Key points**

- Calculate the incremental time required to produce each additional unit using the learning curve principle.
- Prepare the total cost statement using the labour costs applicable for each proposal.
- Find out the selling price by adding the mark up.

(a) A learning curve, with the help of a mathematical expression, depicts the rate at which labour time per unit is reduced when the job is repeated. It illustrates the effect of learning / experience on labour time and cost over a period.

*1 mark*

The theory is based on the concept that, through the learning process, a person acquires skill, confidence, knowledge and ability that help him to perform the work more effectively and efficiently and thereby reduce the time and cost of the work. When tasks are repeated, the worker becomes familiar with them and gains experience that results in accomplishment of the job in lesser time.

*1 mark*

This theory helps managers to predict how costs will change as the job is repeated. Therefore it helps to identify the selling price of the products. Apart from this, it also helps the manager in several other ways:

- It helps to improve his planning process by having a better estimation of the time needed to execute the task.
- It can also assist in control, as the manager now knows the standards of the job, and the ideal time it should take to be completed.
- It can also help to reduce wastage of materials.
- In the budgetary control system, while incorporating labour standards, care should be taken to consider the anticipated time that will be saved.

2 marks
**Maximum marks 4**

**(b)** Every theory has certain drawbacks when it comes to implementing it in real life. Likewise, the learning curve has a few limitations that are as follows:

- The learning curve theory can be successfully applied only in the case of complex and labour intensive procedures. The principle is not at all suitable to machine intensive procedures.

1 mark

- It assumes that the labour rate remains the same over a certain period but, in reality, the labour rate may change.

1 mark

- It is a reality only if the same job / procedure is performed repetitively.

1 mark

- The learning curve calculations are based on the assumption that there will only be an effect when the job doubles, but, in real life, the learning effect exists even if the job has not doubled but is constantly repeated.

1 mark

- It is applicable only to new jobs / industries / workers etc. but not to experienced jobs / industries / workers as, after the steady state has been reached, there isn't a learning effect.

1 mark

- Learning curves are only approximates. The theory states that there will be a consistent rate of decrease in the time required to perform the job, but in reality, the time required is highly unlikely to decrease at a constant rate.

1 mark

- It is not applicable in the case of jobs which are subject to changes, depending on the circumstances, e.g. it's not applicable to managerial work.

1 mark
**Maximum marks 6**

**(c) Cumulative average time**

| No. of Machines | Cumulative Average Time (Hours) | Total Time to Date (Hours) | Incremental Time for Additional machines (Hours) |
|---|---|---|---|
| 1 | 150 |  | 150 |
| 2 | 120 (80% of 150) | 120 x 2 = 240 | 240 – 150 = 90 |
| 4 | 96 (80% of 120) | 96 x 4 = 384 | 384 - 240 = 144 |
| 8 | 76.8 (80% of 96) | 76.8 x 8 = 614.4 | 614.4 – 384 = 230.4 |

**Note 1:** The number of machines produced doubles each time because the learning rate calculates the average time taken between two points as production doubles. That is, as cumulative quantities of production doubles, the average time per unit falls to only 80% of the previous time.

4 marks

# 130: Budgeting

**(i) Quotation for eight machines (including the first one)**

|  | $ |
|---|---|
| Cost of raw materials ($2,550 x 8 machines) | 20,400 |
| Labour cost (614.4 hrs x 10) (note 2) | 6,144 |
| Fixed overheads (50% of labour cost) | 3,072 |
| **Total cost** | **29,616** |
| Profit (25% of cost) | 7,404 |
| **Selling price** | **37,020** |

**Note 2:** From the above table of cumulative average time, we can see that the total time taken for the first 8 machines (including the first one) is 614.4 hours.

$$\text{Price per machine} = \frac{\text{Total price}}{\text{Number of units}}$$

$$= \frac{\$37,020}{8}$$

$$= \$4,627.50$$

2 marks

**(ii) Quotation for second machine**

|  | $ |
|---|---|
| Raw materials | 2,550 |
| Labour cost (90 hrs x $10) | 900 |
| Fixed overheads (50% of labour cost) | 450 |
| **Total cost** | **3,900** |
| Profit (25% of cost) | 975 |
| **Selling Price** | **4,875** |

**Note 3:** According to the cumulative average time calculated in table c, incremental time for additional machines produced is 90 hours

2 marks

**(iii) Quotation for third and fourth machine**

|  | $ |
|---|---|
| Materials ($2,550 x 2 machines) | 5,100 |
| Labour (144 hrs x $10) | 1,440 |
| Fixed overheads (50% of labour cost) | 720 |
| **Total cost** | **7,260** |
| Profit (25% of cost) | 1,815 |
| **Selling price** | **9,075** |

**Note 4:** According to the cumulative average time calculated in table c, Incremental time for additional machines produced is 144 hours.

2 marks
**Maximum marks 10**

### Score More

If the answer is written without explaining the learning curve principle, then you will lose marks. So make sure your answer is very clear and add the learning curve principle.

## 32. Learning curve - Richard Designs

### (a) Total cost of production for 200 identical bedroom furniture sets:

|  | $ | Marks |
|---|---|---|
| Materials cost(W1) | 92,500.00 | 2 |
| Labour cost (W2) | 22,348.60 | 7 |
| Overhead cost (W3) | 28,606.21 | 6 |
| **Total cost** | **143,454.81** | |

**Workings**

**W1 Calculation of material cost**

Material cost for 10 sets = $4,625

Average cost of one set = $4,625/10
= $462.50

*1 mark*

Cost of 200 sets = $462.50 X 200
= $92,500

*1 mark*

**W2 Calculation of labour cost**

Labour cost for producing first set = 36 hrs x $10
= $360

Labour cost per batch for first 75 batches.

$Y = ax^b$ where a=cost for the first batch, x = number of batches and b=learning factor at the 85% learning curve.
$Y = 360x \; 75^{-0.2345}$
= 360 x 0.363327
= $130.798

*2 marks*

Labour cost for first 75 batches = 130.798 x 75
= $9,809.85

*1 mark*

The average cost for the first 75 batches is $9809.85. The labour cost for the 75th batch will be applicable to the remaining batches. Hence, we need to calculate the cost of producing 74 batches and deduct that from the cost of producing 75 batches. The figure thus obtained will be the cost of the 75th batch.

$Y = ax^b$
$Y = 360 \; x \; 74^{-0.2345}$
= 360 x 0.364473
= $131.210

*2 marks*

Labour cost for first 74 batches = $131.210 x 74
= $9,709.55

Cost of the 75th batch = $9,809.85 – $9,709.55
= $100.30

*1 mark*

Total cost for 200 batches:

First 75 batches = $9,809.85
Next 125 batches = $12,537.50
(125 x 100.30)
**Total cost** = **$22,347.35**

*1 mark*

## W3 Calculation of overhead costs

The company uses a high low method for calculation of overhead costs:

$$\text{Variable cost per unit} = \frac{\text{Difference in overhead costs at high and low level production}}{\text{Difference in labour hours}}$$

$$= \frac{\$46,720 - \$45,440}{3,840 - 3,680}$$

$$= \$1,280/160$$

$$= \$8 \text{ per unit}$$

*1 mark*

For calculation of fixed overheads at the production level of Month 2.

Variable cost during Month 2 = 3,680 hrs x $8
= $29,440

*1 mark*

Fixed cost = Total cost for Month 2 – Total variable cost for that month
= $45,440 – $29,440
= $16,000

*1 mark*

Variable cost per year = 40,000 x 8 = $320,000
Fixed cost per year = 16,000 x 12 = $192,000
Total cost for the year = $512,000

*1 mark*

Overhead absorption cost per labour hour = $512,000/40,000
= $12.8

*1 mark*

Total labour hours = Total labour cost/Labour cost per hour
= $22,347.35/$10
= 2,234.74

*1 mark*

Hence, overhead cost for the project = Total labour hours x Overhead cost per hour
= 2,234.74 x $12.8
= $28,604.67

*1 mark*
**Maximum marks 13**

**(b)** Average labour time to produce two bedroom sets = (36hrs x 95%) x 2
= 68.4 hrs.

*1 mark*

The labour time for producing second bedroom set = Average time taken for producing two sets – Time taken for producing first set
= 68.4 – 36
= 32.4 hrs

*2 marks*
**Maximum marks 2**

**(c)** Incremental budgeting is one of the most common methods of budgeting. Under this system, the budget of the previous year is taken as a base. This base is then adjusted for changes expected in the activity levels and other factors during the budget period for which the budget is prepared.

*2 marks*

One of the reasons why incremental budgeting is widely accepted by organisations is that it is a simple, cost and time-saving method of budgeting.

*1 mark*

Additionally, an organisation's personnel usually prefer this system over other methods of budgeting. This is because they have a ready base on which to prepare a budget, rather than preparing the budget from scratch.

*1 mark*

However, incremental budgeting has its own limitations. The main disadvantage of this method is that the majority of the previous year's expenditures remain unchanged in the new budget. As a result, the inefficiencies and wastages of the base period are carried forward. Also, there are more chances of budget slack, as the cost elements are not evaluated for value addition.

*2 marks*
**Maximum marks 5**

Solution Bank: 133

### 33. Learning curve and net cash flow – BFG Ltd

**Strategy**

This question relates to Study Guide C4. This topic has been consecutively examined for three years, December 2008, June 2009 and December 2009.

In part (a), you need to show whether the product S-pro will provide the target net cash flow. Your answer should contain all the necessary workings as the examiner has asked for 'detailed calculations'. In part (b), you need to compare length of time required by using 80% and 90% learning curve. Part (c) asks you to suggest specific actions for BFG to improve net cash flow.

---

**(a) The projected cash flow from product S-pro**

|  | Units | Marks |
|---|---|---|
| Sales | 120,000 |  |
|  | $ |  |
| Sales revenue (W1) | 1,260,000 | 1 |
| **Costs** |  |  |
| Direct materials (W2) | 514,000 | 0.5 |
| Direct labour (W3) | 315,423 | 0.5 |
| Variable overheads (W4) | 126,169 | 0.5 |
| Rent ($15,000 x 12 months) | 180,000 | 1 |
| Total cost | (1,135,592) |  |
| **Net cash flow** | **124,408** | 1 |

BFG Ltd is expecting a cash flow of $130,000 from the product. However, the above table indicates a net cash flow of $124,408, which is lower than the target level. This proves that the product will not generate the target cash flow.

1 mark

**Workings**

**W1 Sales revenue**

Selling price is $1,050 per batch of 100 units.

Therefore, total number batches = 120,000 units/100 units = 1,200

Sales revenue = 1200 units x $1,050
= $1,260,000

1 mark

**W2 Direct materials**

Cost for the first 200 batches = $500 per batch

|  |  | $ | Marks |
|---|---|---|---|
| Cost for 1st 200 batches | (200 x $500) | 100,000 | 1 |
| Cost of 2nd 200 batches | (200 x (90% x $500)) | 90,000 | 1 |
| Cost of remaining 800 batches | (800 x (90% x $450)) | 324,000 | 1 |
| **Total cost** |  | **514,000** |  |

*The remaining batches will cost 90% of the per batch cost of the 2nd 200 batches. Therefore, it is calculated as 90% of $500 i.e. $450*

**W3**

Direct labour cost for the first 700 batches can be determined with the help of the learning curve equation.
$Y = a x^b$
Where,

Y = cumulative average time
a = labour cost of the first batch
x = number of batches
b = learning curve factor

Y = $2,500 x 700$^{-0.3219}$
  = $2,500 x 0.12138441815
  = $303.461045375

2 marks

Total cost for first 700 batches = $303.461045375 x 700 batches
                                 = $212,423

0.5 marks

All remaining batches will have a labour cost equal to the cost of the 700th batch. In order to find out the cost of the 700th batch, calculate the cost of the first 699 batches and deduct it from the cost of the 700 batches.

Y = a x$^b$

Y = $2,500 x 699$^{-0.3219}$
  = $2,500 x 0.12144029041
  = $303.600726025

2 marks

Total labour cost for the first 699 batches = $303.600726025 x 699 batches
                                            = $212,217

0.5 marks

Cost of the 700th batch = Cost of the first 700 batches – cost of the first 699 batches
                        = $212,423 – $212,217
                        = $206

1 mark

Total cost for the 12 months of production i.e. 1,200 batches:

|  | $ |
|---|---|
| First 700 batches | 212,423 |
| Remaining 500 batches (500 x $206) | 103,000 |
| **Total cost** | **315,423** |

1 mark

**W4**
Variable overhead is estimated at $2 per hour of direct labour. Therefore,

Variable overhead = $315,423 x 40%
                  = $126,169

> Variable overhead is $2 per hour whereas labour is paid at $5 per hour. This means that variable overhead rate per hour is 40% ($2/$5 x 100) of the labour hour rate.

0.5 marks
**Maximum marks 12**

(b) The learning curve phenomenon is an important tool for forecasting costs. It can also be used in budgeting. It illustrates the effect of learning / experience on labour time and cost, over a period. To calculate its effect on labour time, the company will need to measure the time taken by the first batch (500 hours) and the time taken by the second batch. It is easy to measure the learning rate when the production doubles between the first and the second batch.

**At 80%**

|  | Hours |
|---|---|
| Labour time for first batch | 500 |
| Average time for two batches @ 80%= (500 x 0.8) | 400 |
| Total time for two batches (400 x 2) | 800 |
| Time taken for second batch (800 - 500) | 300 |

1.5 marks

**At 90%**

|  | Hours |
|---|---|
| Labour time for first batch | 500 |
| Average time for two batches @ 90% (500 x 0.9) | 450 |
| Total time for two batches (450 x 2) | 900 |
| Time taken for second batch (900 - 500) | 400 |

1.5 marks

The above figures indicate that 80% learning rate lowers the time taken by two successive batches by a larger amount. Hence, the learning rate of 80% is a faster rate as compared to the learning rate of 90%.

1 mark
**Maximum marks 3**

© GTG  Solution Bank: 135

**(c) BFG can take a few measures to improve the net cash flow of the product to make it more feasible.**

➢ BFG could take steps to increase the price charged for the product. It is given in the question that market for the product has been identified at an agreed design specification. Therefore, a higher price could be accepted by the market in future. This may result in considerable increase in the cash flow.

1 mark

➢ The company can look for alternative suppliers who can supply raw-materials (substitute material) at lower costs. This would help them to reduce costs, and thus increase cash flow. However, care should be taken not to damage the product's specification.

1 mark

➢ The company can take steps to reduce the labour costs. This can be done by re-engineering the work process, or by simplifying the product design without changing its features to a great extent.

1 mark

➢ Reduction in the variable overheads such as electricity can also help to improve the cash flow.

1 mark

➢ The company can consider training its employees and also improving the quality of people when recruiting in order to improve the learning rate. This can prove to be time consuming and expensive in the short run but will pay off in the long run.

1 mark

➢ BFG could try to negotiate a reduction in the rent. It could also look for alternatives to avoid additional rent.

1 mark
**Maximum marks 5**

## 34. Learning curve – Henry Co

**Strategy**

This question concerns a bid for a new contract by a kitchen fitter. Part (a) asks for factors that the fitter would need to take account of when calculating his bid. Your answer should contain sensible ideas about figures that might have to be included in the bid (without calculations).

Part (b) involves the bid calculation itself (including learning curve calculations). You need to calculate labour costs, variable overheads and fixed overheads.

Part (c) is very simple. It asks you to prove the learning rate, given the data for the time, for the second kitchen to be fitted.

---

**(a) HC should consider the following factors for calculating the bid:**

➢ **Contingency allowance**

As HC is making an estimate of the bid for a new apartment contract, there is a possibility that a significant change may take place. Hence, the company should consider the accuracy of the estimate and the degree of uncertainty which it is subject to. In order to avoid the conflicts that may occur due to these uncertainties, a contingency can be added to the bid.

➢ **Competition**

HC must understand that the builder may have invited a quotation for the same contract from other suppliers also. Therefore, HC should gather information about the competitors who are likely to bid. The company may face tough competition as it has not worked for this builder before.

➢ **Materials and loose tools**

Various fixing material (e.g. screws, nuts and bolts) and the use of tools for fitting the kitchen will possibly be supplied with the kitchen. Therefore, HC should make an allowance for this while calculating the bid.

➢ **Labour supervision**

It is given in the question that the first kitchen will take 24 labour hours to fit. This indicates that allowance for the supervision of labour is considered. Therefore, HC should take such allowance into account. However, if such allowance is included in the overheads, the overheads need to reflect this.

## 136: Budgeting

> **Idle time**

Labour may remain idle or its efficiency may be influenced adversely due to events such as lack of material etc. The effect of such idle time on the labour cost should be considered.

> **Risk of non-payment**

It is mentioned that HC has not worked for the builder before. Therefore, the company should take the risk of non-payment into account. In order to avoid this, HC can insist on part of the payment in advance from the builder.

*2 marks for each point discussed*
**Maximum marks 6**

**Note**

In this answer, we have discussed extra points for students' better understanding. Students can discuss any three of the above points. They can also discuss some additional points such as opportunity cost, likelihood of repeat business etc.

**(b) Bid calculation for HC to use as a basis for the new apartment contract:**

|  | $ |
|---|---|
| Labour cost (W1) | 138,705 |
| Variable overheads (W2) | 73,976 |
| Fixed overheads (W2) | 36,988 |
| **Total cost** | **249,669** |

*2 marks*

**Workings**

**W1 Calculation of labour cost**

The first kitchen will take 24 labour hours to fit.

Labour hours for fitting the first 200 kitchens

$Y = ax^b$
Where,
a = labour hours for the first kitchen,
x = number of kitchens and
b = learning factor at 95% learning curve.

$Y = 24 \times 200^{-0.074}$
   = 24 × 0.675653
   = 16.2156746455 hours

*(Use a scientific calculator to calculate this figure. Don't round off the value of Y.)*

*2 marks*

Total labour hours for the first 200 kitchens = 16.2156746455 hours × 200
= 3,243.13 hours

*1 mark*

The total time taken for the first 200 kitchens is 3,243.13 hours. The labour hours needed for the 200th kitchen will be applicable to the remaining kitchens. Hence, total time for fitting 199 kitchens should be calculated and the total time taken for 200 kitchens should be deducted from it. The figure thus obtained will be the time for fitting the 200th kitchen.

Labour hours for fitting 199 kitchens

$Y = ax^b$
$Y = 24 \times 199^{-0.074}$
   = 24 × 0.6759038
   = 16.2216906091 hours

*2 marks*

Labour hours for 199 kitchens = 16.2216906091 hours x 199
= 3,228.12 hours

1 mark

Hours for fitting the 200th kitchen = 3,243.13 hours - 3,228.12 hours
= 15.01 hours

1 mark

Total time for 600 kitchens:

| | |
|---|---|
| First 200 kitchens | = 3,243.13 hours |
| Next 400 kitchens | = 6,004 hours |
| (400 x 15.01 hours) | |
| **Total hours** | = 9,247.13 hours or 9,247 hours |

1 mark

Total labour cost = 9,247 hours x $15 per hour = $138,705

0.5 marks

**W2 Calculation of overhead costs**

The company uses a high low method for calculation of overhead costs:

$$\text{Variable cost per unit} = \frac{\text{Difference in overhead costs at high and low level production}}{\text{Difference in labour hours}}$$

$$= \frac{\$116,800 - \$113,600}{9,600 \text{ hrs} - 9,200 \text{ hrs}}$$

= $3,200/400 hours
= $8 per hour

1 mark

For calculation of fixed overheads at the low production level (month 2)

Variable cost during month 2 = 9,200 hours x $8
= $73,600

1 mark

Fixed cost = Total cost for month 2 – Total variable cost for that month
= $113,600 – $73,600
= $40,000 per month

Fixed cost per year = $40,000 x 12 = $480,000

*Remember to use the labour hour basis for calculation of the overhead absorption rate*

1 mark

0.5 marks

Overhead absorption rate per labour hour = $480,000/120,000
= $4 per hour

1 mark

Hence, total variable and fixed overheads for a new apartment contract will be
Total variable overheads = 9, 247 hours x $8 per hour = $73,976
Total fixed overheads = 9, 247 hours x $4 per hour = $36,988

1 mark
**Maximum marks 12**

**(c)** Average labour time to fit two kitchens = (24 hours x 95%) x 2
= 45.6 hours.

1 mark

The labour time for fitting the second kitchen = Average time taken for fitting two kitchens – Time taken for fitting the first kitchen
= 45.6 hours – 24 hours
= 21.6 hours

2 marks
**Maximum marks 2**

## 35. Budgeting and forecasting – Track Co

**Strategy**

This question mainly involves numerical calculations for forecasting, with a theoretical part (c) about incremental budgeting.

Part (a) tests your knowledge of time series analysis and part (b) tests your knowledge of regression analysis.

Part (c) requires a description of two advantages and two disadvantages of incremental budgeting.

---

**(a)** In 20Y0, the four quarters will be numbers 5–8, consequently the trend figures for raw cotton to be supplied will be:

Quarter 1 (Q = 5): 46.25 + 0.25(5) = 47.50 tonnes

Quarter 2 (Q = 6): 46.25 + 0.25 (6) = 47.75 tonnes

Quarter 3 (Q = 7): 46.25 + 0.25 (7) = 48.00 tonnes

Quarter 4 (Q = 8): 46.25 + 0.25 (8) = 48.25 tonnes

*1 mark*

Seasonal adjustments are needed thus:

| | |
|---|---|
| Quarter 1: 47.50 – 2.00 | 45.50 |
| Quarter 2: 47.75 + 2.50 | 50.25 |
| Quarter 3: 48.00 + 1.50 | 49.50 |
| Quarter 4: 48.25 – 1.00 | 47.25 |
| **Total tonnage** | **151.50** |

*2 marks for seasonal adjustments*
*1 mark for total tonnage*
**Maximum marks 4**

**(b)** The variable operating and fixed operating costs in 20X9 are calculated as follows:

(figures in $'000)

| Tonnes (X) | Total Cost (Y) | XY | $X^2$ | Marks |
|---|---|---|---|---|
| 47 | 100 | 4,700 | 2209 | 1 |
| 49 | 120 | 5,880 | 2401 | 1 |
| 40 | 95 | 3,800 | 1600 | 1 |
| 32 | 97.5 | 3,120 | 1024 | 1 |
| 168 | 412.5 | 17,500 | 7,234 | 4 |

Y = a + bX

Where,

a is the fixed operating cost and

b is the variable operating cost

X is the number of units

Y is the total cost

Here, b can be calculated as follows:

$$b = \frac{n\Sigma XY - \Sigma X \Sigma Y}{n\Sigma X^2 - (\Sigma X)^2}$$

Here, n is 4 as there are 4 quarters, therefore b is:

$$b = \frac{4(17,500) - (168)(412.5)}{4(7,234) - (168)^2}$$

b = 0.9831 i.e. $983.10 per tonne.

$983.10 was the variable operating cost per tonne for 20X9.

*2 marks*

$$a = \frac{\Sigma Y - b\Sigma X}{n}$$

a= (412.5 – 0.9831 x 168)/4

a= 61.83 i.e. $618,300

This means the fixed operating cost was $618,300 in 20X9.

*2 marks*

### Calculation of variable operating costs and fixed operating costs in 20Y0

For this, we have to make an allowance for inflation in 20Y0.

Therefore,

Variable operating cost in 20Y0 will be $983.10 x 1·0325 = $1,015.05 per tonne

Fixed operating cost in 20Y0 will be $618,300 x 1·0325 = $638,394.75

*2 marks*
**Maximum marks 10**

### (c) Advantages of an incremental budgeting approach

➢ It is a simple, cost and time-saving method of budgeting and therefore widely accepted by organisations. Local government organisations are often complex and using incremental budgeting involves less effort.

➢ Because they are complex, organisations may have very long budget processes. In such cases, the incremental budgeting approach is quicker as it has a ready-made base available on which to prepare a budget, rather than preparing the budget from scratch.

### Disadvantages of incremental budgeting:

➢ If this approach is used, the organisation may be tempted to incur the maximum expenses allowed in this year's budget so that the next year's budget, which will be based on this, will incorporate even higher amounts of expenditure. This will ensure flexibility for the organisation.

➢ The excess expenditure thus incurred will be added to the next year's budget, and so on. This is equivalent to wasting the taxpayers' money.

*1 mark per each correctly mentioned advantage and disadvantage*
**Maximum marks 6**

## Score More

If you do not remember the following two points, you might not earn full marks:

> - In part (a), the use of quarter numbers in the formula should be 5, 6, 7 and 8, and not 1, 2, 3 and 4.
>
> - In part (b), regression analysis is required, not the high-low method for separating fixed and variable costs.

**SOLUTION BANK**

# SECTION D: STANDARD COSTING AND VARIANCE ANALYSIS

### 36. Analysis of variances – Smart Ltd

**Strategy**

You can easily score high marks in this question. It is an ideal question to test the students' overall knowledge on standard costing and variance analysis.

Calculate all the required variances very carefully. It is better to write formulas while calculating variances.

While analysing the performance, give reasons for variances, and calculate the total loss for which the manager is responsible. This helps you to score more marks.

This question asks students to analyse the performance of the two managers. Therefore, remember to give a heading for each.

---

### (a) Calculation of variances

#### (i) Direct material price and usage variances

Direct material price variance = Standard material price for actual quantity - Actual material cost

Material AP price variance = ($1.80 × 61,838 kg) – $108,835 = $2,473.40 (F)
Material AQ price variance = ($1.40 × 31,525) – $40,352 = $3,783 (F)

*2 marks*

Direct material usage variance = (Actual quantity consumed – Standard quantity for actual production) × Standard material price

Material AP usage variance = (61,838 kg – (24,250 units × 2.50 kg)) × $1.80 = $2,183.40 (A)
Material AQ usage variance = (31,525 kg – (24,250 units × 1.25 kg)) × $1.40 = $1,697.50 (A)

*2 marks*

#### (ii) Labour rate and efficiency variances

Labour rate variance = (Standard wages rate per hour – Actual wages rate per hour) × Actual labour hours
= ($1.50 × 50,500 hrs) – $80,800 = $5,050 (A)

*1.5 marks*

Labour efficiency variance = (Standard hours for actual production - Actual hours worked) × Standard rate
= [(2.20 hrs × 24,250 units) – 50,500 hrs] × $1.50 = $2,850 (F)

*1.5 marks*

#### (iii) Fixed overhead expenditure variance = Budgeted fixed overheads – Actual expenditure on fixed overheads
= $31,250 – $32,500 = $1,250 (A)

*1 mark*

#### (iv) Sales variances

Sales volume variance = (Actual sales quantity – Budgeted sales quantity) × Standard contribution per unit
= (24,250 units – 25,000 units) × $7.00 (W1) = $5,250 (A)

> Remember to calculate the standard contribution per unit.

*1.5 marks*

## 142: Standard Costing and Variance Analysis © GTG

Sales price variance = (Actual selling price per unit – Standard selling price per unit) x Actual quantity
= ($16.28 - $16.55) x 24,250 units = $6,547.50 (A)

> It is calculated by dividing actual sales value by actual sales quantity.

1.5 marks

**Working**

**W1 Calculation of standard contribution per unit**

|  | $ Per unit | $ Per unit |
|---|---|---|
| Selling price |  | 16.55 |
| Less: |  |  |
| Direct material |  |  |
| AP 2.5kg at $1.80 per kg | 4.50 |  |
| AQ 1.25 kg at $1.40 per kg | 1.75 |  |
| Direct labour (2.20 hrs at $1.50 per hour) | 3.30 | (9.55) |
| **Contribution** |  | **7.00** |

2 marks
**Maximum marks 12**

**(b)** Variances are analysed to find out the causes or circumstances leading to them, so that management can exercise proper control. Robin, the management accountant has some doubts about the decision taken by his colleagues, the purchasing manager and the production manager relating to the material price and labour rate. Therefore, the performance of these managers is analysed in the following manner:

**Purchasing manager**

It is clearly stated that the purchasing manager has bought inferior quality materials at low costs from new suppliers. Therefore, this results in a saving of $6,256.40 ($2,473.40 + $3,783) due to lower prices. However, the material usage variance is adverse. This shows that more material has been wasted, as compared to the standard, which resulted in a loss of $3,880.90 ($2,183.40 + $1,697.50). The additional waste was obviously due to the low quality of material. Even though the purchasing manager purchased the material at a low price in order to save the company money, it has had a direct adverse impact on the usage of material.

1.5 marks

The decision of purchasing material at a low cost, to save money was wise. However the material should not have been of such a low quality. Due to the inferior material the actual sales fell by 750 units (25,000 – 24,250 units). This could have led to the adverse sales volume variance of $5,250 in the three month period. The sales price may also have dropped to $16.28 per unit due to the poor quality of the product. Therefore, adverse sales price variance occurred showing a loss of revenue of $6,547.50 in the three month period.

It is concluded that the purchasing manger is responsible for a loss of $9,422 ($3,880.90 + $5,250 + $6,547.50 - $6256.40) in consideration of these four variances.

1.5 marks

**Production manager**

The production manager increased the wage rate which resulted in an adverse labour rate variance of $5,050. However, he increased the wages in anticipation of higher labour efficiency. A favourable labour efficiency variance of $2,850 shows that the increase in wages motivated employees to work harder than before. In short, the wage increase improved the morale and productivity of the employees. This variance could have conceivably been higher but for the fact that the employees may have had to put in additional time due to the lower quality material. Therefore, the production manager is mainly accountable for a loss of $2,200 ($5,050 - $2,850) taking into account these two variances.

2 marks
**Maximum marks 4**

**(c)** A standard cost system provides guidance and criteria for operations and performance evaluations. Variance analysis is strictly a tool for controlling and improving operations; it should never be used to find a scapegoat. Research in organisational behaviour has shown that successful operations are often the result of proper rewards. The focus in using a standard cost system should be on influencing behaviour through positive supports and appropriate motivation.

The perception of a standard costing system affects its success or failure. A negative perception or motivation is often the consequence of unreasonable standards, lack of transparency in setting standards, strict control procedures, poor communication, too much pressure, inflexibility, uneven reward systems or excessive importance to earning profits. These situations can make a good standard cost system a failure.

*2 marks*

**The following points can be adopted to prevent this:**

- The standards should be well defined and communicated to all employees so that operational efficiency can be achieved. This helps to attain standards and control costs. Management must make sure that the new scheme does not reward incorrect behaviour.

- The employees can be involved in setting standards and in developing performance measures. The management should always welcome their advice and new thoughts to change work systems. This may result in high levels of employee motivation and an improvement in their efficiency.

- An organisation should set understandable and achievable standards. Otherwise it neither motivates nor rewards employees. Complex financial measures and jargon-heavy reports mean nothing to most employees.

- Performance pay plans must be constantly adjusted to meet the changing needs of employees, customers and the business as a whole. The life expectancy of a plan may be no more than three or four years.

*1 mark for each point discussed*
**Maximum marks 4**

### 37. Variances and budgeting – Morse Plc

**Strategy**

This question covers two important areas of the standard costing system – (i) Flexible budgeting approach and (ii) calculation of variances. Part (a) and (b) of this question is very simple and you can earn high marks. In part (c), the calculation of fixed overhead variances is the only tricky area.

In part (b), remember to split semi-variable costs into fixed and variable overheads. Provide proper workings for this calculation.

For the preparation of the flexed budget, you need to calculate all costs and sales for an activity level of 85,000 units on a proportionate basis.

In part (c), calculate all variances very carefully. Place an emphasis on the calculation of fixed overhead variances.

**(a) Importance of flexing budget in performance management**

A flexed budget is a form of a master budget, which shows the effect of changes in volume on cost structures. Hence, a flexible budget can be used at any output level. A flexed budget therefore helps to estimate how revenue and costs should behave over a range of production volume.

A flexible budget need not necessarily be relevant only for a specific period of time. They can be used either before or after a specific period. This can help managers to make decisions with regards to the volume of production for planning purposes. It can also assist managers in analysing the actual results at the end of the period.

A flexed budget helps to make important comparisons between actual costs incurred and a realistic budget allowance for costs. In a flexible budget, each item of costs is evaluated into fixed and variable elements. When the actual activity level is known, the budget can be flexed to produce a standard cost allowance against which actual costs can be legitimately compared. Unless the actual level of activity is equal to the budgeted level, a fixed budget cannot be used effectively for control purposes. Hence, flexible budgets are helpful for control.

*1.5 marks for each point discussed*
**Maximum marks 4**

## 144: Standard Costing and Variance Analysis

**(b)** The flexed budget will be based on the actual activity level of 85,000 units.

| | $ | $ | Marks |
|---|---|---|---|
| Sales ($1,625,000 x 85/65) | | 2,125,000 | 0.5 |
| **Less:** Cost of sales | | | |
| Direct materials ($318,500 x 85/65) | 416,500 | | 0.5 |
| Direct labour ($364,000 x 85/65) | 476,000 | | 0.5 |
| Variable production overheads ($3.71 x 85,000 units) | 315,350 | | 1 |
| Fixed production overheads (W1) | 300,300 | | 0.5 |
| | | (1,508,150) | |
| **Budgeted profit** | | **616,850** | 1 |

> The company is operating at 85% capacity. Therefore, actual total sales volume is calculated proportionately (65,000 units x 85/65)

**Working**

**W1 Calculation of fixed overheads**

| | $ |
|---|---|
| Semi-variable overheads | 313,950 |
| Less: variable overhead ($3.71 x 65,000) | (241,150) |
| Fixed overhead | 72,800 |
| Add: Fixed production overhead | 227,500 |
| **Total fixed overheads** | **300,300** |

> Don't calculate fixed production overheads proportionately as they remain constant for each level of activity.

*2 marks*
**Maximum marks 5**

**(c) Calculation of variances**

(i) Direct material cost total variance = Standard material cost for actual production − Actual material cost
= $416,500 − $431,800 = $15,300 (A)

*1.5 marks*

(ii) Direct labour cost variance = Standard direct wages for production − Actual direct wages paid
= $476,000 − $467,500 = $8,500 (F)

*1.5 marks*

(iii) Variable overhead total variance = Variable overhead absorbed − Actual variable overhead
= ($3.71 x 85,000 units) − $318,750 = $3,400 (A)

*1.5 marks*

(iv) Fixed overhead efficiency variance = (Standard hours for actual production − Actual hours worked) x Fixed overhead absorption rate
= (25,500 hrs (W2) − 25,700 hrs) x $15.40 (W1) = $3,080 (A)

*1.5 marks*

(v) Fixed overhead capacity variance = Budgeted fixed overheads − (Actual hours x Fixed overhead absorption rate)
= $300,300 − (25,700 hrs x $15.40 (W1)) = $95,480 (F)

*1.5 marks*

(vi) Fixed overhead expenditure variance = Budgeted fixed overhead − Actual expenditure on fixed overhead
= $300,300 − $381,130 = $80,830 (A)

*1.5 marks*

**Workings**

**W1**

Fixed overhead absorption rate = $300,300/19,500 hrs = $15.40 per machine hour

*1 mark*

## Tip

As normally budgeted fixed overheads remain constant for each level of activity, we need to consider budgeted 19,500 machine hours for 65% capacity while calculating the fixed overhead absorption rate.

**W2**

Standard machine hours for actual production
= 19,500 hrs x 85/65 = 25,500 hrs

*Remember that standard machine hours given in the question are for 65,000 units; therefore you need to calculate machine hours for 85,000 units on a proportionate basis.*

1 mark
**Maximum marks 11**

## Score More

While answering part (b), a bad answer would calculate variable overheads for an activity level of 85,000 units as follows:

Variable overheads = $313,950 x 85/65 = $410,550.

Many students calculate the variable overhead as above, which is wrong. They ignore the break up of these overheads into variable and fixed overheads.

To earn good marks in part (c), you should calculate the fixed overhead absorption rate per machine hour very carefully, as well as the actual and budgeted hours for production. Give a formula for each variance to make calculation easier.

A common mistake while calculating variable overhead total variance, is considering semi-variable overheads as "variable overheads absorbed".

---

### 38. Operational changes – Woodezer Ltd

## Strategy

This question is very easy to answer. However, proper time management is required for part (a). As part (b) of this question requires you to analyse the impact of operational changes on the company's profitability, thinking clearly will help you to answer this and earn more marks.

**Key points**

➢ First calculate variances in detail using the information given. Provide a formula for each variance calculation to get good marks. This also makes variance calculation easier.

➢ Don't forget to adjust sales margin variance (sales volume variance and sales price variance) to the budgeted profit in the operating statement.

➢ Understand carefully what variances calculated in part (a) tell you about the operational changes made by Mr Beech and write its impact.

---

**(a) Operating statement**

|  | $ | $ | $ | Marks |
|---|---|---|---|---|
| Budgeted profit |  |  | 112,000 | 1 |
| Sales volume profit variance (W1) |  |  | (22,400) |  |
| Standard profit on actual sales |  |  | 89,600 |  |
| Sales price variance (W2) |  |  | 16,000 |  |
|  |  |  | 105,600 | 0.5 |

*It is calculated as 4,000 units x $28 per unit*

## 146: Standard Costing and Variance Analysis

| Cost Variances | Favourable | Adverse | | |
|---|---|---|---|---|
| Material price (W3) | | 24,000 | | |
| Material usage (W4) | 32,000 | | | |
| Labour rate (W5) | 16,000 | | | |
| Labour efficiency (W6) | | 12,800 | | |
| Variable overhead efficiency (W7) | | 6,400 | | 2 |
| Variable overhead expenditure (W8) | 4,000 | | | |
| Fixed overhead expenditure (W9) | 60,000 | | | |
| Fixed overhead efficiency (W10) | | 25,600 | | |
| Fixed overhead capacity (W11) | 0 | | | |
| Total cost variances | 112,000 | 68,800 | 43,200 | |
| **Actual Profit** | | | **148,800** | 0.5 |

**Note**

This does not form a part of the answer. Had the closing inventory been valued at the actual cost of $180 per unit, the actual profit would have been $144,000 ($148,000- $4,800). However, as the closing inventory was valued at the standard cost i.e. $192 per unit; the actual profit is overstated by $4,800.

**Workings**

**W1**

Sales volume profit variance = (Actual sales quantity – Budgeted sales quantity) x Standard profit per unit
= (3,200 units – 4,000 units) x $28
= $22,400 (A)

1 mark

**W2**

*It is calculated by dividing actual sales by actual sales quantity i.e. $720,000/3,200 units = $225*

Sales price variance = (Actual selling price per unit – Standard selling price per unit) x Actual quantity
= ($225 - $220) x 3,200 units
= $16,000 (F)

1 mark

**W3**

Material Price Variance = (Standard Price - Actual Price) x Actual Quantity
= ($3.2 - $3.5) x 80,000 kg
= $24,000 (A)

1 mark

**W4**

Material Usage Variance = (Standard quantity for actual production - Actual quantity) x Standard price
= [(3,600 x 25 kg) - 80,000 kg] x $3.2
= $32,000 (F)

1 mark

**W5**

Labour rate variance = (Standard wages rate per hour - Actual wages rate per hour) x Actual labour hours
= ($8 - $7) x 16,000 hours
= $16,000 (F)

1 mark

**W6**

Labour efficiency variance = (Standard labour hours for actual production - Actual labour hours worked) x Standard wages rate per hour
= [(4 hrs x 3,600 units) - 16,000 hrs] x $8
= $12,800 (A)

1 mark

**W7**

Variable overhead efficiency variance = (Standard hours for actual production - Actual hours) x Standard variable overhead rate per hour
= [(4 hrs x 3,600 units - 16,000 hrs) x $4]
= $6,400 (A)

1 mark

## W8

Variable overhead expenditure variance = (Standard variable overhead rate − Actual variable overhead rate) x Actual hours worked
= [($4 x 16,000 hrs) - $60,000]
= $4,000 (F)

1 mark

## W9

Fixed overhead expenditure variance = Budgeted fixed overhead - Actual expenditure on fixed overhead
= [(4,000 units x $64) − $196,000]
= ($256,000 - $196,000)
= $60,000 (F)

1 mark

## W10

Fixed overhead efficiency variance = (Standard hours for actual production - Actual hours worked) x Fixed overhead absorption rate
= [(4 hrs x 3,600 units) - 16,000 hrs)] x $16
= $25,600 (A)

1 mark

## W11

Fixed overhead capacity variance = (Budgeted hours − Actual hours) x Fixed overhead absorption rate
= [(4 hrs x 4,000 units) - 16,000 hrs] x $16
= 0

1 mark
**Maximum marks 14**

### (b)
### (i) Motivation and budget setting

The budget set for monthly production for years prior to November 20X8 was 3,400 units. Mr Beech is of the opinion that the target should be high enough to motivate the employees to put in their best possible efforts in terms of higher expected output. Therefore, he has used the budget as a motivational tool and set the budgeted output at the level of 4,000 units per month.

1 mark

This has resulted in the increase of absorption costing profit by $53,600 ($95,200 ($28 × 3,400) - $148,800).

It would appear from the given information that the budget had been set in the past at the level of output achieved in the years prior to November 20X8.

1 mark

Mr Beech appears to have considered that budget targets should be challenging, yet attainable. Therefore, maximising output helps to motivate employees to put in their best efforts. However, beyond a certain level, motivation may fall sharply as the target becomes unachievable. Therefore, the aim to achieve targets as well as motivate employees should be balanced.

1 mark
**Maximum marks 2**

### (ii) Explanations of Variances

An increase in sales price by $5 ($220 - $225) per unit may have decreased the sales quantity to 3,200 units compared to the standard set. This has resulted in the favourable sales price variance and adverse sales volume variance. Therefore, we may possibly conclude that these two variances are inter-related.

1 mark

As Mr Beech has changed suppliers of material, the actual material price per unit is more than the standard by $0.30 ($3.20 - $3.50). Therefore, it has had an adverse effect on the material price variance. It also appears that Mr Beech has purchased better quality materials. The use of better quality material may have resulted in less waste. Hence, it may have contributed to the favourable material usage variance.

1 mark

## 148: Standard Costing and Variance Analysis

Actual payment made to labour is less by $1 ($8 - $7) than the standard labour rate per hour. This has accounted for the favourable labour rate variance. The reduction in the wage rate may have de-motivated the workers which resulted in lower efficiency.

It is also stated that Mr Beech has introduced less skilled labour. As less skilled workers are employed, efficiency is also reduced and they have taken a longer time to achieve a given target. This has affected the volume of production of benches.

*1.5 marks*

Favourable variable overhead expenditure variance has occurred because the actual overhead rate $3.75 per hour ($60,000/16,000 hrs) is less than the standard rate $4 per hour. Normally, variable overheads and fixed overheads are absorbed on the basis of labour hours worked. As labour efficiency is reduced, adverse variable and fixed overhead efficiency variance have occurred.

However, the fixed overhead expenditure variance is favourable. This may be because of a reduction in significant fixed overheads which may have a long-term impact on the business.

*1.5 marks*
**Maximum marks 4**

### 39. Revised budget and variances – Jackson Plc

**Strategy**

This question tests students' awareness of two important areas of performance management:

(i) revision of the budget plan, and
(ii) calculation of variances

Part (a) of this question requires clear thinking to analyse the performance of the accounting manager.
Part (b) and (c), involve understanding the practical problem.

**Key points**

➢ Explain clearly whether the situation which caused the budget revision is out of the company's control or not.
➢ Consider all expected changes in the price and cost, while preparing the revised budgeted statement.
➢ In the calculation of variances, take into account the revised budgeted price and compare it with the actual price.

---

**(a)** Successful budgets should have adequate flexibility to meet changing business conditions. Since budgets are used for planning, operation, co-ordination and control, they should be revised if changes occur in the business environment.

One of the objectives of a budget is to provide a yardstick for performance evaluation. If budgets are not revised in line with the changing environment / conditions, comparing actual results with the budgeted ones will not give appropriate results. Therefore it is necessary to revise budgets and analyse the causes of variance with the adjusted standards (i.e. revised budgets).

*1 mark*

**A budget can be revised under the following circumstances**

1. Emergence of unforeseen and unanticipated situations.

*1 mark*

2. Changes in internal factors, such as production forecast, sales forecast, capacity utilisation, etc.

*1 mark*

3. Changes in external factors, such as market trends, nature of the economy, prices of inputs and resources, consumer tastes and fashions and input cost structure.

*1 mark*

4. Errors made while preparing the budget. They may be discovered, causing the budgeted figures to be rectified.

*1 mark*

The material price and the labour rate are increasing due to inflation. The increase in the market price of raw materials and labour charges are outside the control of Jackson Plc. As these are uncontrollable factors the organisation needs to revise its original budget.

If Jackson Plc does not revise the budget, it will not be realistic, and thus can have a direct impact on the profitability of the company. This means, if a change in one of the above factors is found to have a substantial impact on the future outcome of the organisation, the budget is allowed to be revised. Consequently the selling price of the product will have to be adjusted. Therefore, Brown was correct to suggest a revision in the budget plan.

1 mark
**Maximum marks 5**

### (b) Revised budget for 20X8 based on inflation

|  |  | $ | Marks |
|---|---|---|---|
| Budgeted output and Sales (a) | 5,000 units @ $468 per unit (W1) | 2,340,000 | 0.5 |
| Material | 5,000 units @$225 per unit (W2) | 1,125,000 | 0.5 |
| Labour charges | 5,000 units @ $56.25 per bag (W3) | 281,250 | 0.5 |
| Variable overheads | 5,000 units @ $28.125 per hour (W4) | 140,625 | 0.5 |
| **Fixed overheads** |  |  |  |
| Administrative expenses |  | 165,000 | 0.5 |
| Selling expenses |  | 91,000 | 0.5 |
| Distribution expenses |  | 64,000 | 0.5 |
| **Total budgeted cost (b)** |  | 1,866,875 |  |
| **Total budgeted profits (a - b)** |  | 473,125 | 0.5 |

*As additional selling expenses of $40,000 are expected to be incurred, it is added here. $51,000 + $40,000 = $91,000*

**Workings**

Revised costs and selling prices per unit are calculated as follows:

**W1 Selling price** = $390 + (20% of $390)
= $468

0.5 marks

**W2 Material price** = $13.64 + (10% of $13.64)
= $15 per metre

Material price per bag = $15 per metre x 15 metres = $225

1 mark

**W3 Labour rate** = $6 per hour + $3 per hour
= $9 per hour

*Remember to calculate the 15% increase in the variable overheads on the revised labour rate per hour.*

Labour rate per bag = $9 per hour x 6.25 hours = $56.25 per bag

1 mark

**W4 Variable overheads** = $3.15 per hour + (15% of $9 per hour)
= $4.50 per hour

Variable overheads per bag = $4.5 per hour x 6.25 hours = $28.125 per bag

1 mark
**Maximum marks 5**

### (c) Calculation of variances

1. Direct material price variance = (standard material price per metre − actual material price per metre) x total material used for actual production units
   = ($15 per metre - $16.75 per metre) x 63,000 metres (W1)
   = $110,250 (A)

1 mark

2. Direct material usage variance = (standard material usage – actual material usage) x standard material price per metre
= (67,500 metres (W1) - 63,000 metres) x $15 per metre
= $67,500 (F)

1 mark

3. Direct material cost variance = Direct material price variance + Direct material usage variance
= $110,250 (A) + $67,500 (F)
= $42,750 (A)

1 mark

4. Direct labour rate variance = (standard labour rate per hour – actual labour rate per hour) x actual labour hours
= ($9 per hour - $8.20 per hour) x 29,250 hours (W1)
= $23,400 (F)

1 mark

5. Direct labour efficiency variance = (standard labour hours for actual production – actual labour hours worked) x standard labour rate per hour
= (28,125 – 29,250) x $9 per hour
= $10,125 (A)

1 mark

6. Direct labour cost variance = Direct labour rate variance + Direct labour efficiency variance
= $23,400 (F) + $10,125 (A)
= $13,275 (F)

1 mark

7. Variable overhead expenditure variance = (standard variable overhead rate per hour – actual variable overhead rate per hour) x actual hours
= ($4.50 – $4.75) x 31,500 hours (W1)
= $7,875 (A)

1 mark

8. Variable overhead efficiency variance = (standard hours for actual production – actual hours used) x standard variable overhead rate per hour
= (28,125 hours – 31,500 hours) x $4.50 per hour
= $15,187.50 (A)

1 mark

9. Total variable overhead variance = Variable overhead expenditure variance + Variable overhead efficiency variance
= $7,875 (A) + $15,187.50 (A)
= $23,062.50 (A)

1 mark

**Working**

**W1**

|  | Standard for actual production | Actual |
| --- | --- | --- |
| Total material | 15 metres x 4,500 units = 67,500 metres | 14 metres x 4,500 units = 63,000 metres |
| Total labour hours | 6.25 hrs x 4,500 units = 28,125 hrs | 6.5 hrs x 4,500 units = 29,250 hrs |
| Total variable overheads hours | 6.25 hrs x 4,500 units = 28,125 hrs | 7 hrs x 4,500 units = 31,500 hrs |

1.5 marks
**Maximum marks 10**

© GTG                                                                                                                                          Solution Bank: 151

## 40. Sales variances – Simple Co

### Strategy

In this question, more than 60% part is based on a practical framework. The question requires an understanding of sales variances.

### Key points

- Remember to allocate the fixed overheads using the traditional method in the calculation of standard profit per unit.
- Adopt a step-by-step approach for the calculation of standard profit and actual profit at standard mix, or actual mix.
- In the reconciliation statement, add all favourable variances to, and deduct all adverse variances from, the standard profit to reach to the actual profit.
- Consider carefully what the figures of the sales volume and profit indicate about sales performance. It is also good to give suggestions for improving the sales performance.

### (a) Calculation of standard profit per unit

|  | Oil Pump $ | Gas pump $ | Diesel pump $ |
|---|---|---|---|
| Selling price (a) | 91.00 | 97.50 | 117.00 |
| Less: |  |  |  |
| Direct material | 35.10 | 26.65 | 31.52 |
| Direct labour | 21.12 | 33.80 | 29.58 |
| Fixed production overhead (W1) | 8.78 | 17.55 | 23.40 |
| Standard cost (b) | (65.00) | (78.00) | (84.50) |
| **Standard profit (a-b)** | **26.00** | **19.50** | **32.50** |

1.5 marks

Budgeted sales quantity in standard mix at standard profit

| Product | Quantity | Standard profit $ | Total profit $ |
|---|---|---|---|
| Oil Pump | 10,000 | 26.00 | 260,000 |
| Gas pump | 13,000 | 19.50 | 253,500 |
| Diesel pump | 9,000 | 32.50 | 292,500 |
|  | **32,000** |  | **806,000** |

1.5 marks

Actual sales quantity at actual profit margin (at actual selling price less standard cost)

| Product | Quantity | Actual profit $ | Total profit $ |
|---|---|---|---|
| Oil Pump | 9,500 | 29.25 | 277,875 |
| Gas pump | 13,500 | 22.75 | 307,125 |
| Diesel pump | 8,500 | 39.00 | 331,500 |
|  | **31,500** |  | **916,500** |

1.5 marks

Actual sales quantity at actual mix at standard profit

| Product | Quantity | Standard profit $ | Total profit $ |
|---|---|---|---|
| Oil Pump | 9,500 | 26.00 | 247,000 |
| Gas pump | 13,500 | 19.50 | 263,250 |
| Diesel pump | 8,500 | 32.50 | 276,250 |
|  | **31,500** |  | **786,500** |

1.5 marks

## 152: Standard Costing and Variance Analysis

Actual sales quantity at standard mix at standard profit

| Product | Quantity | Standard profit $ | Total profit $ |
|---|---|---|---|
| Oil Pump | 9,844 | 26.00 | 255,944 |
| Gas pump | 12,797 | 19.50 | 249,542 |
| Diesel pump | 8,859 | 32.50 | 287,917 |
|  | 31,500 |  | 793,403 |

Alternative approach to actual sales quantity in standard mix at standard profit
= Actual quantity x average standard profit per unit
= 31,500 units x $25.1875 per unit
= $793,403

*It is calculated by dividing the total standard profit, as calculated above, by the total budgeted sales quantity.*

1.5 marks

**Calculation of variances**

(i) Sales profit margin variance = $916,500 - $786,500 = $130,000 (F)
(ii) Sales volume profit variance = $786,500 - $806,000 = $19,500 (A)
(iii) Sales mix profit variance = $786,500 - $793,403 = $6,903 (A)
(iv) Sales quantity profit variance = $793,403 - $806,000 = $12,597 (A)

2 mark

**Working**

**W1 Calculation of overhead absorption rate**

Budgeted machine hours = (10,000 x 1.95) + (13,000 x 3.90) + (9,000 x 5.20)
= 117,000 hours

*AS company follows absorption costing method, fixed overheads are allocated on machine hours basis.*

Overhead absorption rate = $526,500/117,000 hours
= $4·50 per machine hour

1 mark
**Maximum marks 9**

**(b) Reconciliation statement**

| Reconciliation | Favourable $ | Adverse $ | $ | Marks |
|---|---|---|---|---|
| Standard profit |  |  | 806,000 | 1 |
| **Variances** |  |  |  |  |
| Sales profit margin variance | 130,000 (F) |  |  | 0.5 |
| Sales mix profit variance |  | 6,903 (A) |  | 0.5 |
| Sales quantity profit variance |  | 12,597 (A) |  | 0.5 |
|  | 130,000 (F) | 19,500 (A) | 110,500 (F) | 0.5 |
| Actual sales at actual price less standard cost |  |  | 916,500 | 1 |

(c) The sales mix profit variance is the difference between the actual sales quantity in the actual mix at standard profit and the actual sales quantity in the standard mix at standard profit. It describes the effect on the profit of variations from the standard proportion.

1 mark

The overall sales mix profit variance calculated in part (a) is adverse. This indicates that the actual sales mix contained more lower-margin products and fewer higher-margin products. The following table will illustrate this in detail:

| Product | Standard mix | Actual mix | Difference | Standard profit | Total profit $ |
|---|---|---|---|---|---|
| Oil Pump | 9,844 | 9,500 | (344) | $26.00 | 8,944.00 (A) |
| Gas pump | 12,797 | 13,500 | 703 | $19.50 | 13,708.50 (F) |
| Diesel pump | 8,859 | 8,500 | (359) | $32.50 | 11,667.50 (A) |
|  | 31,500 | 31,500 |  |  | 6,903.00 (A) |

1 mark

The above table shows that the sales volume of a gas pump is more than the budgeted sales volume. However, it was sold at the least profit of $19.50 when compared to other products. On the other hand, lower quantities of products like oil and diesel pumps were sold at the higher standard profits per unit than the budgeted sales volume.

*1 mark*

If products are interrelated or substitutes for each other, the calculation of individual sales mix profit variance for each product will be meaningful. Otherwise it wrongly conveys that the actual profit varies from the standard due to the change in sales mix. In fact, only deviations from the planned volumes for individual products need to be investigated if products are not inter-related. In this case the products are not substitutes and so are not interrelated. Therefore, the individual sales mix profit variances may not be useful.

*1 mark*

### (d) Comment on sales performance

The analysis of overall sales volume of the products is reduced by 500 units (32,000 – 31,500 units). This may be because of higher sales prices charged compared to the standard that has been set. However, the company has acquired additional profit of $110,500. On the whole, this shows that the company has performed well.

A reduction in price could have maintained the standard sales level. Additionally, the improved quality of support staff may have helped to maintain the sales level. At the same time, the actions of competitors should be taken into consideration to comment on the performance of the company. In a tough competitive market, merely maintaining budgeted sales could be appreciated as a good achievement, provided that the budgets were set appropriately.

*3 marks*

### Score More

While answering part (a), students generally make mistakes in the calculation of standard profit per unit. Many students fail to consider the fixed overheads of $526,500 which will results in less marks.

To score more, students should be very careful about the formulae while calculating sales variances.

Remember that sales volume profit variance is the sum of the sales mix and sales quantity profit variance. Therefore, you should consider either sales mix and quantity profit variance or sales volume profit variances to reach to the actual profit.

---

### 41. Analysis of variances – Tasty Treat Inc

### Strategy

This problem involves not just calculation of the variances, but also interpretation of the different kinds of variances.

**Key points**

➢ A clear explanation of the meaning of variances helps you to evaluate the performance of the production manager, in light of the variances and the sales report.
➢ Do not get confused between mix and yield variances. Write the formula correctly for every variance calculation.

---

**(a)** Explaining the variances, and ascertaining the controllability of the variances by the production manager

**Material Price Variance**

A direct material price variance occurs when raw materials are purchased at a price different from the standard price. If the actual raw material price is greater than the standard raw material price, it is indicative of incurring higher costs for the procurement of raw materials, therefore the variance is adverse (A).

*1 mark*

### 154: Standard Costing and Variance Analysis

Price variances are controllable only to some extent, because Tasty Treat can choose its material suppliers. But the company will not settle for bad quality, even if the price of those goods is low. Also, factors outside the control of the company influence the cost of the raw material, e.g. the demand and supply of wheat, sugarcane, etc. But, in essence, the production manager has no control over the price of raw materials, as the purchase manager handles the transactions related to purchases.

1 mark

**Material Mix Variance**

Material mix variance is the difference between the material cost in the flexible budget based on actual input used at actual mix and the material cost in the flexible budget based on actual input used at standard (budgeted) mix. Standard costs are used in constructing these flexible budgets.

The variance is favourable (F) when it has a positive effect on operating income i.e. when actual mix on actual input is less than standard mix on actual input. Otherwise, the variance is adverse (A).

1 mark

Mix variance is exclusively under the control of the production manager. She has the absolute authority to order a change in proportions.

1 mark

**Material Yield Variance**

The material yield variance is the difference between the material cost in the flexible budget based on actual input used in the standard (budgeted) mix, and that amount in the flexible budget, based on the standard input allowed in the standard mix. Standard costs are used to construct the flexible budgets.

This variance is favourable (F) when it has a positive effect on operating income i.e. when the cost of actual input used in the standard mix is greater than the cost of standard input allowed in the standard mix. Otherwise the variance is adverse (A).

This variance identifies the change in raw material costs due to a change (from standard) in input quantity when used in the standard mix.

1 mark

Yield variance is under the control of the production manager, as she is responsible for the operation of the production department. For example, Jill can take steps to minimise waste during production, resulting in higher yield.

1 mark
**Maximum marks 6**

**(b) Evaluation of the production manager's performance**

Jill's performance can be evaluated according to the following parameters:

**Price wise evaluation**

Material price variance is favourable only in the first month and adverse in the next two months. As discussed above, adverse variance occurs when actual price is more than the standard. This shows that material prices are rising over the period. As Jill has no control over the material price, her performance should not be evaluated taking these variances into consideration.

1.5 marks

**Mix wise evaluation**

The rising material prices may have forced the production manager to make the mix cheaper. Therefore, the proportion of the ingredients used to make the cookies has changed considerably in order to control cost. This may result in a poor quality product, due to which the sales are falling. One of the implications of a cheaper mix is cheaper product quality, which is unacceptable.

1.5 marks

**Yield wise evaluation**

The production manager has produced a favourable yield over three months. The actual proportion of ingredients may be more productive than the standard proportion. This is good for the company, provided the quality aspect is taken into consideration.

1.5 marks

## Overall evaluation

In view of the Sales Report, we can assume that the new mix of ingredients is adversely affecting the quality of the cookies. People want their children to have the best ingredients available. , therefore, the sales of Tasty Treat cookies are seen to be slipping. The production manager needs to understand that efficiency and cost effectiveness are important, but not by jeopardising the quality of the product.

1.5 marks
**Maximum marks 5**

### (c) Variances

#### (i) Material Price Variance

Material Price Variance = (Standard material price - Actual material price (W1)) x Actual quantity

0.5 marks

For Wheat flour

($0.80 – $0.85) x 123,000 Kg = $6,150 (A)

0.5 marks

For Butter

($4 – $4.3) x 7,350 Kg = $2,205 (A)

0.5 marks

For Sugar

($0.5 – $0.48) x 183,000 Kg = $3,660 (F)

0.5 marks

**Note:** calculation for Actual Material price is shown in W1.

#### (ii) Material Mix Variance

Material Mix Variance = (Standard mix of raw materials on actual input - Actual mix of raw materials on actual input) x Standard cost per unit of raw materials

For Wheat flour
(137,568 kg – 123,000 kg) x $0.80 = $11,654.40 (F)

0.5 marks

For Butter
(7,643 kg – 7,350 kg) x $4 = $1,172 (F)

0.5 marks

For Sugar
(168,139 kg – 183,000kg) x $0.50 = $7,430.5 (A)

0.5 marks

**Note:** Calculation for Standard Mix of Material on actual inputs is shown in W2.

#### (iii) Material Yield Variance

Material Yield Variance = (Standard yield for actual mix – Actual yield for actual mix) x Standard weighted average cost per unit of all material in the mix

1 mark

= (101,902.44 kg – 102,500kg) x $2.205 = $1,317.6 (F)

1 mark

**Note:** Calculation for Standard Yield for Actual Mix is shown in W3.

**Workings:**

**W1 Actual Price = Actual total cost for the raw material / Actual Quantity**

| Raw Material | Actual Total Cost (a) $ | Actual Quantity (b) Kg | Actual Price (a/b) $ |
|---|---|---|---|
| Wheat Flour | 104,550 | 123,000 | 0.85 |
| Butter | 31,605 | 7,350 | 4.30 |
| Sugar | 87,840 | 183,000 | 0.48 |

1 mark

## W2 Standard mix of Raw Materials on Actual Input

Total Input:

| Wheat Flour | 123,000 kg |
|---|---|
| Butter | 7,350 kg |
| Sugar | 183,000 kg |
| **Total** | **313,350 kg** |

**Standard Mix for Actual Input for:**

$$\text{Wheat flour} = \frac{313{,}350 \text{ kg} \times 1.35 \text{ kg}}{3.075 \text{ kg}} = 137{,}568 \text{ kg}$$

> This is the total of standard input required for one unit i.e. 1.35 kg + 0.075 kg + 1.65 kg = 3.075 kg

$$\text{Butter} = \frac{313{,}350 \text{ kg} \times 0.075 \text{ kg}}{3.075 \text{ kg}} = 7{,}643 \text{ kg}$$

$$\text{Sugar} = \frac{313{,}350 \text{ kg} \times 1.65 \text{ kg}}{3.075 \text{ kg}} = 168{,}139 \text{ kg}$$

*1.5 marks*

## W3

**Standard Expected Output**

Standard inputs for 1 kg of cookies = 3.075 kg (W2)

Actual total inputs = 313,350 kg (W2)

Therefore Standard Expected Output = 313,350 kg / 3.075 kg = 101,902.44 kg

*1.5 marks*
**Maximum marks 9**

## 42. Variances – Lumina Inc

**Strategy**

Part (a) and (b) of this question require you to calculate the variances in detail, and part (c) is a discursive question.

The following important points will help you to score high marks in this question.

> Standard contribution per lamp is not given. Calculate this by deducting standard cost per unit from standard selling price per unit.

> Give workings in detail for the standard mix of raw materials on actual input and actual yield for actual mix. Also provide a separate working for actual profit.

> Consider budgeted and actual fixed overheads in the reconciliation statement.

---

**(a) Calculation of variances**

**(i) Sales volume contribution variance**

Sales Volume Contribution Variance = (Actual sales – Budgeted sales) x Standard contribution per unit (W1)
= (48,000 units – 50,000 units) x $4.875
= $9,750 (A)

*1 mark*

**(ii) Sales Price Variance**

Sales price variance = (Actual selling price per unit – Standard selling price per unit) x Actual quantity sold
= ($18.15 – $18) x 48,000 units
= $7,200 (F)

> This is calculated as actual total sales/actual total quantity sold.

*1 mark*

### (iii) Material price, mix and yield variances for both raw materials

Material price variance = (Standard material price – Actual material price) x Actual material quantity

For glass tubing
= ($1.70 – $1.64) x 182,926 g
= $10,974 (F)

*This is equal to actual total material price/actual total material quantity.*

0.5 marks

For tungsten filaments
= ($1.20 – $1.25) x 100,800 g
= $5,040(A)

0.5 marks

Material mix variance = (Standard mix of raw materials on actual input (W2) – Actual mix of raw materials on actual input) x Standard cost per unit of raw materials

For glass tubing
= (177,329 g – 182,926 g) x $1.7
= $9,515 (A)

1 mark

For tungsten filaments
= (106,397g – 100,800 g) x $1.2
= $6,716 (F)

1 mark

Material yield variance = (Standard yield for actual mix (W2) – Actual yield for actual mix (W3)) x Standard cost per unit of raw material

For glass tubing
= (177,329 g – 180,000 g) x $1.7
= $4,541(F)

1 mark

For tungsten filaments
= (106,397 g – 108,000 g) x $1.2
= $1,924 (F)

1 mark

### (iv) Labour rate, efficiency and idle time variances

Labour rate variance = (Standard wages rate per hour – Actual wages rate per hour) x Actual labour hours
= ($6 – $6.1) x 28,800 hrs
= $2,880 (A)

*This is calculated by dividing actual total labour cost by actual total labour hours paid for.*

0.5 marks

Idle time variance = (Hours paid – hours worked) x Standard wage rate per hour
= (28,800 hrs – 28,350 hrs) x $6
= $2,700 (A)

1 mark

Labour efficiency variance = (Standard labour hours for actual production – Actual labour hours worked) x standard wages rate per hour
= [(0.675 hrs x 48,000 units) – 28,350 hrs] x $6
= $24,300 (F)

0.5 marks

## 158: Standard Costing and Variance Analysis

**Workings**

**W1 Standard Contribution per unit**

|  | $ | $ |
|---|---|---|
| Standard sales price |  | 18.00 |
| Less: |  |  |
| Glass tubing ($1.70 x 3.75 g) | 6.375 |  |
| Tungsten filament ($1.20 x 2.25 g) | 2.70 |  |
| Labour ($6 x 0.675 hrs) | 4.05 |  |
|  |  | (13.125) |
| **Standard Contribution** |  | **4.875** |

Total Standard Contribution ($4.875 x 50,000 units) = $243,750

1 mark

**W2 Standard mix of raw materials on actual input (i.e. Standard yield for actual mix)**

182,926 g + 100,800 g = 283,726 g

Glass tubing = 283,726 g x $\frac{3.75 \text{ g}}{6 \text{ g}}$

= 177,329 g

*This is the total of standard input required for one unit i.e. 3.75 g + 2.25 g = 6 g*

Tungsten filaments = 283,726 x $\frac{2.25 \text{ g}}{6 \text{ g}}$

= 106,397 g

1 mark

**W3 Actual yield for actual mix**

Standard quantity of materials = 48,000 units x 6 g = 288,000 g

Glass tubing = 288,000 x $\frac{3.75 \text{ g}}{6 \text{ g}}$

= 180,000 g

Tungsten filaments = 288,000 x $\frac{2.25 \text{ g}}{6 \text{ g}}$

= 108,000 g

1 mark
**Maximum marks 8**

**(b) Reconciliation of Budgeted and Actual Profit**

*Remember budgeted profit is equal to budgeted contribution less budgeted fixed costs.*

|  |  |  | Marks |
|---|---|---|---|
| Budgeted Profit |  | 181,250 | 0.5 |
| Budgeted Fixed production overheads |  | 62,500 | 0.5 |
| Budgeted contribution (W1) |  | 243,750 |  |
|  |  |  |  |
| Sales volume contribution variance | 9,750(A) |  |  |
| Sales Price Variance | 7,200 (F) | 2,550 (A) |  |
|  |  | 241,200 |  |
| Material Price Variances |  |  | 0.5 |
|   Glass Tubing | 10,974 (F) |  |  |
|   Tungsten Filaments | 5,040 (A) |  |  |
|  |  |  |  |
| Material Mix Variances |  |  | 0.5 |
|   Glass Tubing | 9,515(A) |  |  |
|   Tungsten Filaments | 6,716(F) |  |  |

**Continued on the next page**

| Material Yield Variances | | | 0.5 |
|---|---|---|---|
| Glass Tubing | 4541(F) | | |
| Tungsten Filaments | 1,924(F) | | |
| | | | |
| Labour Rate Variance | 2,880(A) | | |
| Idle Time Variance | 2,700(A) | | |
| Labour Efficiency Variance | 24,300(F) | 28,320(F) | 1 |
| | | | |
| Actual contribution | | 269,520 | 0.5 |
| Actual Fixed production overhead | | (64,000) | 0.5 |
| **Actual Profit (W4)** | | **205,520** | 1 |

**W4 Actual Gross Profit**

| | $ | $ |
|---|---|---|
| Actual Sales | | 871,200 |
| Less: Actual costs | | |
| Glass tubing | 300,000 | |
| Tungsten Filaments | 126,000 | |
| Labour | 175,680 | (601,680) |
| Actual Contribution | | 2,69,520 |
| Less: Actual Fixed Overheads | | (64,000) |
| **Actual Profit** | | **205,520** |

1.5 marks
**Maximum marks 5**

**(c)** Although it is accepted that standard costs are predetermined costs or cost estimates in a particular set of circumstances or conditions, there are differences of opinion on the circumstances or conditions that should be considered for setting standards. As a result, several types of standard costs are used in practice. Standards may be classified as:

**Current standards**

Current standards are subject to alterations in prevailing conditions during the period the standards are to be used. Since current standards may require periodic revision, these standards normally remain valid for the accounting period under consideration.

1 mark

**Basic (or static) standards**

Basic standards are not intended for revision in the short run and therefore, they may not reflect current conditions. These standards are suitable for industries where technical processes and operations are fully established and do not change materially over a number of years.

1 mark

**Normal Standards**

Normal standards are the average standards that are anticipated to be attained over a future period of time, preferably long enough to cover a trade cycle. Normal standards are useful for long-term planning and decision making.

1 mark

**Ideal Standards**

Ideal standards are set considering the ideal prevailing conditions and demand a high degree of efficiency and performance. Ideal standards consider consumption of the minimum quantity of material at the lowest price, labour at the minimum rate and time, and overhead at the maximum efficiency.

Ideal standards are mostly theoretical and found to be unachievable most of the time. In an automated production plant where efficient methods of production and production control exist, ideal standards may be most suitable.

1 mark

# 160: Standard Costing and Variance Analysis

**Attainable Standards**

Attainable or expected standards take into account the conditions and circumstances expected to prevail during the period for which the standard is set. Allowances for wastage and idle time are provided for in the standard. Expected standards are more realistic than ideal standards.

*1 mark*

**Effect of standards on employee motivation**

Basic standards remain unchanged for a long time, and so, may become too easy to achieve. This will not be demanding, and will not motivate the employees in any way.

Ideal standards are those that can be achieved under ideal conditions, which are not likely to occur for any significant period. These standards are too difficult to achieve, thereby, decreasing employee motivation.

Attainable standards are realistically set standards, and can be achieved with optimum efficiency. These standards will enhance employee motivation.

*1 mark for each point discusses*
**Maximum marks 7**

> **Tip**
>
> You may also discuss the effects of standards on employee motivation while explaining various standards to earn good marks.

## 43. Variances – Nice-look Ltd

> **Strategy**
>
> You can easily earn high marks in this question. The question has a variation in that it asks you to calculate the market size and market share variances.
>
> In part (a), remember to calculate a budgeted average contribution per unit. Don't confuse the market share variance with market size variance. Write formulae for the calculation of variances to earn high marks.
>
> In part (b), the question requires you to calculate variances only for one product. Remember that the standard contribution per unit of Jasmine is given, therefore don't waste your time in calculating the same figure again. While calculating sales variances, only consider the actual and budgeted sales of Jasmine.
>
> Part (c) is a theory question and requires you to explain the key purposes of a budgeting system. Mentioning all purposes step by step should be enough to earn more marks. A proper heading should be given to each point.

**(a) Calculation of Market size and Market share variance**

Market size variance = Budgeted market share percentage x (Actual industry sales volume in units – Budgeted industry sales volume in units) x Budgeted WACM (W1)
= 10% x (25,000 units – 22,250 units) x $12.06 (W1) = $3,316.50 (F)

> This is calculated by dividing total sales volume by estimated total market for perfumes i.e. 2,225 units/22,250 units = 10%

*2 marks*

Market share variance = (Actual market share percentage – Budgeted market share percentage) x Actual industry sales volume in units x (Budgeted WACM)
= (9% - 10%) x 25,000 units x $12.06 per unit (W1) = $3,015 (A)

*2 marks*

> This is calculated by dividing actual total sales volume by actual total market for perfumes i.e. 2,250 units/25,000 units = 9%

> **Tip**
> You can verify your answer for market share variance and market size variance by calculating total sales volume variance in the following way:
>
> Total sales volume variance = (Total actual sales – Total budgeted sales) x Standard contribution per unit
> = (2,250 units – 2225 units) x $12.06 = 301.50 (F)
>
> Total sales volume variance = Market share variance + Market size variance
> = $3,015 (A) + $3,316.50 (F) = $301.50 (F)

**Workings**

**W1 Calculation of budgeted average contribution per unit**

$$\text{Budgeted average contribution} = \frac{\text{Total budgeted contribution}}{\text{Total budgeted sales volume}}$$

= $26,825/2,225 units = $12.06 per unit

*1 mark*
**Maximum marks 5**

**(b) Calculation of variances**

**(i) Sales variances**

Sales volume contribution variance = (Actual sales – Budgeted sales) x Standard contribution per unit
= (700 units – 750 units) x $12 per unit = $600 (A)

*1.5 marks*

Sales price variance = (Actual selling price per unit – Standard selling price per unit) x Actual quantity sold
= ($147 - $145.50) x 700 units = $1,050 (F)

*1.5 marks*

**(ii) Material variances**

Material price variance = (Standard material price - Actual material price) x Actual material quantity
= ($2.50 - $2.40 (W1)) x 32,550 ml = $3,255 (F)

*1.5 marks*

Material usage variance = (Actual quantity consumed – Standard quantity for actual production) x Standard price
= [32,550 ml – (700 units x 45ml)] x $2.50 = $2,625 (A)

*1.5 marks*

**(iii) Labour Variances**

Labour rate variance = (Standard labour rate per hour - Actual labour rate per hour) x Actual labour hours
= ($14 - $10.50 (W2)) x 1,400 hrs = $4,900 (F)

*1.5 marks*

Labour efficiency variance = (Standard labour hours for actual production - Actual labour hours worked) x Standard wages rate per hour
= [(90/60 min x 700) – 1,400 hrs] x $14 per hour = $4,900 (A)

> Remember that standard labour hour per unit is given in minutes. Therefore, we need to convert minutes into hours.

*1.5 marks*

## Workings

**W1**

$$\text{Actual material price per unit} = \frac{\text{Total material cost}}{\text{Material actually consumed}}$$

= $78,120/32,550 ml = $2.40 per ml

*1 mark*

**W2**

$$\text{Actual labour rate per hour} = \frac{\text{Total direct labour}}{\text{Total hours}}$$

= $14,700/1,400 hrs = $10.50 per hr

*1 mark*
**Maximum marks 9**

**(c)** The main purposes of a budgeting system are planning, co-ordination, communication, control, motivation and performance evaluation.

### Planning

One of the main purposes of a budgeting system is to ensure that planning takes place in the organisation. A budget is a formal expression of the future plan. It helps in determining the individual goal of each activity or department and planning their actions to achieve this goal. Budgets provide premises for detailed operational plans to be followed during the budget period. A fixed master budget is used as a basis for the overall planning of an organisation.

### Co-ordination

The activities of the organisation should be carried out with proper coordination so as to enable the organisation to achieve its objectives. The budgeting system helps to achieve coordination among various activities because, during a budgeting process various organisational objectives are identified and the links between these are examined. This enables overall consistency between budgeted activities, which is in turn reassessed before the master budget is agreed by senior managers. If such a framework of the budgeting system is absent, then the departmental or divisional managers might take decisions that do not prove to be optimal in achieving overall organisational objectives.

### Control

One of the most important purposes of a budgeting system is to assist in controlling costs in the organisation. This is done by comparing actual costs with budgeted costs. If there is a difference between two, the variance is examined in order to determine the reason for the difference between actual performance and planned performance. This helps in taking corrective action to ensure the organisational objectives are met.

### Motivation

An important aspect of the budgeting system is to set targets for various levels of employees. If targets are challenging and realistically set, they can be achieved with optimum efficiency. This helps to motivate the employees to work hard and improve their performance, in order to achieve these targets. On the other hand, unattainable targets can have a reverse effect on the employees. It has the potential to reduce motivation. Another key factor is the degree of participation of the employees in the budget-setting process. Rewards, bonuses, commissions etc. are given to employees who have been able to achieve the target level set for them.

### Performance evaluation

Performance evaluation of employees is a key aspect of any organisation. Employee performance is often evaluated on the basis of the budgetary targets that have been set for them and how far they have been achieved and they are appropriately rewarded. The departments can also evaluate their own performance with the help of budgets.

**Note:** candidates can discuss any three of the above purposes.

*2 marks for each point discussed*
**Maximum marks 6**

## 44. Planning and operational variances – Kid-world

> **Strategy**
>
> Part (a) of this question requires you to calculate planning and operational variances. Remember to calculate revised standard costs before calculating variances. Give the formula for each variance to earn good marks.
>
> In part (b) you don't need to calculate direct material and labour variances again by using the formula. It can be calculated simply by adding planning and operational variances.
>
> Part (c) requires you to provide a theoretical answer on the factors to be considered for investigation of variances. Structure the answer point-by-point and link it to the case given in the question. This will help you to earn high marks.

### (a) Revised standard costs

Direct material price = $5.57 per kg
Direct material usage = 7.05 kg x 0.95 = 6.70 kg

*1 mark*

Direct labour rate = ($84.60/3 hrs) + $1.13 = $29.33 per hr
Direct labour hour = 3 hrs x 0.90 = 2.70 hrs

*1 mark*

**Planning variances**

Planning variances are required to be calculated because of the revision of standard costs. It is calculated by comparing original standard cost with revised standard costs.

Planning variances are calculated as under:

**Direct material price variance** = (Original material rate – Revised material rate) x Actual material quantity
= ($5.41– $5.57) x 52,000 units x 6.58 kg = $54,745.60 (A)

*1.5 marks*

**Direct material usage variance** = (Original budgeted material usage – Revised material usage) x Original standard material price
= [(7.05 kg – 6.70 kg) x 52,000 units] x $5.41 (W1) = $98,462(F)

*1.5 marks*

**Direct labour rate variance** = (Original budgeted labour rate – Revised labour rate) x Actual labour hours
= [($28.20 – $29.33) x 52,000 units] x 3.05 hrs = $179,218 (A)

*1.5 marks*

**Direct labour efficiency variance** = (Original budgeted labour hours – Revised labour hours) x Original standard labour rate
= [(3 hrs – 2.70 hrs) x 52,000 units] x $28.20 (W1) = $439,920 (F)

*1.5 marks*

**Operational variances**

Operational variances are calculated to analyse the deviation of actual costs from revised standard costs. Therefore, it is a difference between the actual costs and revised standard costs.

The operational variances are calculated as follows:

**Direct material price variance** = (Revised standard material price – Actual material price) x Actual material usage
= [($5.57 – $5.78) x 52,000 units] x 6.58 kg = $71,853.60 (A)

*1.5 marks*

**Direct material usage variance** = (Revised standard material usage – Actual usage) x Standard price
= [(6.70 kg – 6.58 kg) x 52,000 units] x $5.41 (W1) = $33,758.40 (F)

*1.5 marks*

**Direct labour rate variance** = (Revised labour rate − Actual labour rate) x Actual labour hours
= [($29.33 − $29.60) x 52,000 units] x 3.05 hrs = $42,822 (A)

*1.5 marks*

**Direct labour efficiency variance** = (Revised standard labour hours − Actual hours) x Standard labour rate
= [(2.70 hrs − 3.05 hrs) x 52,000 units] x $28.20 (W1) = $513,240 (A)

*1.5 marks*

**Working**

**W1 Original material price per kg and labour rate per hour are calculated as under:**

Material price per kg = $\dfrac{\text{Material price per unit}}{\text{Material usage per unit}}$

= $38.14/7.05 kg
= $5.41 per kg

Labour rate per hour = $\dfrac{\text{Labour rate per unit}}{\text{Labour hours per unit}}$

= $84.60/3 hrs
= $28.20 per hr

*1 mark*
**Maximum marks 11**

**(b) The direct material and labour variances based on standard cost data are calculated by adding the relevant planning and operational variances.**

|  | Planning Variances ($) | Operational Variances ($) | Total Variances ($) | Marks |
|---|---|---|---|---|
| Direct material usage variances | 98,462.00 (F) | 33,758.40 (F) | 132,220.40 (F) | 0.5 |
| Direct material price variances | 54,745.60 (A) | 71,853.60 (A) | 126,599.20 (A) | 0.5 |
| **Total direct material cost variances** | **43,716.40 (F)** | **38,095.20 (A)** | **5,621.20 (F)** | 0.5 |
| Direct labour efficiency variances | 439,920.00 (F) | 513,240.00 (A) | 73,320.00 (A) | 0.5 |
| Direct labour rate variances | 179,218.00 (A) | 42,822.00 (A) | 222,040.00 (A) | 0.5 |
| **Total direct labour cost variances** | **260,702.00 (F)** | **556,062.00 (A)** | **295,360.00 (A)** | 0.5 |

**Maximum marks 2**

> **Tip**
>
> You can verify your answer in the following way:
>
> Total direct material cost variance = Standard material cost for actual production − Actual material cost
> = [$38.14 − ($5.78 x 6.58 kg) per unit] x 52,000 units = $5,595.20 (F)
>
> A difference of $26 ($5,621.20 − $5,595.20) is due to rounding off.
>
> Total direct labour cost variance = Standard direct wages for actual production − Actual direct wages paid
> = [$84.60 − ($29.60 x 3.05 hrs) per unit] x 52,000 units = $295,360 (A)

(c) Controlling variances and improving operations can be carried out once the variance is ascertained and investigated. The organisation should take up an investigation at the right stage and undertake corrective action. While deciding whether a variance should be investigated or not, the following factors should be considered:

➢ **Size**

Investigating large variances and taking necessary corrective action can help to save a large amount of costs. Companies usually have a policy laid out for investigating all variances which exceed a certain size. This minimum size of variance can be determined by statistical decision models. For example, the policy of Kid-world requires investigation of all variances that exceed beyond 25% of the total adverse variances, and only then will the adverse material price variances be investigated.

*2 marks*

➢ **Adverse or favourable**

A variance could affect the organisation either adversely or favourably. Most organisations give attention to adverse variances and investigate the reason for it. This is necessary for the smooth functioning of the organisation. However, each variance, whether adverse or favourable, should be investigated. Investigating favourable variances might help to identify budgetary slack or ways in which the budgeting process can be improved. They might also point out that the budget is easy to follow and achieve. Hence, the budget can be made much more challenging in order to increase the motivational effect of the budget.

For example, the significantly high favourable direct material usage variance of Kid-world needs to be investigated, as it may be due to a budgetary slack. It points out that the budget is easy to follow, and can be made more challenging.

*2 marks*

➢ **Historic pattern of variances**

Variances that have occurred for the first time and have not taken place historically could be considered for investigation, even if they are not large. Organisations might use statistical tests of significance in order to identify such variances.

*1.5 marks*

➢ **Reliability and quality of data**

Organisations can reap the benefits of investigation in variances only if the data obtained and the recording system of the organisation is reliable and of dependable quality. If the data itself is not accurate, the calculation of variances may give misleading results.

*1 mark*

➢ **Cost versus benefits**

It is meaningful to undertake an investigation of those variances that are likely to bring in higher benefits as compared to the costs of investigation. In the case of Kid-world, the adverse direct material price variance may be investigated and corrected by purchasing in bulk quantities. This action will incur lower costs and there will be greater benefits arising from it.

*1.5 marks*
**Maximum marks 7**

## 45. Reconciliation of budgeted and actual profit – Ash Plc

**Strategy**

Part (a) asks you to prepare an operating statement reconciling budgeted profit with actual profit, calculating variances in as much detail as allowed by the information provided.

Part (b) is a theoretical question in which you need to explain the use of operating statement for management in controlling costs - fixed and variable.

## (a) Operating statement for product RS8

|  | $ | $ | $ | Marks |
|---|---|---|---|---|
| Budgeted profit (W1) |  |  | 18,339.30 | 0.5 |
| Sales volume profit variance (W2) |  |  | 258.30 | 0.5 |
| Standard profit on actual sales |  |  | 18,081.00 |  |
| Sales price variance (W3) |  |  | 1,050.00 | 0.5 |
| Actual sales less standard cost |  |  | 17,031.00 | 0.5 |
| **Cost Variances** | Favourable | Adverse |  |  |
| Material price (W4) |  | 273.00 |  |  |
| Material usage (W5) | 252.00 |  |  |  |
| Labour rate (W6) | 105.00 |  |  |  |
| Labour efficiency (W7) |  | 252.00 |  |  |
| Variable overhead efficiency (W8) |  | 73.50 |  | 2 |
| Variable overhead expenditure (W9) |  | 157.50 |  |  |
| Fixed overhead expenditure (W10) |  | 252.00 |  |  |
| Fixed overhead efficiency (W11) |  | 315.00 |  |  |
| Fixed overhead capacity (W12) | 252.00 |  |  |  |
| Total cost variances | 609.00 | 1,323.00 | (714.00) |  |
| **Actual Profit (W13)** |  |  | **16,317.00** | 1 |

*Note: Budgeted profit can also be calculated as 2,100 units x $8.61 per unit.*

**Workings**

**W1 Calculation of budgeted profit**

|  |  | $ Per unit |
|---|---|---|
| Selling price |  | 15.00 |
| Direct material: |  |  |
| M3 | 0.6 kg @ $1.55 per kg | 0.93 |
| M7 | 0.68 kg @ $1.75 per kg | 1.19 |
| Direct labour | 14 mins @ $7.20 per hour | 1.68 |
| Variable overheads | 14 mins @ $2.10 per hour | 0.49 |
| Fixed overheads | 14 mins @ $9 per hour | 2.10 |
| Total cost |  | (6.39) |
| **Standard profit** |  | **8.61** |

Total budgeted profit = $8.61 per unit x (497 hours x 14min/60)
= $8.61 per unit x 2,130 units
= **$18,339.30**

2 marks

**W2**

Sales volume profit variance = (Actual sales quantity – Budgeted sales quantity) x Standard profit per unit
= (2,100 units – 2,130 units) x $8.61
= $258.30 (A)

1 mark

**W3**

Sales price variance = (Actual selling price per unit – Standard selling price per unit) x Actual quantity
= ($14.50 - $15) x 2,100 units
= $1,050 (A)

1 mark

**W4**

Material Price Variance = (Standard Price – Actual Price) x Actual Quantity

For M3 = ($1.55 - $1.60) x 1,050 kg
= $52.50 (A)

*It is calculated by dividing actual material cost by actual quantity e.g. $1,680/1,050 kg = $1.60 per kg*

For M7 = ($1.75 - $1.90) x 1,470 kg
    = $220.50 (A)

Total material price variance = $52.50 (A) + $220.50 (A)
                = $273.00 (A)

1.5 marks

**W5**

Material Usage Variance = (Standard quantity for actual production – Actual quantity) x Standard price

For M3 = [(2,100 x 0.6 kg) – 1,050 kg] x $1.55
    = $325.50 (F)

For M3 = [(2,100 x 0.68 kg) – 1,470 kg] x $1.75
    = $73.50 (A)

Total material usage variance = $325.50 (F) + $73.50 (A)
                = $252 (F)

1.5 marks

**W6**

Labour rate variance = (Standard wages rate per hour – Actual wages rate per hour) x Actual labour hours
        = [$7.20 – ($3,675/525 hours)] x 525 hours
        = $105 (F)

1 mark

**W7**

Labour efficiency variance = (Standard labour hours for actual production – Actual labour hours worked) x Standard wages rate per hour
        = [(14 mins x 2,100 units) – 525 hours] x $7.20
        = $252 (A)

1 mark

**W8**

Variable overhead efficiency variance = (Standard hours for actual production – Actual hours) x Standard variable overhead rate per hour
        = [(14 mins x 2,100 units – 525 hours)] x $2.10
        = $73.50 (A)

1 mark

**W9**

Variable overhead expenditure variance = (Standard variable overhead rate – Actual variable overhead rate) x Actual hours worked
        = [($2.10 x 525 hours) - $1,260]
        = $157.50 (A)

1 mark

**W10**

Fixed overhead expenditure variance = Budgeted fixed overhead – Actual expenditure on fixed overhead
        = [(497 hours x $9)] – $4,725
        = $252 (A)

1 mark

**W11**

Fixed overhead efficiency variance = (Standard hours for actual production – Actual hours worked) x Fixed overhead absorption rate
        = [(14 mins x 2,100 units) – 525 hours] x $9
        = $315 (A)

1 mark

**W12**

Fixed overhead capacity variance = (Budgeted hours – Actual hours) x Fixed overhead absorption rate
        = 497 hours – 525 hours x $9
        = $252 (F)

1 mark

## 168: Standard Costing and Variance Analysis

### W13 Calculation of actual profit

|  | $ Per unit |
|---|---|
| Sales ($14.50 x 2,100 units) | 30,450 |
| **Less:** Costs |  |
| Direct material: |  |
| M3 | 1,680 |
| M7 | 2,793 |
| Direct labour | 3,675 |
| Variable overheads | 1,260 |
| Fixed overheads | 4,725 |
| Total costs | (14,133) |
| **Standard profit** | **16,317** |

*2 marks*
**Maximum marks 14**

### (b)

#### (i) Controlling variable costs

> The operating statement presents the favourable and adverse variances separately. This helps the manager to clearly identify areas which deviate to a great extent from the standard set. Therefore, the manager can concentrate only on these significant areas in order to bring the actuals back in line with the standards.

In order to compare the actual cost with the standard cost of actual production, the operating statement considers the effect of the sales volume and the price difference between the actual and standard.

> Variable costs can be controlled in the short term. The operating statement showing the variable cost variances can easily detect the areas where management can take effective actions to control the costs. For example, the operating statement indicates adverse material price variance of $273. The management can reduce this by purchasing substitute materials at low price, purchasing them from other suppliers etc. However, care should be taken so that the quality of the product would not suffer due to such purchase of material.

*1 mark for each point discussed*
**Maximum marks 3**

#### (ii) Controlling fixed production overhead costs

> The operating statement reports the fixed production overhead variance as it helps to reconcile budgeted profit with actual profit. However, as the fixed production overheads (sunk costs) cannot be controlled in the short term, the manager will not be able to take action to bring the adverse variances back in line with the standards.

*Remember, fixed costs are not controllable in the short term.*

> The occurrence of an adverse fixed production overhead expenditure variance may be the effect of poor budget planning. Further investigation of overheads may indicate whether any of its components are controllable or not. The operating statement can assist the management in this way.

> Fixed production overhead volume variance indicates the difference between the actual production and planned production. The fixed production overhead volume variance occurs due to the process of absorption costing as it is a function of both, the production and the sales volume.

The operating statement plays an important role in reporting the information about the deviations between the actual and standard activity levels. This helps management in the decision-making process.

*1 mark for each point discussed*
**Maximum marks 3**

### Score More

In part (a), you could lose marks if you use marginal costing, as here the standard cost information provided includes fixed production overhead per unit, which means that absorption costing was in use.

In part (b), if your answer explains how the variances calculated might have arisen (poor material, unskilled labour, new machines, and so on), again you may lose marks. You need to be aware of the budgetary control cycle and how the operating statement fits into the control process.

## 46. Sales variances – Spike Co

### Strategy

This question requires proper understanding of budgets. In the answer to part (a), you should state that the budgets can be revised to eliminate planning errors.

However, it should also be considered that revision of budgets overlooks poor operational performance behind the curtain of planning errors.

Your answer should support both the criteria separately.

Part (b) is computational and requires application of basic variance formulae. Remember, part (c) requires analysis of sales volume variance into market size and market share components, not opinions.

Part (d) expects explanation of meaning and implications of the data computed in parts (b) and (c).

Your answer should express that a business that fails to meet its sales budget by only 2.2% in the face of a market that has shrunk by 11%, could hardly be totally criticised.

---

**(a)** Successful budgets should have adequate flexibility to meet the changing business conditions, since budgets are used as a tool for controlling the costs. One of the objectives of a budget is to provide a yardstick for performance evaluation.

If budgets are not revised in line with the changing environment / conditions, comparing actual results with the budgeted ones will not give appropriate results. Therefore, it is necessary to revise budgets and analyse the causes of variances with the adjusted standards (i.e. revised budgets).

However, revision of budgets should not be allowed in cases where the conditions are within the control of the manager.

**A budget can be revised under the following circumstances:**

- emergence of unforeseen and unanticipated situations

- changes in internal factors, such as production forecast, sales forecast, capacity utilisation, etc.

- changes in external factors, such as market trends, nature of the economy, prices of inputs and resources, consumer tastes and fashions and input cost structure

- errors made while preparing the budget: they may be discovered, causing the budgeted figures to be rectified

2 marks

## Materials

**Arguments in favour of revision of budget**

- As a local supplier went into liquidation, the company's buyer purchased the material from another supplier at a higher price. This situation is outside the control of the company. As the company could not have expected this while preparing the original budget, it is allowed to revise the budget accordingly.

- As the buyer is aware that the situation is outside his control and is demanding revision of the budget, the revision is allowed.

1.5 marks

**Arguments against revision of budget**

- The buyer may have failed to negotiate the price of materials. Therefore, he incurred a higher cost for the materials needlessly.

- The buyer may not have investigated other available suppliers in the market who could have offered a lower price.

1.5 marks

The nature of the problem is such that it is outside the control of the company. This is a prime cause for the revision of the budget. Therefore, the buyer should not be penalised for this. If the company does not revise the budget, it will not be realistic. Therefore, the revision of budget is allowed.

1 mark
**Maximum marks 4**

## Labour

**Arguments in favour of revision of budget**

- It was the board's decision to recruit only top graduates in order to increase productivity. This has resulted in increasing the costs. As this situation exists due to the board's decision and not the departmental manager's, the additional cost to the departmental budget is out of the control of the manager. Hence, the revision of the budget is allowed.

1.5 marks

**Arguments against revision of budget**

- Before complaining to the board, the departmental manger should have taken efforts to improve the efficiency of labour. However, he complained directly in the board report. This may have resulted in mere approval of the board for the change.

As the situation is entirely within the control of the company, the budget revision is not allowed.

- The reason for the change in policy may be that the department would benefit from the increased productivity. As the department benefits from this change, it should accept the increased costs.

1.5 marks

As the board made the final decision which resulted in the change of policy, this was outside the control of the manager. Hence, a budget revision is allowed.

1 mark
**Maximum marks 4**

**(b) Calculation of variances**

- **Sales volume contribution variance**

Sales Volume Contribution Variance = (Actual sales – Budgeted sales) x Standard contribution per unit
= (176,000 units – 180,000 units) x $7
= $28,000 (A)

2 marks

➢ **Sales Price Variance**

Sales price variance = (Actual selling price per unit – Standard selling price per unit) x Actual quantity sold
= ($16.40 – $17) x 176,000 units
= $105,600 (A)

*2 marks*

**(c) Calculation of market size and share variances**

**Market size variance**

= Budgeted market share percentage x (Actual industry sales volume in units- Budgeted industry sales volume in units) x Budgeted WACM

> Budgeted market share percentage is calculated by dividing total sales volume by estimated total market for diaries i.e. 180,000 units/1,800,000 units = 10%

= 10% x (1.6m units – 1.8m units) x $7 = $140,000 (A)

*2 marks*

**Market share variance**

= (Actual market share percentage – Budgeted market share percentage) x Actual industry sales volume in units x (Budgeted WACM)

> Actual market share percentage is calculated by dividing actual total sales volume by actual total market for perfumes i.e. 176,000 units/1,600,000 units = 11%

= (11% - 10%) x 1.6m units x $7 per unit = $112,000 (F)

*2 marks*

The total sales volume can be analysed in the following way:

Total sales volume variance = Market share variance + Market size variance
= $140,000 (A) + $112,000 (F)
= $28,000 (A)

This is exactly equal to the sales volume variance which is calculated in part (c).

*1 mark*
**Maximum marks 4**

**(d) Comment on sales performance**

The selling price is reduced by $0.6 per unit ($17 - $16.4). This resulted in loss of sales revenue amounting to $105,600 as compared to the standard sales.

The company may have felt that reduction in price would help to maintain the standard sales level.

The overall sales volume of the products is reduced by 4,000 units (180,000 – 176,000 units). This results in the business losing $28,000 of profit.

The reduction in the sales volume may be because of the shrinking market for diaries.

Therefore, it would not be fair to say that the sales department has not performed well.

Although the market for diaries has been shrinking due to their wide availability, the company has performed well.

This is because actual market share percentage increased by 1% as compared to budgeted market share. The company successfully crossed the revised budgeted level (10% of 1.6m) of sales by selling more units (176,000) in the period.

Considering the shrinking market, the company performed better than expected.

Another reason for maintaining the expected sales level could be the reduction in selling price. Additionally, the improved quality of support staff may have helped to maintain the sales level. At the same time, the actions of competitors should be taken into consideration when commenting on the performance of the company. In a tough, competitive market, merely maintaining budgeted sales could be appreciated as a good achievement, provided that the budgets were set appropriately.

1 mark for each point discussed
**Maximum marks 4**

# SOLUTION BANK

## SECTION E: PERFORMANCE MEASUREMENT AND CONTROL

### 47. Performance Evaluation - Serene Bay

**Strategy**

This is a discursive question. It requires comments on performance of the business on both counts, financial, as well as non financial. In such questions, you should be able to identify the critical information and analyse it. Some indicators should be analysed together with other indicators.

In this question, you can score easy marks. Just by calculating the percentage of increase or decrease, you can assess the general performance and get a few marks. However, in order to score high marks, proper analysis is needed.

---

**(a) Financial Performance of Serene Bay**

From the financial data given above it is apparent that the company has performed well in 20X8, compared to 20X7.

The following is a detailed discussion of the financial performance of Serene Bay:

➢ The total turnover shows a 5% [($945 – $900) / $900 x 100] growth. This is an indication of a growing business. It also shows that the turnover from special events is up by 50%. [($300 – $200) / $200 x 100]. This is very encouraging, but the cost attributable to special events should also be taken into consideration.

2 marks

➢ The total turnover only increased by $45,000. The turnover from special events increased by $100,000. This means the increase of $45,000 in total turnover is because of special events. The turnover other than that from special events has decreased by $55,000 ($100,000 - $45,000). The decrease in the normal restaurant activities is not a good indicator. The management has to concentrate on the core activities, and take measures to increase the turnover from them.

*This is a very important point, and can be easily overlooked. Read this carefully as this is how you should relate more than one indicator and then analyse the data*

2 marks

➢ The costs attributable to special events are up approximately by 91%. [($230 – $120) / $120 x 100]. In 20X7, the cost attributable to special events was 60% ($120/$200 x 100) which increased to $ 77% ($230/$300 x 100) in 20X8. This is a significant increase, and management should consider cost control. As a result, even if the turnover from special events has increased, the profit from them has actually decreased by $10000 (WN1).

2 marks

➢ The total profit has increased by 30% [($169 – $130) / $130 x 100]. This is in spite of a decrease in the turnover from normal business activities, and a decrease in profit from special events. Therefore it can be concluded that either the management has successfully controlled the costs related to the normal activities, or the base of overhead allocation is such that more and more overheads are allocated to the special events. Therefore management should be more cautious while selecting overhead allocation basis.

2 marks
**Maximum marks 8**

## Working

### W1

**Profit from Special Events**

> It is good to write working notes for every calculation, even in answers to discursive problems.

|  | 20X7 ($'000) | 20X8 ($'000) | Increase in 20X8 ($'000) |
|---|---|---|---|
| Turnover from special events | 200 | 300 | 100 |
| Cost attributable to special events | (120) | (230) | 110 |
| Therefore profit from special events | 80 | 70 | (10) |

### (b) Performance related to non financial factors

For effective performance management, non-financial indicators are equally important. The non financial information will give a much greater insight into the performance of the restaurant, and its future viability.

The four perspectives of a balanced scorecard are financial performance, internal business process, customer satisfaction and learning and growth. Of these, the financial performance is already discussed above. Performance of the restaurant considering the other perspectives can be evaluated as follows:

#### ➢ Internal Business Process

The average service delay at peak times has increased by 66.66% [(25mins – 15mins) /15mins x 100] from the previous year. This is in spite of a decrease in the normal business activities. As discussed above, it seems that the cost of normal business activities has reduced as compared to 20X7. This could be due to reducing the number of chefs and waiters. If this is the case, then management should reconsider this decision, as. A delay in serving time may lead to customer dissatisfaction and consequently can result in a further decrease in demand.

*1 mark*

The idle time has decreased by 10% [(540-486) mins / 540 x 100]. This decrease is not significant, and needs to decrease further, to better utilise the resources. The employees can be motivated to be more productive by announcing incentives for completing the work in time.

> Idle time and delay at peak hours can be related. This will help you to score well.

Idle time can be utilised to make pre-preparations wherever possible, to avoid delays during peak times. For example, the chefs can order the ingredients and keep them ready for popular dishes, waiters can lay the tables and keep the menus handy before the peak hours.

*1 mark*

The increase in the reported cases of food poisoning is alarming. This is surprising, as the owner emphasises on the quality of the food served. Also, this leaves a very bad impression in the minds of the customers. This could affect the popularity of the restaurant. The importance of cleanliness and hygiene should be explained to the chefs and the helpers. In addition to loss of popularity, Serene Bay could incur financial loss, if the aggrieved customers decide to sue.

*1 mark*

#### ➢ Customer Satisfaction

In spite of the cases of food poisoning, customers visiting the restaurant regularly have increased by 66.66% [(15 – 9)/9 x 100]. This is a sure sign of the popularity the restaurant enjoys, and also that the regular customers are satisfied with the service of Serene Bay. This may also be due to price competitiveness, over other restaurants in that league. However, it seems that the restaurant failed to attract new customers. This is evident from the decrease in normal business as discussed earlier. The management should re-consider its marketing policies.

*1 mark*

Complimentary letters from satisfied customers have also increased, further affirming the popularity of Serene Bay. It is a known fact, that customers take the effort to write such letters only if they are extremely satisfied with the experience. However, this has not helped the restaurant in terms of generating more profits.

*1 mark*

The average bill amount per customer has increased by 70% [($51-$30) / $30 x 100] which is a very considerable increase. This may be due to an increase in the rates on the menu. By increasing rates, Robert may be trying to capitalise on the growing popularity. A subtle increase would have gone down well with the customers, but increasing the rates by 70% might prove to be dangerous. This may be the reason why the turnover from normal business has gone down. The price increase should ideally be gradual, so that the customers' response can be gauged.

*1 mark*

> **Learning and Growth**

Special theme evenings were introduced from the current year. This is a good step. New ideas give an edge over other restaurants in this competitive business. This shows that the management can come up with innovative ideas in the future. However, in the absence of data, it cannot be ascertained how the concept was received by the patrons. Robert should decide whether to continue with the special theme evenings after considering details such as, turnover, profit, and customer response.

*1 mark*

New entrées in the menu introduced during the year have gone down by half, than that of the previous year. It shows that efforts were made to introduce new dishes on the menu only during 20X7 when the restaurant was initially taken over by Robert. To stay ahead of the competition, Serene Bay needs to experiment with new recipes. This can be done by enrolling the chefs in cooking classes, or announcing a prize for the best new recipe of the month, etc.

*1 mark*

Total proposals submitted to cater for special events have gone up significantly which resulted in increased turnover from the events. The costs incurred for submitting these proposals may be included in the costs attributable to special events. This may be the reason for the significant increase in the costs of the events.

*1 mark*

From the financial aspect, the growth of Serene Bay looks promising. The only concern is that Robert needs to concentrate more on the core restaurant business rather than the special events.

The position of Serene Bay, after taking the non financial factors into consideration, seems to be good. The serious concerns are a decrease in the normal business, a significant increase in price and the food poisoning cases, which need to be looked into.

> Do not forget to write this concluding paragraph. This is specifically asked for, and carries marks.

Considering both, the financial as well as the non financial information, Serene Bay emerges as a successful business. However, Robert should not take the success for granted and get carried away by the success. He should continue making innovations and increase the items on the menu. He should remember that this is a highly competitive field.

*3 marks*
**Maximum marks 12**

## 48. Balanced scorecard and building block - Fresh Foods

**Strategy**

Of the three sub-questions in this question, sub-question (a) and (c) are theory based. However, in sub-question (c), do not suggest general improvements. The suggestions should be related to the company.

In the case of sub-question (b), the information given in the problem is not categorised into the various perspectives of the balanced scorecard. In order to answer this, you should know how performance is assessed in the balanced scorecard i.e. perspectives used in the balanced scorecard, and you should also be able to categorise the items in the perspectives.

Once this is done, discuss each item separately and write a short conclusion after each perspective. You should also provide a conclusion as to the overall performance of Fresh Foods.

### (a) Balanced scorecard

The concept of a balanced scorecard is that no one measure of performance can evaluate the performance of an organisation. For comprehensive evaluation, multiple measures, including financial and non-financial, need to be taken into consideration. Realising this need for a balanced measurement system, Robert S Kaplan and D.P. Norton developed the balanced scorecard system. It links the short-term operational goals of an organisation to its long-term objectives and strategy by forcing control and monitoring of day to day operations. It defines the entire roadmap of lead indicators for achieving the goals and constantly reveals what is happening in an organisation.

This system measures the performance of an organisation in the following main areas:

- Customer perspective: considers customers' perception of the organisation using measures such as customer satisfaction.

- Financial perspective: considers financial performance using measures such as gross profit, ROI and NPV.

- Internal business process: considers strengths and weaknesses in the business process to come up with ways to improve the work process. Measures used include error rate, ability to meet deadlines etc.

- Learning and Growth: considers innovations by the organisation to ensure the growth prospect of the organisation. Measures used include number of new products introduced during the year, time taken to develop next generation product etc.

Thus, the emphasis of the balanced scorecard is on progress and improvement, rather than meeting any specific standards. It links the short term operational goals of an organisation to its long term objectives, by controlling its day to day operations.

| | |
|---|---|
| Explaining meaning of balanced scorecard | 1 mark |
| Importance of balanced scorecard | 1 mark |
| Stating perspectives of balanced scorecard | 1 mark |
| Examples of measures | 1 mark |

**Building blocks model**

Fitzgerald and Moon developed the building blocks model to measure performance in service industries. In the model there are three blocks, dimensions, standards and rewards. According to the model, the organisation should come up with the performance measures which can be categorised in the six dimensions given in the model. Once the dimensions of performance have been selected, performance standards are set to facilitate performance evaluation. Finally, the rewards should be designed which should be linked to the performance i.e. achievement of the standards

The model is very comprehensive as it takes into account six different areas in which performance can be assessed. In addition, since performance is assessed based on the standards, and the reward system is linked to the achievement of the standards, it takes care of the behavioural issues arising from a reward system. The model requires that employees should be involved in setting standards, and the standards should be achievable and fair to all.

While setting a rewards policy, clarity, motivation and controllability should be focused on.

According to this model, controllable performance can be measured in the following six ways:

- **Financial performance:** include indicators like profitability, capital structure, etc.
- **Competitiveness:** includes growth in sales, capturing market share, etc.
- **Quality of service:** such as reliability, competence, customer relation, etc.
- **Flexibility:** includes ability to provide service in appropriate speed, responsiveness to deliver service according to customer specifications, etc.
- **Resource utilisation:** indicates how efficiently resources may be utilised.
- **Innovation:** considers both innovation in the process of providing service and innovation in the service content.

Financial performance and competitiveness indicate performance (success / failure) as an outcome of the decisions and actions taken in the past.

The other measures indicate competitive performance (success / failure) at present and accordingly are relevant for current performance measurement.

| | |
|---|---|
| Explaining meaning of building blocks model | 1 mark |
| Importance of the model | 1 mark |
| Stating blocks in the model | 1 mark |
| Example of measures | 1 mark |
| **Maximum marks** | **6** |

**(b) Evaluation of the performance of Fresh Foods on the basis of the balanced scorecard:**

**Financial perspective**

➢ **Revenue:** the growth in revenue of Fresh Foods has shown an increase from 4% in 20X7, to 5.5% in 20X8. This is good, but considering the target growth rate of 6%, it can be said that the company needs to take steps to increase the revenue, either by increasing the selling price of their products or by increasing the volumes

*1 mark*

➢ **Selling price:** average selling price per product has increased by around 6% [($235 - $220)/$220 x 100], as compared to the previous year. This may explain the growth in revenue. Considering the industry average selling price, which is higher than Fresh Foods, it can be seen that the company may further increase the selling price of its products to increase the revenue, and thus achieve the targeted growth rate of 6%. In addition, it may have to reconsider the sales mix to ensure that an emphasis on the sale of the higher priced products is kept in mind. This will lead to an increase in the average selling price.

*Linking two points given in the problem will earn you better marks.*

On the other hand, this price competitiveness may be the reason for the revenue growth in the first place. The management should consider all these aspects before deciding to increase the prices.

*2 marks*

Although the target for revenue growth has not been met, overall, the performance of Fresh Foods from the financial perspective seems to be good.

*0.5 marks*
**Maximum marks 3**

**Customer perspective**

➢ **Number of customers (only malls):** the number of malls buying Fresh Foods products has increased by 25% [(25-20)/20 x 100] in 20X8, when compared to the previous year. This increase is more than the expected increase, which was 22% (20%+10% of 20%). This is a very encouraging sign. It seems that either the existing customers are satisfied or Fresh Food has advertised the product in the right way. This customer satisfaction shows that quality of the product and service may be good resulting in the increasing popularity of the products and also the customer base.

*2 marks*

➢ **Customer retention rate:** customer retention rate has gone up from 46% in 20X7 to 50% in 20X8. This is impressive and confirms the reason for the increasing number of malls buying Fresh Foods' products. This exceeds the targeted increase of 48.3% (46% + 5% of 46%) by 1.7% (50% - 48.3%).

Taking into consideration the increase in the client base as well as the increase in the client retention rate, it can be said that Fresh Foods is successful in meeting the expectations of their clients. This may also be one of the reasons for the impressive growth in revenue.

*Again, here two points can be linked.*

*2 marks*
**Maximum marks 3**

**Business processes perspective**

➢ **New products:** Fresh Foods has come up with four new products in 20X7 and 20X8 each. However, looking at the target of six products, there was a decrease in the new products launched, by two products. Since an industry average is not available, it is difficult to comment on whether the new products launched are sufficient or not. This is because the nature of the business is such that there is scope for introducing new products and it is essential to have more of the new products.

*1.5 marks*

➢ **Wastage:** wastage of raw material has increased from 3% in 20X7 to 5% in 20X8. This is unacceptable, especially in the light of the industry average of 3% which is low compared to Fresh Foods. Moreover, competitors seem to have taken steps to control their wastage, as the industry average wastage declines from 3% in 20X7, to 2.5% in 20X8.

It could be that the employees have become increasingly careless in their work. In addition, the possibility of pilferage of the raw material cannot be denied. This is a serious issue, and the management should pinpoint the causes and work on them to minimise it. It is also probable that Fresh Foods is sourcing more produce than what can be processed and sold to the malls. Fresh agricultural products are susceptible to deterioration very quickly and this may have contributed to the increase in the wastage. The company could study the controls on raw material, and the practices of its competitors to minimise wastage.

If wastage is successfully controlled, it will lead to a reduction in costs, resulting in an increase in profit.

2 marks

The above two points show that Fresh Foods has to concentrate on its business processes as this is core activity and in the long-term this can affect the whole business and the financial performance of Fresh Foods.

0.5 marks
**Maximum marks 3**

**Learning and growth perspective**

> **Employee retention rate:** The employee retention rate has gone down by 0.5% (78% - 77.5%). Although this is a very low percentage, this shows the dissatisfaction of the employees. Fresh Foods hoped to increase the retention rate to 79%. It seems that since the work has increased more than the target, indicated by the increase in malls buying Fresh Foods products, employees may have been pressurised to work more without an adequate improvement in the rewards.

The management of Fresh Foods needs to look into the reasons for the fall in the employee retention rate and take steps to control it.

2 marks

> **Time taken to develop new products:** Targeted average time for bringing a new product into the market was two months. However, Fresh Foods took around three months for this, which is 50% [(3 months – 2 months)/2 months x 100] higher. Fresh Foods should improve on technology and manufacturing knowledge to reduce the time taken to develop and introduce new products

1 mark

Based on the above analysis, it can be concluded, that Fresh Foods is a growing and successful business. The products are price competitive and the customers are satisfied. The only concern is the wastage of material and employee retention rate, which needs to be controlled. In addition, Fresh Foods needs to continue with the innovation and develop new and different food products to maintain its success.

*Remember to give a conclusion on the overall performance, as it carries marks.*

1.5 marks
**Maximum marks 3**
**Maximum marks 12**

**(c) Two ways to improve the performance measurement system of Fresh Foods.**

It can be seen that Fresh Foods measures its financial performance based on the average selling price per product and the revenue growth, as the indicators. It should also think of using better indicators such as return on Investment (ROI), which calculates the net profit earned in relation to the total investment made, or the capital employed and residual income (RI), which considers investments by comparing the profit with the notional income on the investment.

1 mark

In the case of evaluation of performance based on the customer perspective, customer complaints also need to be considered. This is a very important measure of performance. By studying the reasons behind dissatisfaction of the customers, Fresh Foods can improve its performance.

1 mark
**Maximum marks 2**

## 49. Not-for profit organisations, behavioural issues - Osho Spiritual Centre

> **Strategy**
>
> Time management is very important for this question as it comprises four sub-questions. Sub-question (a), is comparatively easy but is a base for the answer of sub-question (b). For answering sub-question (a), each target should be compared with the actual information given.
>
> For answering sub-question (b), read and understand the bonus policy properly. Use the analysis of sub-question (a) to determine the Richard's eligibility for bonus. Do not forget to write behavioural issues arising from the bonus policy and relate them to Richard.
>
> Sub-question (c) and (d) are theoretical but to earn high marks, you should relate them to the given case.

---

**(a)** The financial performance of the Riverdale branch seems to be good, but when compared with the targets, there appears to be scope for improvement.

Revenue for the year exceeds the target. Therefore it can be said that the branch's performance in relation to sales looks promising. The actual revenue is around 104% (176,450 / 169,000 x 100) of the targeted revenue. This may be because Richard constantly strives for higher quality standards of the services offered, which may result in an increase in the number of clients.

2 marks

The actual profit is 95%% [$28,200 / 30,000 x 100] of the targeted profit. This is very low, considering the sales exceed the target. In addition, this situation can be traced to Richard's passion for quality, as higher quality services come at a price. So in spite of increased revenue, Richard fails to increase the branch's profits.

2 marks

The actual remuneration paid to the yoga teachers exceeds the allowable remuneration. The actual remuneration is $150($54,000 / 360 days), which is 7.14% [($150- $140) / 140 x 100] higher than the targeted, $140. This increase contributes to the increase in operating costs, which is responsible for lowering the profits.

As we know Richard emphasises on quality of service, it appears that he may have engaged better qualified yoga trainers with a view to enhancing the quality of the yoga sessions. This will be beneficial in the long term, as it will help to build a strong client base.

2 marks

Exercise room hire expenses also are higher than the targeted. Actual room hire cost per day is $55 ($19,800 / 360 days), as opposed to the targeted $50. Therefore these costs are increased by 10% [(55 – 50) / 50 x 100]. Again, Richard may have rented a room better equipped for yoga training sessions. It may also be that he is paying a higher rent for a normal room. In that case, he should take steps to cut the costs.

2 marks<br>**Maximum marks 8**

**(b)** As the actual revenue is 104% of the targeted revenue, Richard may qualify for a bonus of 10% of the annual remuneration provided the other three conditions are fulfilled.

Profit is exactly 95% of the targeted profit. Since this is exactly 95% Richard is still eligible for the bonus provided the other two conditions are fulfilled.

Remuneration to the trainers per working day is $150 which is more than $147, and hire expenses of the exercise room per working day are $55 which is more than $52.5. Since these two conditions are not met, Richard will not be eligible for any bonus in spite of earning more than the targeted revenue.

> Do not forget to mention Richard's eligibility for bonus considering the other two targets.

2 marks

In spite of high revenue and customer satisfaction, Richard will not be eligible for a bonus. This will definitely de-motivate Richard. In future Richard may not concentrate on quality which will be bad for the company as a whole. It seems that Lily Geller has 'myopia' i.e. short sightedness, as all the targets given by her are quantitative in nature which focuses on short-term performance. The quality of service aims at long-term performance which has not been considered by Lily Geller. Other managers may also concentrate only on short-term performance measures, as the bonus policy is linked to them. As a result the focus of the whole organisation will only be on short-term performance measures.

**180: Performance Measurement and Control**

This policy can have a negative impact on the future of the business. The branch managers, in their anxiety to achieve the profit targets to earn a bonus, may cut down costs and the resultant negative effect on the quality may be felt as the number of clients patronising the yoga centre may reduce.

*2 marks*
**Maximum marks 4**

(c) Non quantifiable objectives can be defined as those that are difficult to measure and express in monetary terms. These objectives are observed more in the case of not for profit organisations. For example, SYF's objective to spread awareness of the yoga practice. The problems of having non-quantifiable objectives in not for profit organisations are discussed below:

- It is very difficult to define these objectives, as they cannot be measured in monetary terms.

- As more than one of these objectives is seen in not for profit organisations, it is also difficult to say which one of the objectives is the key objective. As in the case of SYF, with three major objectives, it would be difficult to determine which of these is actually the key focus of the organisation.

  > Remember to relate your answer to the case given in the problem.

- Too much subjectivity is involved in the assessment of the non-quantifiable objectives. For example, in the objectives of SYF, to serve maximum members, provide service at minimum fees etc. it is very difficult to determine what is maximum and minimum.

- Unlike quantifiable objectives, it is very difficult to judge whether these objectives can be achieved. For example, the spreading of awareness of yoga among people cannot be measured. It cannot be said that the existing awareness of yoga among is because of the efforts of SYF.

*1 mark for each point discussed*
**Maximum marks 4**

(d) Measurement of performance for a not for profit organisation will be different from a commercial business, as their objectives are different. The main objective of a commercial organisation is maximisation of profits. This is not the case for not for profit organisations, as the name suggests. Their main objectives depend on the purpose for which they are formed. Performance will be measured on the basis of these objectives, rather than financial objectives as in the case of commercial organisations.

Not for profit organisations may also have some financial objectives (which are not the key objectives). Like in the case of SYF, one of the objectives may be earning enough profits/surplus to cover all the operating expenses and transfer some amount to a fund to be used to spread awareness of yoga, by conducting lectures, rallies, etc.

The financial data from OSC and SYF cannot be compared, as their objectives (as discussed above) are different.

The main objective of OSC is to earn maximum returns on the investment made. But as SYF is a not for profit organisation, its objective will differ from that of OSC, in the sense that SYF will not seek to make profits alone. This can be seen from the profit figures of the two organisations. SYF makes around 7.6% of profit, in relation to sales, whereas OSC makes more than 14% of profit in relation to sales, which is two times the profit of SYC.

Also, SYC is involved in spreading awareness of yoga. Although Osho is also indirectly involved in spreading the awareness, this is not one of the objectives of Osho.

Another objective of OSC is upgrading the quality of services offered. SYF will also be concerned about the quality of services, but not at the cost of an increase in fees. This can be seen by observing the operational costs of the two divisions.

*1 mark for each point discussed*
**Maximum marks 4**

## 50. Financial and non-financial performance indicators - Concept Academy

### Strategy

This is a discursive question. You should calculate various ratios to show increase / decrease in sales and costs.

While discussing points, you should remember that this is the first year of sale and Concept Academy is new in the market with competition from well-established competitors.

In sub-question (b), do not forget to consider the competitor's data wherever available.

Sub-question (c) appears to be a theoretical question but in order to earn good marks you should relate the non-financial indicators to Concept Academy.

---

**(a)** In order to assess the financial Performance of Concept, it is necessary to discuss changes in the sales, various costs and profits.

**Sales**

> Do not forget to give allowance for first year of sale and for the existence of well-established competitors

The sale in the first quarter itself is impressive and it further increases by $2.95m i.e. 56% [($8.20-$5.25)/$5.25 x 100] in quarter 2. This is a remarkable growth, in spite of Concept being a new company and working in a highly competitive market. It can be said that Concept has made a good start. This shows the competence of the management and of the marketing department.

1 mark

**Cost of sales**

The cost of sales has been increased by 76% [($4.40 - $$2.50)/$2.50 x 100] in quarter 2. In quarter 1, it was around 48% ($2.50/$5.25 x 100 of sales and in quarter 2, it became 54% ($4.40/$8.20 x 100), which is not good. Since cost of writing (amortised cost) is the same in both quarters, the increase may be attributed to printing costs. Since the books are printed only when ordered, sometimes Concept may have to pay for urgent printing. Therefore, management should see whether contacts and contracts can be made with the printers in order to control the cost and also to ensure availability of the printer. In addition, a stock of a few books can be maintained to avoid rush at the last moment.

> Cost of sales and gross profit may be discussed together. The only thing to bear in mind is to cover all the relevant points. Even if more than one point is discussed under one heading, marks will be given for each point discussed.

Another reason for the increased cost of sales/sales ratio could be a decrease in the selling price due to pressure from competitors. As a result more books would have been printed and sold at a price lower than the price in quarter 1.

> See Score more

3 marks

**Gross profit**

The actual gross profit has increased by around 38% [($3.80 - $2.75)/$2.75 x 100]. This would be due to an increase in the sales volume. However, gross profit margin in quarter 1 was around 52% ($2.75/$5.25 x 100) of sales, which then decreased to around 46% [$3.80/$8.20 x 100] of sales. The probable reasons i.e. increase in printing cost and reduced selling price are discussed in detail above. In the absence of information on the industry average, it is difficult to comment on the gross profit percentage earned by Concept.

2 marks

### Tip

While discussing individual costs, it is better to calculate their percentage with the total cost.

---

**Forum development costs**

Forum development cost forms around 39% ($1.50/$3.80 x 100) of the total cost in quarter 1 and around 32% ($1.30/$4.05 x 100) in quarter 2 which is very high. Although it decreased by around 13% [($1.50 - $1.30)/$1.50 x 100] in quarter 2, it is expected to decrease further in future. In future only the running cost will exist, which will be much lower than the development cost. If we do not consider the forum development cost (being a one time cost) the performance of Concept is good.

> Remember to discuss the future effects, if any.

In addition, it can be concluded that Concept will perform better in future as the forum will bring in more and more business in the future.

*2 marks*

**Administration costs**

In quarter 2, administration costs are increased by 41.66% [($1.20 - $1.70)/$1.20 x 100] which is unusually high and alarming. Administration cost is the major cost in the total cost, constituting around 32% ($1.20/$3.80 x 100) in Quarter 1 and 42% ($1.70/$4.05 x 100) in quarter 2 (if forum cost is amortised it will be even more). The management should investigate the causes and should immediately take measures to control it.

*1 mark*

**Distribution costs**

Distribution costs amount to less than 10% ($0.35/$3.80 x 100) of the total cost and increased only by around 29% [($0.35 - $0.45)/$0.35 x 100] in quarter 2. This is significantly lower than the growth in sales. These costs seem to be well controlled.

*1 mark*

**Marketing costs**

Marketing costs are around 20% ($0.75/$3.80 x 100) in the first quarter and decreased to around 15% ($0.60/$4.05 x 100) in the quarter 2. However, as given in the question, these costs will not be high in the future, and it can be assumed that profits will increase over the period.

*1 mark*

**Conclusion**

Although Concept has not yet earned profit during the first two quarters, it can be concluded that the financial performance of Concept is good. Assuming that the forum and marketing expenses will bring in more business in the future, it can be concluded that Concept will do well in financial terms.

*1 mark*
**Maximum marks 10**

**(b) Number of inquiries converted into actual sales**

In quarter 1, around 57% (125,830 / 220,850 x 100) of the inquiries were converted into the actual sales. However in quarter 2, only around 48% (189,450 / 391,960 x 100) of enquiries were converted into sale. In spite of the decline, it is above the industry average of 45% which is good. However, the management should try to convert maximum enquiries into the actual sales.

*1 mark*

**On-time delivery**

In the first quarter, on-time delivery is 95% which is good considering that the business is in its initial stages, books are printed as and when ordered and sales are made worldwide. However, in the second quarter it has started struggling with making on-time delivery. This may lead to customers becoming dissatisfied. This may be avoided by keeping a few books in stock and entering into longer term contracts with delivery agencies.

*See score more*

*2 marks*

**Sales return**

Sales return is very rare in this industry and since this is increasing in quarter two, it should be looked into seriously. If the reason for sales return is the quality of the book, then it is a serious issue and should be considered by the management.

*1 mark*

**Customer complaints/ handling of customer complaints**

In a book, human errors are bound to happen. However, they should not be intolerable. In addition, formatting mistakes may be acceptable but technical mistakes can mislead students. Therefore, mistakes should be analysed properly and corrective action should be taken.

Although customer complaints in quarter 1 were less than the industry average, they have increased in quarter 2 and there is a chance of it increasing further. This is because students may not have finished reading the whole book (or all the books) so they could contact Concept again as and when they find mistakes.

*Do not forget to consider industry average here.*

In addition, the handling of mistakes is also very important considering the reputation of the company. An errata sheet may be made available to the students. It seems that Concept is lacking here but this should be given priority.

*2 marks*

**Forum visitors**

Within two quarters, the forum became popular considering the number of forum visitors. In quarter two it has increased by more than double. However, Concept should try to creatively convert those visitors into customers. Developing a forum shows that the management is very innovative and good at marketing. However, additional support is required for gaining business from it.

*1 mark*

Considering these teething problems, Concept is performing very well and has a good future. However, it should concentrate on certain issues such as errors in its books, and on-time delivery.

*0.5 marks*
**Maximum marks 6**

(c) Financial indicators play a key role in assessing the performance of an entity. However, not every aspect of a business activity can be expressed in terms of money; therefore, in order to assess performance using various aspects of business activities, it is necessary to consider non-financial indicators in addition to financial indicators. For example, the quality of books cannot be assessed by using financial indicators. For this, errors in books, compliment letters from students, student reviews on the book posted on the forum etc. should be used.

Accordingly, product quality, delivery, reliability, after sales service and customer satisfaction are key competitive variables for the performance measurement of an organisation. The non-financial measures of performance include measures of quality and customer satisfaction and measures of internal performance. Non-financial performance indicators include both quantitative and qualitative factors.

Financial indicators focus on short-term performance which may not be helpful in determining long-term performance. Non-financial indicators, especially quantitative indicators, allow a more detailed and finer analysis and offer explanations for financial data. For example, in the case of Concept Academy, had the information on the number of books sold been given, it would have enabled us to analyse the reason for the increase in cost of sales.

Non-financial indictors, especially qualitative ones, focus on long-term organisational performance. For example, if the quality of the books produced by Concept is very good, one can predict that it will earn a good reputation over the period and will perform very well in the long-term.

Non-financial indicators also help in determining the strength and weaknesses of an organisation which can be used for improving performance. For example, the quality of books may be a strength in Concept, but delays in reply to students' queries (may be generally or on the forum) is a weakness. This will help the management to improve in the areas of weaknesses.

Non-financial performance indicators are critical success factors and must also play a role in evaluating the performance of an organisation. However, the non-financial performance indicators given by Concept are not sufficient and more indicators such as the number of books sold and the feedback from the students should be included.

*1 mark for each point discussed*
**Maximum marks 4**

---

**Score More**

Just calculating the ratios and giving a very short explanation will get you very few marks.

For example, **on time delivery:** in the first quarter, on-time delivery is 95% as compared to 88% in the second quarter, which is good.

**Cost of Sales:** The cost of sales has been increased by 76% [($4.40 - $2.50)/$2.50 x 100] in quarter 2. In quarter 1, it was 48% ($2.50/$5.25 x 100 of sales and in quarter 2, it became 54% ($4.40/$8.20 x 100).

## 184: Performance Measurement and Control

> **Tip**
> The examiner expects you to make a qualitative assessment of each item of performance measurement. For example,
>
> **On time delivery:** just briefly commenting on the information given will only earn you one mark. But analysing why it has happened, and suggesting simple ways to improve the situation, will always get you higher marks.
>
> **Cost of Sales:** only showing the calculations for the increase in the cost of sales will earn you a mere half mark. Commenting on this increase, whether good or bad, will get you one mark! Furthermore, giving reasons (hypothetical) for such an increase, and suggesting ways to solve problems, will get you higher marks.

### 51. Divisional performance assessment and ROI - Mystique Ltd

> **Strategy**
> Part (a) – Based on the given information the most obvious measures other than ROI to be used should be the GP ratio and NP ratio. Apart from this the RI method may also be used. Make sure that you calculate each ratio to provide a basis for further discussion in the answer. The answer to the second part should contain the reasons for HOW the given measures help us assess the financial performance, and also WHY they can sometimes be misleading.
>
> Part (b) - The disadvantages of divisional performance should be related to the given case and explanations should be provided. It should also be stated how this comparison of the two stores may not be much help for planning e.g. the capital investment itself is not same, sales are different etc.

**(a)**

|  | Store A $'000 Calculations | Store A Ratio | Store B $'000 Calculations | Store B Ratio | Marks |
|---|---|---|---|---|---|
| **Calculation of ROI** $ROI = \dfrac{Profit}{Investment} \times 100$ | 75/585 x 100 | 12.82% | 50/360 x 100 | 13.88% | 1 |
| **Gross profit ratio** $GP = \dfrac{GP}{Sales} \times 100$ | 362/860 x 100 | 42.09% | 285/675 x 100 | 42.22% | 1 |
| **Net profit ratio** $NP = \dfrac{NP}{Sales} \times 100$ | 75/860 x 100 | 8.72% | 50/675 x 100 | 7.41% | 1 |
| Charge on income (Investment x Desired rate of return) | 585 x 10% | 58.50 | 360 x 10% | 36 | 1 |
| Residual income (Income – Charge on income) | 75 – 58.5 | 16.5 | 50 - 36 | 14 | 1 |

The financial performance of the stores has been assessed on the basis of ROI, gross profit ratio and net profit ratio.

> **Tip**
> Comparing direct sales is also a measure that can be used to assess financial performance apart from the above.

**Return on income**

The ROI for store B is greater at 13.88% even with a comparatively low investment. This is indicative that store B is capable of generating profits at a higher rate for Mystique, even with low investment. Hence, it should concentrate on this store for achieving higher profits.

Taking a decision based on only on ROI may be misleading. This is because ROI does not apply to long term investments but takes into consideration only short term investments.

2 marks

**Gross profit ratio**

The gross profit ratio for both the divisions is greater than 40%, which is more than the general trend of the GP ratio for Mystique i.e. 40%. Hence, both the divisions are doing well, in fact better than expected. It suggests that the trading expenses are being managed efficiently due to economies of scale being experienced from bulk purchases.

However the administrative and other operating expenses are likely to be on the higher side in the stores. Therefore considering the GP ratio as a measure of profitability may be misleading.

2 marks

**Net profit ratio**

The net profit ratio can be considered as a more appropriate measure than GP ratio for assessing financial performance in case of the stores since it reflects the profitability after incurring all operating expenses which are greater in the stores.
The net profit ratio for Store A is higher at 8.72%. However the difference in the NP ratios for both the stores is small, and hence the operating expenses are more or less similar for both the stores. The difference in the gross profit and the net profit is 33.37% for store A and 34.81% for store B. This again suggests that these stores spend similar amounts in percentage terms on operating expenses.

*Important to explain NP ratio since Mystique operates through stores that have high operating expenses*

Both the stores are located in the same city, but at different locations. The operating expenses and demand conditions at these locations may have an impact on the operating expenses. The difference of 1.31% between these ratios may be attributed to this reason.

The investment made in the stores is completely ignored in the calculation of the NP ratio. Hence it cannot be considered as a good measure for financial performance.

2 marks

**Residual income**

The residual income method provides you with the absolute values for income that you earn from an investment, compared to the standard expected rate of return. Hence, this shows that the stores are actually earning $16,500 for store A and $14,000 for store B more than what we expect to earn from our investment.

However comparing absolute values is not a good measure to assess divisional performance as it neither considers the investment made in the stores nor the size of operations.

In order to judge the performance of a division, a set of performance parameters have to be considered together rather than depending on one specific ratio in isolation.

2 marks

**Maximum marks 13**

**(b)** The performance evaluation of divisions or stores is usually done on the basis of predetermined standards, budgets or plans. However, performance of divisions can also be done with the help of other measures like return on investment (ROI), residual income (RI), etc. These are then compared among divisions to analyse their efficiency / inefficiency and to take corrective action accordingly.

*1 mark*

However, there are some issues in adopting this method:

### 1. Selecting the correct measure

There are a number of measures / tools that can be used to analyse performance of divisions. A few measures are based on profitability while others are on quality or quantity. Selection of the right tool is essential for reaching the correct conclusions. For example, the net profit ratio only considers the profitability and does not take into consideration the amount of investment in the firm. In the above case however it has proved to be a fairly accurate measure since Mystique operates through stores.

*1 mark*

### 2. Different working conditions

Each division faces a different working condition. The performance varies in these conditions. Some of them are:

**Work culture**

It does not simply vary among different organisations, but can also vary among divisions. These differences have an effect on the performance of the division. For example, Mystique's Store A might have an informal work culture whereas, Store B might have a more formal work culture. This also depends to a great extent on the approach of store management and the store managers.

**Geographical location**

This can again affect the amount of sales at each of these stores. Each of these, either individually or collectively affect the performance of the division. In the case of Mystique Ltd, one reason why Store A has higher sales than Store B, could be that people prefer to make their electronic purchases around Trafalgar Square rather than Oxford Street.

**Investment**

The amount of investment plays a huge role in the firm's profitability. In the case of Mystique this could mean investment in setting up a store with the appropriate ambience, the infrastructure for display etc. In the case of Store A the investment is higher as opposed to store B. This may be linked to their higher revenue. The demography of the location where the store is located also plays a vital role in investment decisions.

*3 marks*

### 3. Scale of operations

Before comparing divisional performance allowance should be given to the difference in their size of operations. If the scale of the operations is not similar, then the conclusion thus achieved does not hold value. For example, if Store A is operating at a relatively larger scale as compared to Store B, then it would hold a higher bargaining power in the external world. This can affect the profitability ratios.

*1 mark*

### 4. Transfer pricing difficulties

This plays a key role in evaluating a division's performance. Although information on internal transfers is not given in the question it may happen that one of the stores requires some products at short notice and cannot receive them from the centralised warehouse. In such case the decision on transfer price may affect divisional performance.

*1 mark*

### 5. Different regulations

If different divisions are located in different cities or countries, the rules and regulations applicable might differ. Hence, this will directly influence the functioning and performance of a division. This might not hold true in the case of Store A and Store B as they are located in the same city.

*1 mark*
**Maximum marks 7**

## 52. Transfer pricing and external considerations in performance measurement – Elegant Ltd

**Strategy**

This question contains two sub-questions (a) and (b).

Sub-question (a) is a combination of calculations and analytical discussions and contains two requirements:

- whether to sell 4,000 units internally or sell all 12,500 units externally; and
- behavioural issues if it decides to sell internally.

In order to make the decision, profitability from Graceful's product (when sold externally and when sold internally) should be calculated and compared.

Remember that the second requirement does not depend on Elegant's decision. Even if Elegant decides not to sell internally, the issues arising from internal transfer need to be discussed.

Sub-question (b) is theory based. However, for such questions it is advisable to relate the answer with the case given. If it is not possible then general examples can be given to show the examiner that you understand the concept. This will help you earn higher marks.

---

**(a) Profit earned by Graceful if sales are made externally**

|  | (Per unit) $ | Marks |
|---|---|---|
| Selling price (a) | 95.00 | 0.5 |
| Variable costs |  |  |
| Direct materials | 44.00 | 0.5 |
| Direct wages | 15.00 | 0.5 |
| Variable overheads (W1) | 10.00 | 1 |
|  | 69.00 | 0.5 |
| Fixed overheads (W2) | 5.60 | 1 |
| Total Cost (b) | (74.60) | 0.5 |
| **Profit** (a - b) | **20.40** | 0.5 |

Total profit = $20.40 per unit x 12,500 units
 = $255,000

0.5 marks

*It is always better to give workings. This is because even if you make a mistake while carrying the figure to the main answer, you will get marks for the workings.*

**Workings Notes:**

**W1**

$125,000 variable overheads for 12,500 production hours; therefore absorption rate is $10 for Graceful division.

0.5 marks

**W2**

The remaining $70,000 ($195,000 - $125,000) are fixed overheads for 12,500 production hours; therefore absorption rate is $5.60 for Graceful division.

0.5 marks

Per unit profit earned by Graceful if sales are made internally = 25% x total cost
 = 25% x $74.60
 = $18.65

1 mark

Stylish division will make a profit of $5.75 ($120 - $114.25) on the product by selling it for $120 per unit and after incurring total cost of $114.25 ($74.60 + $18.65 + $21).

1 mark

Therefore, the total profit from the product will be $24.40 ($18.65 earned by Graceful and $5.75 earned by the transferee division). From Elegant's perspective it is beneficial to work further on the product and then sell it in the market since it earns a total profit of $ 271,000 [(8,500 units x $20.40) + (4,000 units x $24.40)]. Therefore, Graceful should transfer 4,000 units internally instead of selling in the external market.

2 marks

*Remember, $24.40 profit is only for 4,000 units.*

However, the manager of Graceful division may not be happy with the decision of selling internally. This is because selling internally will affect the performance of the division and he will lose the profit by $1.75 ($20.40 - $18.65) per unit for 4,000 units.

*1 mark*

In addition, according to the bonus policy, the manager of Graceful will get a bonus only if his profit exceeds the target of $250,000. If he sells in the external market he is exceeding the target by $5,000 ($255,000 - $250,000) and eligible for the bonus. However, due to company policy he will have to sell internally and earn a profit of $ 248,000 [($20.40 x 8500 units) + ($18.65 x 4,000 units)] which is below the target. This may de-motivate the manager of Graceful.

> Do not forget to discuss bonus policy while discussing behavioural issues.

*2 marks*
**Maximum marks 12**

**(b)** The performance of an entity / division cannot be measured effectively based on internal parameters in isolation.

An effective performance management system is one that allows external considerations such as market conditions and existence of competitors.

Not all entities in an industry or divisions work in the same environment. They work under different political, economical, technological, environmental, legal and socio-economical environments. In addition, competitors, customers, suppliers etc also have an impact on the performance of an entity / division.

*1 mark*

Two divisions of Elegant, Stylish and Classy are working in two different countries. Therefore it is not advisable to assess their performance without considering the environment in which they are working.

**Reputation**

The product or Elegant may be well known in one country and not so well-known in another country. As a result, a division where the product / Elegant is known will get advantage of it over another division.

> This is how the discussion can be related to the given case.

*1 mark*

**Competition**

A division may be facing acute local competition and another division may not be facing competition to such an extent. In this case also the division which has less or no competition will gain advantage over the other division.

*1 mark*

**Availability of raw material / labour at a lower rate**

The availability of the raw material and labour will also influence the performance of the division. If inputs are available at a lower rate, the division will get the cost benefit and will definitely earn good profit.

*1 mark*

**Government policies**

Government policies such as taxation policies, fiscal policies etc. have an impact on the performance of the entity. For example, in a country liquor may be prohibited in some parts, whereas in another country there may not be such a restriction. As a result the market size / target customers will vary.

> Since the product in which Elegant deals is not known, general examples can be given to explain the point.

*1 mark*

**Socio-cultural environment**

The population of a country, demographic pattern, overall societal trends etc. also affect the performance of an entity. For example, in countries where both parents work, there is a need for day-care facilities for kids etc.

*1 mark*

**Technology**

A country may be more technologically advanced than another country. If Stylish and Classy's product is a technology based product, then it may have more demand in a country which is more technologically advanced than the other. However, it may be other way around too, i.e. a country which is technologically advanced may have a more advanced product (with advanced features) than that of Elegant. In such a case, the division in that country will suffer.

*1 mark*

© GTG
Solution Bank: 189

### Economic conditions

If the economy of a country is developing very fast, it will be beneficial for the division working in that country.

1 mark

### Legal and environmental

In some countries there are strict regulations regarding the environment. For example, in the UK, the Climate Change Levy has been in force since 20X1. If one of the divisions is working in such countries, it will have to bear more cost and this will affect its performance. In addition, certain products, say tobacco / tobacco based products are banned, and this prohibition affects the performance of the entity.

1 mark

> Do not forget to give a conclusion since it carries marks.

From the above discussion, it is clear that there are several external factors which have an impact on the performance of an entity. Therefore, Robert's view is correct and performance should not be assessed in isolation. However, this does not mean that inter-division comparison should not be made at all. Inter-division comparison is a good measure and should be adopted but allowance should be made for external considerations.

1 mark
**Maximum marks 8**

## 53. Return on investment – Smart Mart

### Strategy

This question is divided in two sub-questions. In sub-question (a) a lot of calculations are required. Therefore it is necessary to spend some time on deciding the presentation. The presentation should be concise and simple to understand. Do not forget to calculate the average for the fours years, and also to give your opinion on whether to open a new division.

Sub-question (b) is a theoretical question, but in order to score good marks, you should relate it to Smart Mart.

### (a) Estimated performance statement for four years

|  | Year 1 | Year 2 | Year 3 | Year 4 | Marks |
|---|---|---|---|---|---|
| Sales volume (W1) | 30,000 | 28,500 | 28,500 | 27,075 | 1 |
|  | $ | $ | $ | $ |  |
| Sales price per unit (W2) | 30 | 33 | 31.35 | 31.35 | 1 |
| Revenue | 900,000 | 940,500 | 893,475 | 848,801 | 1 |
| Direct costs (W3) | (540,000) | (513,000) | (513,000) | (487,350) | 1.5 |
| Gross profit | 360,000 | 427,500 | 380,475 | 361,451 | 1 |
| Indirect expenses | (150,000) | (200,000) | (200,000) | (200,000) | 0.5 |
| Depreciation (W4) | (150,000) | (150,000) | (150,000) | (150,000) | 0.5 |
| Net profit | 50,000 | 77,500 | 30,475 | 11,451 | 1 |

> As gross profit will vary with the change in sales value, it will not remain 40% for the years two, three and four.

> **Tip** Do not forget to calculate the cost of sales for each year, as it varies with the change in sales volume. In order to calculate the cost of sales, for the subsequent year, calculate per unit cost based on the information given for the first year. For further details see W3.

Average Gross profit = $360,000 + $427,500 + $380,475 + $361,451
= $1,529,426 / 4 years
= $382,356.50

> ROI can also be calculated as
> = Return on sales x Asset turnover

1 mark

Average Net profit = $50,000 + $77,500 + $30,475 + $11,451
= $169,426 / 4 years
= $42,356.50

1 mark

**190: Performance Measurement and Control** © GTG

$$ROI = \frac{Profit}{Average\ investment}$$

Average investment is the average assets employed, which is calculated as follows:

$$Average\ assets\ employed = \frac{Assets\ at\ the\ beginning\ of\ the\ year + Assets\ at\ the\ end\ of\ the\ year}{2}$$

Year 1 = $50,000/[($600,000 + $450,000)/2]
= 9.52%

0.5 marks

Year 2 = $77,500/[($450,000 + $300,000)/2]
= 20.66%

0.5 marks

Year 3 = $30,475/[($300,000 + $150,000)/2]
= 13.54%

0.5 marks

Year 4 = $11,451/[($150,000 + $0)/2]
= 15.27%

0.5 marks

Average ROI = (9.52% + 20.66% + 13.54% + 15.27%)/4
= 14.75%

0.5 marks

**Conclusion**

*Do not forget to give a conclusion; otherwise you will lose the allotted marks!*

|  | Estimated average for the first four years | Benchmark |
|---|---|---|
| Gross profit | $382,356.50 i.e. $3.82m | $3 m |
| Net profit | $42,356.50 i.e. $0.42 m | $0.50 m |
| ROI | 14.75% | 15% |

*See Score More*

The above table shows that gross profit and net profit are more than the benchmark; therefore acceptance of the project can be suggested. The estimated ROI for the first four years is slightly less than the benchmark; however the difference is so negligible that Neil may decide to open the new division.

1 mark

**Score More**

If, instead of giving the comparison for conclusion, it is simply given in sentences, e.g. average gross profit for the first four years is $382,356.50 i.e. $3.82m against the benchmark of $3m, average net profit for the first four years is $42,356.50 i.e. $0.42 m against the benchmark of $0.40m etc, the answer will not be incorrect, but it will be badly constructed. The presentation should be concise and simple.

**Workings**

**W1 Sales volume**

Year 2 = 30,000 units – (30,000 x 5%)
= 28,500 units

0.5 marks

Year 4 = 28,500 units – (28,500 units x 5%)
= 27,075 units

0.5 marks

**W2 Sales price**

Year 2 = $30 + ($30 x 10%)
= $33

0.5 marks

Year 3 = $33 – ($33 x 5%)
= $31.35

0.5 marks

### W3 Cost of sales

It is given that gross profit in the first year is 40%. This means that the cost of sales is 60% in the first year which comes to $540,000 ($900,000 x 60%).

Direct costs per unit will remain constant which, in the first year is $18 ($540,000/30,000 units).

0.5 marks

Therefore, cost of sales in

Year 2 and 3 = $18 x 28,500 units
= $513,000

0.5 marks

Year 4 = $18 x 27,075 units
= $487,350

0.5 marks

### W4 Depreciation

Investment of $400,000 to be depreciated over four years comes to $100,000 ($400,000 / 4 years)

0.5 marks
**Maximum marks 12**

### (b) Advantages of ROI

#### (i) Versatility

When calculating ROI, various aspects such as revenues and costs as well as investments are considered. It is therefore more logical to evaluate the performance of divisions using ROI.

1 mark

#### (ii) Comparability

Since ROI considers the investment made in the division, it provides better comparability of various divisions of different sizes. As a result it is widely used for assessing divisional performance

1 mark

#### (iii) Flexibility

ROI can be modified in accordance with the circumstances.

1 mark

#### (iv) Simplicity

It is very simple to calculate. All the required figures can be taken from the financial records.

1 mark

#### (v) Expressed in percentage

Unlike other measures such as residual income, gross profit and net profit, ROI is expressed in percentage terms and not in absolute terms. Therefore it calculates the relative profitability and provides good comparability.

1 mark

### Disadvantages of ROI

#### (i) Ignores time value of money

ROI ignores the time value for money. The value of money changes over time. For example, the value of a dollar / pound today is different from the value of a dollar / pound tomorrow, or what it was two years ago. Therefore, the purchasing power of the unit of money undergoes a change.

In the case of Smart Mart, Neil has to decide whether to open a new division, if Neil decides to take the decision only on the basis of ROI, it may result in taking the wrong decision. In addition, all the measures used by Neil, such as gross profit, bet profit and ROI do not consider the time value for money. He should have at least one benchmark such as NPV, to help him decide whether or not to open a new division.

*This is how a theoretical answer can be related to the given case study.*

1 mark

### (ii) Ignores risk associated with the project

ROI also ignores the risks associated with the project. The more the return, the more is the risk. ROI considers only high return and not the risk associated with the product. It is very important for Neil to consider the risk associated with opening a new division, considering the ROI calculated is already just below the benchmark.

*1 mark*

### (iii) Inconsistency

ROI can be modified to fit the situation. This may be a disadvantage, as the flexibility can be used to manipulate the results. For example, the terms income and investment can be interpreted in various ways. Income may be taken as before or after interest and tax. Similarly, investment may be considered as the net value of assets, or the gross value of assets. Therefore, Neil needs to critically asses the base for calculation of the ROI.

*1 mark*

### (iv) Short-term analysis

The calculation of ROI only considers short-term investments. Long-term costs such as maintenance, upgrades etc. are ignored.

*1 mark*

### (v) Variation in calculations

If performance of the divisions is evaluated, based on ROI, and if the policies (such as depreciation) of all the divisions of Smart Mart are different, it will be difficult to compare the performance of one division with another. The decision of whether to open a new branch cannot be taken.

*1 mark*
**Maximum marks 8**

## 54. Performance management - Lavender

**Strategy**

This question consists of two parts. Part (a) is discursive, and requires you to assess the financial performance of Lavender. The actual and targeted financial information given is for a different number of units. This may be overlooked, so read the question carefully.

Part (b) has two requirements. One is based on calculations while the other involves discussions based on the calculations. Be careful while calculating the profit for the initial forecast, as the estimated profit under different strategies is based on it.

After calculating the estimated profit under the initial forecast as well as under all the strategies, you need to evaluate each strategy separately, and deduce which strategy will be the most beneficial to Lavender under the current conditions, as well as under a long term view.

### (a) Financial performance of Lavender

**Sales**

The number of units sold in 20X8 is less than the target by 3.33% [(150,000–145,000)/150,000 x 100]. The sales for the year are also lower by 3.33%, as the selling price per unit, $900 ($135.00m/150,000 units) or ($130.5m/145,000 units), is constant. It shows that demand for the product has probably gone down compared to the year when the target was decided. Although the decrease is negligible, this may be the beginning of a trend of decreasing demand.

*2 marks*

> **Tip** Since the number of units actually sold is less than the targeted amount, it is meaningless to compare the actual costs of the individual items of variable cost with the targeted costs given. For example, if we compare the targeted material and labour costs, $47.50m, (for 150,000 units) to the actual material and labour costs, $46.40m (for 145,000 units), it will not show the true picture. Therefore targeted costs for 145,000 units should be calculated and compared with the actual costs. (Refer W1)

© GTG                                                                                                                                    Solution Bank: 193

**Material and labour costs**

Material and labour cost is more than the targeted amount by 1.08% (W1). This may be due to the following:

- increase in the material and labour rates
- increase in idle time
- increase in material wastage

2 marks

**Assembly and distribution costs**

Assembly costs show an increase if compared to the targeted amount, by 0.68% (W1). Distribution costs also show an increase by around 1.43% (W1).

The total variable costs increased by 0.99%. It can be said that all variable costs have increased. The causes need to be looked into, and steps taken to control the costs. Although all the variable costs show an increase, the increase is not significant. The estimated or targeted cost figures are very close to the actual. This shows that the management has set achievable targets.

2 marks

**Fixed costs**

Although there is no change in the total fixed costs, it has an impact on the profit for the period. This is because, the per unit fixed cost increases with a decrease in the sales volume. This means that if 150,000 units were sold, the fixed cost per unit would be $ 353.33 ($53.00m/150,000 units). However, since only 145,000 units were sold, the per unit fixed costs is $365.52 ($53.00m/145,000 units).

1 mark

> **Tip** Since fixed costs remain constant for a period irrespective of change in the sales volume, there is no need to calculate proportionate fixed costs for the targeted sales.

The overall financial performance of Lavender is not encouraging. Sales are going down, and costs are increasing. Unless the company takes proactive steps to improve the performance, the future viability does not appear promising.

1 mark
**Maximum marks 6**

**Working**

**W1 Increase / Decrease in costs**

> Targeted costs for 150,000 units are given. Remember to calculate the targeted costs for 145,000 units, before comparing them with the actual costs.

|  | Targeted for 150,000 units $m | Targeted for 145,000 units $m | Actual $m | Increase/ Decrease $m | Increase/ Decrease % |
|---|---|---|---|---|---|
| Material and Labour | 47.50 | 45.90 (145,000/150,000 x 47.5) | 46.40 | 0.5 increase | Increase by 1.08% (0.5/45.9 x 100) |
| Assembly | 15.00 | 14.50 (145,000/150,000 x 15) | 14.60 | 0.1 increase | Increase by 0.68% (0.1/14.50 x 100) |
| Distribution | 5.00 | 4.83 (145,000/150,000 x 5) | 4.90 | 0.07 increase | Increase by 1.43% (0.07/4.83 x 100) |
| Total Variable costs | 67.50 | 65.25 (145,000/150,000 x 67.5) | 65.90 | 0.65 increase | Increase by 0.99% (0.65/65.25 x 100) |

## 194: Performance Measurement and Control

**(b) Estimated profit for 20X9**

|  | Initial forecast | Strategy 1 | Strategy 2 | Strategy 3 |
|---|---|---|---|---|
| Sales volume (**W1**) | 150,000.00 | 160,500.00 | 150,000.00 | 150,000.00 |
| Selling price (**W1**) | 900.00 | 855.00 | 950.00 | 900.00 |
|  | $'m | $'m | $'m | $'m |
| Sales revenue | 135.00 | 137.23 | 142.50 | 135.00 |
| **Costs:** |  |  |  |  |
| Variable cost |  |  |  |  |
| Material and labour (**W2**) | 50.40 | 50.40 | 51.41 | 50.40 |
| Assembly | 15.10 | 15.10 | 15.10 | 15.10 |
| Distribution | 5.07 | 5.07 | 5.07 | 5.07 |
| Strategy 3 (cost reduction) (**W3**) |  |  |  | (10.59) |
| Total variable cost | 70.57 | 70.57 | 71.58 | 59.98 |
| Fixed costs |  |  |  |  |
| Assembly | 41.00 | 41.00 | 41.00 | 41.00 |
| Distribution | 11.00 | 11.00 | 11.00 | 11.00 |
| Administration | 1.10 | 1.10 | 1.10 | 1.10 |
| Design cost – Strategy 2 ($20m / 4 years) |  |  | 5.00 |  |
| Cost reduction technique – Strategy 3 ($50m / 5 years) |  |  |  | 10.00 |
|  | 53.10 | 53.10 | 58.10 | 63.10 |
| Total cost | (123.67) | (123.67) | (129.68) | (123.08) |
| **Profit** | **11.33** | **13.56** | **12.82** | **11.92** |
| Marks | 4 | 2 | 2 | 2 |

> For strategy 3, there will be no change in the sales volume and selling price

> The administration cost according to the initial forecast $1.10 ($1.00m + $0.10m) will remain the same under all the strategies.

**Workings**

**W1 Sales volume and price under Strategy 1**

|  | $ |
|---|---|
| Estimated selling price | 900 |
| Less: Reduced by 5% ($900 x 5 / 100) | (45) |
| Selling price per unit under strategy 1 | 855 |
|  | **Units** |
| Initial target for sales volume | 150,000 |
| Add: Resulting increase by 7% (150,000 units x 7 / 100) | 10,500 |
| Increased sales volume under Strategy 1 | 160,500 |

**W2 Material and labour cost under initial forecast**

|  | $ |
|---|---|
| Material and labour cost per unit in 20X8 ($46.40 / 145,000 units) | 320.00 |
| Add: 5% increase [320 x 5/100] | 16.00 |
| Forecasted material and labour rate for 20X9 | 336.00 |
| Sales volume (units) | 150,000 |
| Total material and labour cost | 50.40m |

**Material and labour cost under Strategy 2**

|  | $ |
|---|---|
| Material and labour cost per unit in 20X8 ($46.40 / 145,000 units) | 320.00 |
| Add: 5% increase [320 x 5/100] | 16.00 |
| Forecasted material and labour rate for 20X9 | 336.00 |
| Add: 2% increase under strategy 2 ($336 x 2/100) | 6.72 |
| Material and labour rate for strategy 2 | 342.72 |
| Sales volume (units) | 150,000 |
| Total material and labour cost | 51.41m |

**W3 Variable costs under Strategy 3**

|  | $m |
|---|---|
| Total variable costs according to the initial forecast: |  |
| Material and labour | 50.40 |
| Assembly | 15.10 |
| Distribution | 5.07 |
|  | 70.57 |
| Reduction by 15% ($70.57 x 15 / 100) | 10.59 |

**Strategy 1**

In strategy 1, the selling price decreased by 5% of the price in 20X8. This resulted in an increasing of demand by 7%. The above table of estimated profit shows that this strategy will earn maximum profit [i.e. $2.23 ($13.56-$11.33) over the forecasted profit] as compared to the other strategies. However in the long-term, it may not be possible to decrease the selling price as material and cost is increasing. As a result, this strategy may not be profitable in the long-term.

In addition, demand has increased by 7% in response to the decrease in the selling price. However, in the long-term, demand may fall below 160,500. Reasons for this could be bikes with additional features introduced by the competitors, a change in the mind set of the customers (they may be willing to spend more for a bike with good features).

1.5 marks

**Strategy 2**

Adding a feature in a product is a good strategy considering the following:

- It gives a competitive advantage.
- Customers prefer a company that updates its product from time to time.
- The profit will increase by $1.49 ($12.82 - $11.33), over the profit forecasted for 20X9.

However, the only concern in the long-run will be that the competitors may also introduce the feature in their product (if the feature becomes successful) after which this strategy will not work.

1.5 marks

**Strategy 3**

In strategy 3, Lavender is planning to purchase a cost-reduction technique. Although, when compared with the results of other strategies, it is found that an increase in profit from the strategy is lower than the others [i.e. just $0.59 ($11.91-$11.33)]. However it can be used over a longer period of time. The technique may be helpful to control the cost and therefore beneficial in the long-term.

1.5 marks
**Maximum marks 14**

## 55. Performance measurement – Pace Co

### Strategy

Part (a) requires an assessment of the performance of a store over a four year period with specific requirements to refer to ROI as a method of assessment. You are also asked to consider how performance could be manipulated along with some calculations on the performance of another store.

Part (b) specifically needs to be presented in a columnar form. Here, you need to calculate forecasted profits for the next four years.

In part (c) you need to calculate the volume of sales required based on the ROI.

---

**(a)** In order to assess the performance of store W, following measures of performance can be used.

|  | 2005 | 2006 | 2007 | 2008 |
|---|---|---|---|---|
| ROI (W1) | 13% | 17.5% | 16.7% | 20% |
| Sales growth (W2) |  | 0% | -10% | -5.6% |
| Gross profit ratio (W3) | 40% | 35% | 35% | 30% |
| Net profit ratio (W4) | 6.5% | 7% | 5.6% | 4.7% |
| Overheads (GP – NP) | $67,000 | $56,000 | $53,000 | $43,000 |
| Bonus paid (W5) | no | yes | yes | yes |

2 marks

**Gross profit ratio**

The gross profit ratio has been reducing over the last 4 years. This may be the result of sales price pressure or increase in the cost of sales. The cost of sales may rise due to increase in material prices or labour expenses. Store W has achieved the normal gross profit margin of 40% only once (in 2005) during the last four years, hence it can be concluded that its performance is below expectations.

> Remember to consider this clue which is given in the question, for assessing W's performance.

1.5 marks

**Net profit ratio**

The net profit ratio is a more appropriate measure than GP ratio for assessing the financial performance. It reflects the profitability after incurring the operating expenses. The net profit margin of store W has been falling over the given period of time as a result of fall in the gross profit margin. This indicates poor performance of the store.

1.5 marks

**Sales growth**

It is stated that PC operates in a market which has been growing steadily. However, the sales of the company have been reducing over the last four years. The sales growth rate is -10% and -5.6% in 2007 and 2008 respectively, which highlights the inefficient performance of the store. The negative sales growth rate may be because of poor volumes or poor prices of products.

1.5 marks

**Overheads**

The company has exercised good control over overheads as they have been decreasing over the last four years. However, the reduction in overheads may be the reason for poor sales.

1 mark

**ROI**

The ROI has been impressive during the last four years. Store W has ROI exceeding the target (15%) in all the given years except in the year 2005. This is simply because of reduction in the assets as depreciation is charged. Moreover, ROI has been increasing in spite of a decrease in profit margins. This indicates the assets employed are efficiently utilised to generate profits.

> Don't forget to state that ROI is rising as the book value of assets is reducing due to depreciation.

1.5 marks

### Bonus

Bonus is paid in the year when the ROI exceeds the target. The bonus is paid in all the given years except in the year 2005. This means that the store has successfully achieved the targets in most of the years.

0.5 marks

### Conclusion

The rising ROI does not reflect the true performance of store W. This is because sales are falling even though the market is growing, the GP ratio is below the normal level and NP is also falling.

0.5 marks

### W1 ROI

$$ROI = \frac{Profit}{Net\ asset} \times 100$$

**2005**
$$ROI = \frac{\$13,000}{\$100,000} \times 100 = 13\%$$

**2006**
$$ROI = \frac{\$14,000}{\$80,000} \times 100 = 17.5\%$$

ROI for 2007 and 2008 is to be calculated in the same manner.

1 mark

### W2 Sales growth rate

$$2005 = \frac{\$180,000 - \$200,000}{\$200,000} \times 100 = -10\%$$

$$2006 = \frac{\$170,000 - \$180,000}{\$180,000} \times 100 = -5.6\%$$

1 mark

### W3 Gross profit (GP) ratio

$$GP = \frac{GP}{Sales} \times 100$$

$$2005\ GP = \frac{\$80,000}{\$200,000} \times 100 = 40\% \quad 2006\ GP = \frac{\$70,000}{\$200,000} \times 100 = 35\%$$

The gross profit ratio for 2007 and 2008 is to be calculated in the same manner.

1 mark

### W4 Net profit (NP) ratio

$$NP = \frac{NP}{Sales} \times 100$$

$$2005\ NP = \frac{\$13,000}{\$200,000} \times 100 = 6.5\% \quad 2006\ NP = \frac{\$14,000}{\$200,000} \times 100 = 7\%$$

The net profit ratio for 2007 and 2008 is to be calculated in the same manner.

1 mark

### W5 Bonus

Bonus is paid to store managers if annual ROI exceeds the target. Target has been achieved in 2006, 2007 and 2008 and hence bonus is paid during these years.

0.5 marks
**Maximum marks 9**

**(b) Estimated performance statement for four years**

|  | 2009 | 2010 | 2011 | 2012 |
|---|---|---|---|---|
| Sales volume (W1) (in units) | 18,000 | 10,800 | 21,700 | 21,780 |
|  | $ | $ | $ | $ |
| Sales revenue (W2) | 216,000 | 237,600 | 248,292 | 235,877 |
| Gross profit (W3) | 86,400 | 95,040 | 91,476 | 79,061 |
| Overheads | 70,000 | 70,000 | 80,000 | 80,000 |
| Net profit (GP – overheads) | 16,400 | 25,040 | 11,476 | (939) |
| Net Investment (investment – depreciation) | 100,000 | 75,000 | 50,000 | 25,000 |
| ROI (NP/investment) | 16.4% | 33.39% | 22.95% | -3.8% |

4 marks

**Workings**

**W1 Sales volume**

2009 = 18,000
2010 = 18,000 + (18,000 x 10%) = 19,800
2011 = 19,800 + (19,800 x 10%) = 21,780
2012 = 19,800 + (19,800 x 10%) = 21,780

2 marks

**W2 Sales revenue**

2009 = 18,000 x $12 = $216,000
2010 = 19,800 x $12 = $237,600
2011 = 21,780 x [$12 – ($12 x 5%)] = $248,292
2012 = 21,780 x [$11.4 – ($11.4 x 5%)] = $235,877

2 marks

**W3 Gross profit**

2009 = $216,000 x 40% = 86,400
2010 = $237,600 x 40% = $95,040
2011 = $248,292 x (40 – 5/0.95) = $91,476
2012 = $235,877 x (40 – 5 - 4.75)/100(0.95)(0.95) = $79,061

2 marks
**Maximum marks 8**

**(c)** Bonus is paid if the target of 15% ROI is achieved in 2012.

This requires net profit of $3,750 ($25,000 x 15%)
Gross profit = $3,750 + 80,000 (overheads) = $83,750

1 mark

Sales = gross profit/gross profit margin
= $83,750/33.518% = $249,866

1 mark

The selling price = $10.83 ($235,877/21,780 (W1))
Sales volume = 23,072 units ($249,866/$10.83)

1 mark
**Maximum marks 3**

**Score More**

You should avoid the following mistakes to score more:
1. Concentration on only one or two measurements when more than those are possible.
2. Commenting on increase or decrease in ratios while assessing the performance. You should comment on the reason for the increase or decrease rather than stating how much it has changed.

## 56. Non-financial performance indicators – Ties Only

### Strategy

This question requires qualitative assessment of the financial performance in part (a) and non-financial performance in part (b). Along with calculation for performance measurement, you need to give qualitative comments on them. This question is similar to question 4 given in the Pilot Paper.

---

In order to assess the financial performance of Ties Only, it is necessary to discuss changes in the sales, various costs and profits.

### Sales

Ties Only has made a good start with sales revenue of $420,000 in the first quarter. The sales have risen to $680,000 giving a growth rate of 62% [($680,000 - $420,000)/$420,000 x 100]. Hence, Ties Only has performed well inspite of being new in this competitive industry. This shows the competence of management and the marketing department.

*1 mark*

### Cost of sales

The cost of sales has increased by 69% [($340,680 - $201,600)/$201,600 x 100] in quarter 2. In quarter 1, the cost of sales was around 48% [($201,600/$420,000) x 100] of the sales in quarter 1. It increased to 50% [($340,680/$680,000) x 100] in quarter 2, which is not good. The reason for the increase in the cost of sales to sales ratio could be a decrease in the selling price due to pressure from competitors. As a result, sales in the second quarter would have been made at a price lower than the price in quarter 1.

*1.5 marks*

### Gross profit

The gross profit of the company has declined by two points. It was 52% ($218,400/$420,000) in quarter 1 and 50% [($339,320/$680,000) x100] in quarter 2. The decline in gross profit margin should be taken into consideration seriously in order to avoid the same reduction in future. The fall in gross profit may be due to price pressure in the competitive market. Ties Only may have reduced the pricing terms to compete and this may have affected the gross profit margin. Another reason for the fall in gross profit margin may be the increase in costs. As the sales have increased rapidly, the company may have purchased material at a high price in order to satisfy the demand.

*2 marks*

### Website development

Website development cost forms around 34% [($120,000/$351,263) x 100] of the total cost in quarter 1 and around 23% [($90,000/$394,760) x 100] in quarter 2 which is very high. Although it decreased by around 25% [($90,000 - $120,000)/$120,000] in quarter 2, it is expected to decrease further in future. This is because in future only the running cost will exist, which will be much lower than the development cost. If we do not consider the development cost (being a one time cost) the performance of Ties Only is good.

> Remember to consider the future effects.

*1.5 marks*

### Administration costs

Administrative costs have increased by 50% [($150,640 – $100,500)/$100,500 x 100] in quarter 2, which is unusually high and alarming. Administration cost is a major portion of the total cost, constituting around 29% [($100,500/$351,263) x 100] in quarter 1 and 38% [($150,640/$394,760) x 100] in quarter 2. The management should investigate the causes and should immediately take action to control it.

*1 mark*

### Distribution costs

The distribution cost is a relatively small cost compared to other costs and the proportion of this cost to sales is 4.9% (distribution cost/sales) which is constant in both the quarters. These costs seem to be well controlled.

*1 mark*

### Launch marketing costs

Launch marketing cost amounts to 14% [($60,000/420,000) x 100] of sales in quarter 1. This has decreased to 6% [($40,800/$680,000) x 100] in quarter 2. Launch marketing cost will continue to decrease and will be replaced by general marketing over time. Launch marketing is more expensive compared to general marketing and hence the profits will improve in the long term.

*1.5 marks*

## 200: Performance Measurement and Control

**Other costs**

Other costs are under control as they depend upon the volume of production.

1 mark

**Conclusion**

Although Ties Only has not yet earned profit during the first two quarters, it can be concluded that the financial performance of the company is good. Assuming that the website development and marketing expenses will bring more business in the future, it can be concluded that Ties Only will do well in financial terms.

2 marks

**Maximum marks 12**

### (b) Assessment of business using non-financial indicators

**Website hits**

Ties Only is a new business and operates in a competitive market. In spite of this, it has achieved a growth rate of 25% [($863,492 -$690,789)/ $690,789 x 100] in website hits within a short period. Considering this, it can be said that it has had an impressive start. If the same growth rate continues, the website hits would be over 1.3 million in the last quarter of the year.

1.5 marks

**Number of ties sold**

The conversion rate in quarter 1 is 4% [($27,631/$690,789) x 100] which has increased to 4.5% [(38,857/$863,492) x 100] in quarter 2. Conversion rates in both the quarters are higher than the industry average conversion rate (3.2%). This proves that the company is competitive.

The average price for the ties can be calculated as follows:

Quarter 1 = $420,000/27,631 = $15.20 per tie
Quarter 2 = $680,000/38,857 = $17.50 per tie

This shows that the sales price does not have much impact on gross profit, and hence the reason for fall in the gross profit must be something other than this.

2 marks

**On time delivery**

In the first quarter, on-time delivery was 95% which is impressive, considering that the business was in its initial stages. However, in the second quarter the company has started struggling with making on-time delivery. This is only 89% in quarter 2. This may lead to customer dissatisfaction. Ties Only needs to take serious action to avoid delay in delivery.

1.5 marks

**Sales returns**

Sales returns are common in this industry. The rate of sales returns has increased to 18% in quarter 2, which is above the industry average (13%). It shows that the performance of the company is declining. Delivery of wrong or damaged goods would increase the customer dissatisfaction. If the reason for sales return is the quality of the product, then it is a serious issue and should be considered by management.

1.5 marks

**System downtime**

System downtime has increased to 4% in quarter 2 compared to quarter 1, which adversely affects online sales. If this problem continues, the company might lose the online customers in the long term. The reason for system downtime may be insufficient investment at the time of development of the site or heavy pressure on the site due to an increase in customers.

1.5 marks

Considering all the above indicators, Ties Only is performing well and growing fast. However, it needs to solve the issues related to delivery, website and quality of the product.

1 mark

**Maximum marks 8**

**Score More**

This question typically asks you to comment on the financial and non-financial performance of the company.

If you give only suggestions for improving performance, you will lose marks.

# FORMULAE SHEET

**Learning curve**

$Y = ax^b$

Where,

Y = cumulative average time taken per unit to produce x units
a = the time taken for the first unit of output
x = the cumulative number of units
b = the index of learning (log LR/log 2)
LR = the learning rate as a decimal

**Regression analysis**

$y = a + bx$

Where,

$$b = \frac{n\sum xy - \sum x \sum y}{n\sum x^2 - (\sum x)^2}$$

$$a = \frac{\sum y - b\sum x}{n}$$

$$r = \frac{n\sum xy - \sum x \sum y}{\sqrt{n\sum x^2 - (\sum x)^2}\sqrt{n\sum y^2 - (\sum y)^2}}$$

**Demand curve**

$P = a - bQ$

$$b = \frac{\text{change in price}}{\text{change in quantity}}$$

a = price when Q = 0

$MR = a - 2bQ$

**Formulae Sheet**